Deconstructing Italy

RESEARCH SERIES / NUMBER 91

DECONSTRUCTING ITALY: ITALY IN THE NINETIES

Salvatore Sechi, Editor

UNIVERSITY OF CALIFORNIA AT BERKELEY

Library of Congress Cataloging-in-Publication Data

Deconstructing Italy : Italy in the nineties / Salvatore Sechi, editor.
p. cm. — (Research series ; no. 91)
Includes bibliographical references.
ISBN 0-87725-191-6
1. Italy—Politics and government—1976– 2. Italy—Economic conditions—1976– 3. Italy—Social conditions—1976– I. Sechi, Salvatore. II. Series: Research series (University of California, Berkeley. International and Area Studies) ; no. 91.
JN5451.D35 1995
945.092'9—dc20 95-31268
CIP

Printed in the United States of America

Cover design by Lisa M. Bryant

CONTENTS

Old and New Problems

The Political Actors

NOTES ON CONTRIBUTORS

Salvatore Sechi is Professor of Contemporary History at the University of Ferrara and was Director of the Istituto Italiano di Cultura in San Francisco.

Pino Arlacchi is Professor of Applied Sociology at the University of Florence and deputy of the Partito Democratico della Sinistra.

Guido Baglioni is Professor of Sociology at the University of Milan and the head of CESOS (the Center for Social and Trade Union Studies).

Edmondo Berselli is Executive Editor of *Il Mulino* (Bologna) and commentator for the Roman daily *Il Messaggero.*

Carlo Guarnieri is Professor of Italian Political Systems at the University of Bologna.

Piero Ignazi is Professor of Comparative Politics at the University of Bologna and commentator for the daily *Il Sole—24 Ore.*

Marco Jacquemet received a doctorate in anthropology from the University of California at Berkeley in 1991. He has taught widely and is currently working on a book about the situation in Italy today.

Renato Mannheimer is Professor of Political Science at the University of Genoa and commentator for *Corriere della Sera,* as well as many television programs.

Gianfranco Pasquino is Professor of Political Science at the University of Bologna and Adjunct Professor of Political Science at the Bologna Center of Johns Hopkins University.

Alessandro Pizzorno is Professor of Sociology at the University of Milan and at New York University.

Pippo Ranci is Professor of Economic Policy at the University of Milan.

Sergio Romano was a member of the Italian foreign service and served as ambassador to the USSR until 1989. Currently he writes for *La Stampa* and *Epoca* and teaches international relations at Bocconi University in Milan.

Gian Enrico Rusconi is Professor of Political Science and Chair of the Department of Political Studies at the University of Turin.

Giacomo Sani is Professor of Political Science and Chair of the Department of Social and Political Studies at the University of Pavia.

Chiara Saraceno is Professor of Sociology and Chair of the Department of Social Sciences at the University of Turin.

Giulio Tremonti is Professor of Tax Law at the University of Pavia and was minister of finance in the government headed by Silvio Berlusconi.

INTRODUCTION

Salvatore Sechi

This volume stems from an international conference, "Deconstructing Italy," which was held at the end of March 1993 and sponsored by the Istituto Italiano di Cultura of San Francisco (of which I was director in 1991–93), together with the Department of Italian, the Department of Political Science, and the Center for Western European Studies at the University of California at Berkeley.

Rather than simply editing the conference papers, I thought it would be valuable to set them in the context of the grave ethical-political (and identity) crisis that has beset Italy for the past few years. The country is in part Phoenician and in part Alpine. It creates a double temptation: either to fling onself down on the Levantine shores of Africa, or to reach for the mountains of Europe. The geographic metaphor raises the question which has plagued Italians since at least the beginning of "Tangentopoli" (the kickback scandals) almost three years ago: Are we facing a crisis of transformation or the decline of democracy? The complex answers to this daunting question are what link these papers together.

The crisis and transformation of Italian democracy are closely intertwined. The "Italian case" consists of a series of troubling elements. The first is that Italy can be defined as a democracy only with difficulty. Whereas in other Western countries the governments can work from right to left and left to right, this has never been the case in Italy. Second, criminal activity and corruption are extremely widespread. Third, by inhibiting the alternation in power and the turnover of ruling elites, the political system closes in on itself and favors the preservation of the existing order over innovation. Fourth, the emergence of a central group (the Polo della Libertà e del Buongoverno) represents a break from the First Republic only from the point of view of the social bloc (centered on the productive middle class) and the anti-establishment culture. But from a political point of view, it is a phenomenon of renewal in continuity. In Italian history this has an old and infamous name: transformism. A more recent term, from the title of the brilliant novel by Giuseppe Tomasi di Lampedusa, could be "leopardism" (*gattopardismo*). The fundamental concept is similar: everything must change in order for everything to remain the same.

The durability of this genetic code is easily demonstrated. In two years and eight months, judges in Milan investigated 2,150 people—for the most part politicians, entrepreneurs, and financiers. More than 90 percent of those investigated who went to trial were convicted, and approximately 100 billion lire were recovered. Those convicted were guilty of illegally financing parties; violating tax regulations and building codes; and corruption, extortion, and misappropriation of funds (among other things). Although these convictions and the recent fiscal reforms passed by the Berlusconi government are aimed at countering endemic tax evasion, speculation, and building scandals, they are only a superficial solution for the serious fiscal crisis of the state.

In recent years we have seen the deterioration of the old political parties and classes; the victory of a new political lineup of movements and nonparties (Forza Italia, Alleanza Nazionale, La Lega); the formation of a new elite; a harsh, quibbling, and unbridled conflict among state institutions (the Presidency of the Council against the Presidency of the Republic; the Minister of Justice against the Milan judges and the Union of Magistrates, etc.); and a mad storming of institutions of power.

If we weigh all the pros and cons, the postfascist Second Republic seems remarkably similar to the antifascist First Republic. In a climate of continual controversy (very similar to the Italian merry wives), contentiousness, and instability, after seven months, Berlusconi, abandoned by the Lega, had to resign. The revolt against the past which brought him to power confirmed the existence of a class contrast (between the social strata who pay taxes and those who do not, those who pay too much and those who do not pay enough, etc.), but it largely translated into a simple turnover of men. Party officials and professional politicians have been replaced by the technicians of civil society: doctors, lawyers, teachers, small businessmen and women, magistrates, journalists. Seventy to eighty percent are college graduates (mostly in law or economics). They are largely male, of northern descent, under 50 (in the House, under 45), with a declared (but underestimated) average annual income of 125 million lire gross.

These are old acquaintances in Italian parliamentary history since 1882. Sociologically they recall the fauna of pre-1914 parliaments dominated by the Piedmontese premier Giovanni Giolitti. It is not by chance that the Turin daily paper *La Stampa* called them "old-fashioned notables." In the worst cases, they repeat the vices of their First Republic predecessors—an undisciplined babble of voices, contradictory messages, and the promotion of unqualified people to positions as ministers, managers, and public officials in radio, television, the banks, the police and intelligence services, the EC, public corporations, etc. All over there is a vulgar exhibition of the vanities of the *nouveau riche*.

Never was a government more fatuous and unreliable. Nor can one recall another that has abandoned itself with such regularity to the old psychodramas—dear to the Communists and the fascists—of presumed plots and conspiracies of foreign powers or indigenous groups (such as the Banca d'Italia, the magistrates, Opus Dei, or the freemasons) against parliament and legitimate government. This siege mentality overflows in all branches of the government. It appears in the form of an obsessive lament for the nonalignment of all the state pawns to the new political majority. It is a conception of the vote and democracy similar to that in card games of *asso-piglia-tutto* (ace takes all). It fails to recognize the fact that the state is different from the government, or that it is one thing to command and another to govern.

THE ILLEGAL SYSTEM

Italian "diversity" lies in feeling anomalous in comparison with other European countries.[1] The postwar cycle of boom and modernization fractured the Italian social body into corporatisms, particularisms, and out-and-out egoisms. It created an impetuous spirit of fission. Its protagonists are not organized by class, caste, or status, but small, raging interests of groups, agencies, and social factions.

Instead of harmonizing into a dynamic equilibrium, the diverse segments of Italian society have "collaborated in creating and extending an infernal summation of incompatabilities and fractures, sectarianisms and privileges."[2] These are the poisonous fruits of postwar economic development, free of every democratic rule, as was the dynastic-familistic capitalism which guided it. The political and entrepreneurial elites were greatly influenced by this context (here analyzed by Pippo Ranci).

In public conferences and seminars before the Tangentopoli explosion, the representatives of the business world (Agnelli, De Benedetti, etc.) sang the praises of the ethics of capitalism in Jansenist-Weberian tones, contrasting it to the demonic character of politics. In reality this self-justification failed to recognize the Smithian nature of Italian entrepreneurs. In an editorial, *Corriere della sera,* the northern industrial bourgeois daily, correctly noted the following:

> Italian capitalism for many years had been used to living every day with a lack of real controls, with politically negotiable restraints, with extremely manipulable legislation which could be eluded, with false budgets, false markets, and the lack of any sense of competition—all of which made the line between legal and illegal increasingly uncertain.[3]

A scholar of business history has written extensively about the economy of corruption, considered a unique mechanism which links economics and politics.[4]

In a period of economic development without democratization, in which potential social conflicts led to the consociation of the political left, "divvying up," and kickbacks, the elite had no scruples regarding criminal activity. From the early 1980s, when the services of the welfare state were generalized (Chiara Saraceno discusses an aspect of this in this volume), corruption spread from contracting and building licenses in municipalities to budgets allocated for zones damaged by earthquake, from hospitals to banks, and finally to large public corporations. Kickbacks from 5 to 15 percent were paid to ministers, counselors, and political mediators (such as the administrative secretaries of the parties). Impunity was assumed and therefore ensured. This illicit activity involves all sectors and all levels of income—from the blue-collar worker who breaks the law to build his or her home (one in five is illegal) to the building speculator, from the large (public and private) manager to customs officials, from the big designers and stylists to doctors, from restaurants to the heights of republican institutions, from government parties to those of the opposition, including magistrates, business experts, and journalists.

Italy is today in a sea of theft, contraband, illegal work, wrongful acts, patronage, and tax evasion, as Luciano Gallino, editor of the *Manuale di sociologia,* has put it.

> This is a country of widespread criminal activity. We are a phenomenon almost unique among contemporary societies. Note the ease with which insurance fraud is committed and the fake welfare recipients and fraudulent scholarships—a vicious circle that Italians do not have the courage or strength to break, also because such widespread criminal activity guarantees many social benefits.[5]

Except for employees, the majority of the Italian population (as Giulio Tremonti demonstrated when he became minister of finance) lives on tax evasion and the benefits—even if insufficient—of a welfare state among the most generous in the world.

According to the magistrates of Mani Pulite (Clean Hands), the diffusion of illicit or criminal practices was endemic by the 1980s. Deputy Attorney General Piercamillo Davigo described this as an imminent political danger:

> The question of governability is the same as the question of legality. If the government cannot trust the public administration, if the minister cannot be sure of the vigilance of the customs officials, if corruption penetrates the institutions on a widespread level, how can one govern?[6]

Why should a state that (a) tolerates (and is an accomplice to) tax evasion, the victory of the Mafia (see the analyses of Pino Arlacchi and Marco Jacquemet) over the state in at least three regions (Sicily, Calabria, Campania); (b) bows to string-pulling and the "Italian style" comedies of cooperation-farce in hiring public administration personnel; (c) applies with "discretion" the principle of compulsory penal action; (d) happily practices every type of pardon and confirmation; (e) detains in prison for years (and therefore convicts in advance) some ten thousand people (about half of whom are eventually found innocent in court); (f) complies with the demands of blue-collar workers or employees who are paralyzing production; (g) does not protect citizens but rather oppresses them—why should such a state suddenly remember it is constitutionally bound and fortify itself with sufficient means to cut short illegal behavior? Government appointments, transfers, promotions, etc. depend on high- and low-level officials chosen by the parties. Therefore, in government investigations and inquiries, the sovereignty of the former is limited by the latter. In this context, the importance of the constitutional state, particularly the part that handles the punishment of crimes and misdemeanors, is trivialized.

It is true that Italians love to hide behind their judges. But even that arm of the law has moved slowly against the generalized system of corruption. The district attorney of Milan is alone in actually prosecuting criminals. No less than other Italians, the magistrates are well aware of widespread illegal, if not criminal, practices, as practically all citizens are their beneficiaries or protagonists. The "recommendation," the "favor," are considered minor sins. People will ask politicians or anyone else who has influence for help in procuring a job, advancing a career, transferring an employee from one administration (or city) to another, etc. It is common sense—that is, absolutely natural—to violate the principle of the equality of all citizens, to alter a rule for one's relatives and friends, and thus short-circuit the guarantees of a constitutional state.

This attitude intensifies the inclination of Italians to act as if the laws do not apply to them. In this they are supported by theorists (and magistrates), according to whom the certainty of the law is a myth. After formalism and legalism, Italian juridical culture now docks at the port of sociologism. The so-called alternative use of the law, the role of temporary judges with respect to legislation, the resolution of controversies sought in "social reality" and in judicial creativity, are now central to the legal system.

But this is only half of the story. Together with a disregard for the rules, Italians have a quasi-fetishistic cult for them. It is a paradox, as if there were two different territories or a country inhabited by two different populations. With a stupifying zeal, Italians line up diligently for long hours in front of those places of torture and insanity that are public offices and apply the laws and official regulations, including even those that are clearly iniquitous, such as the tax laws and the health regulations. In the summer of 1993 "they paid the tax for the family doctor, not only without knowing to whom this applied—the dead or living, newborns or ghosts—but also after having been carefully reassured by the ministry concerned that the omission of payment would not have led to penalties of any kind."[7] They demonstrate the same attitude of indifferent heroism, a quasi-religious resigned acceptance, when faced with continuous tax increases on gas (already 77.5 percent of the price), scores of heavy property taxes, and an obligation to admit to possessing exotic animals:

> That in many cities long lines of citizens formed, anxious to report to the authorities not only the jaguar reared in the living room, but also their mother-in-law's mink stole, their great-grandfather's tortoiseshell glasses, the ivory keys of the family piano, demonstrates only one thing: Italians evidently believe that the legislature can now ask of them whatever it pleases, even to paint themselves yellow on odd days.[8]

Meanwhile, the minister of finance has made it known to the honest taxpayers, oppressed by an implacable treasury, that they can sleep easy because he has determined the taxability of the illegal income of architects not registered in the professional register, unlicensed merchants, professionals, business people employed in black market activities, and usurers.

This is a criminal economy which, according to a report of the Confederation of Commerce, in 1993 produced an income of approximately 72 thousand billion lire. In no other country in the world, except in the most ferocious dictatorships, do citizens think that the state can ask anything of them. This has a corollary crucial to understanding the national culture: Italians believe that the laws are unjust and irrational, like natural catastrophes or a cynical destiny. But this also means that, together with the millions of citizens who are terrorized by the laws and apply them zealously, there are just as many who violate them systematically. We are truly a nation of heroes and scoundrels.

INCOMPLETE DEMOCRACY OR SIMULACRUM OF DEMOCRACY?

Parallel to the failure of the constitutional state, Italy has developed a patronage system of proportions never before seen in its history. This patronage system is an efficient machine, a true apparatus of consensus because some of the participants in its legal and illegal forms are elected counselors and ministers even if they use the exchange vote. Thus representative democracy does not obstruct—indeed it perhaps facilitates—the growth of patronage behavior.[9] Those who disagree must ask whether after its liberation from fascism (25 April 1945) Italy would again have become a democracy if it had not paid the price of such corruption. As Alessandro Pizzorno explains, it has also had its noble aims, such as breaking the forty-year stranglehold on power of the Christian Democratic Party. In effect, the medium-sized Socialist Party felt it had to seize the resources of the state (postal services, agency budgets, kickbacks on public works contracts, acquistion of hospital and office equipment, etc.) to replace the resources that, when it was in opposition, were furnished by its Communist allies. It succeeded in this thanks to financing from the Soviet Union and to transfers of monetary and human resources from the central administration and thousands of regions, provinces, and municipalities.

The judicial attacks on the nation's most powerful politicians and businessmen could be directly followed by Italians on television. Neither the private management of Fiat, Montedison, Enimont, Olivetti, and Fininvest (Silvio Berlusconi's company), nor the great boyars of public industry could save themselves from devastating accusations. According to Sergio Romano, "as in the most tumultuous and uncontrolled phases of the great revolutions, the gap that separates the desk of power and the bench of the accused was narrowed terribly."[10] In fact, plausible accusations involved the head of state, the heads of the secret service, customs officials, journalists, treasury agents (paid to shut their eyes to tax evasion), business consultants, and magistrates. The hearings became sessions of a general collective unconscious. The roots of criminal activity in Italy are found in the bowels of civil as well as political society. One cannot consider the course of Tangentopoli a sufficient cleansing, a sort of collective absolution. The trials of those in power have become trials of the Italians as a people, as a nation. According to ex-head of state Francesco Cossiga,

> We must reestablish, culturally, why we are a state, nation, community, or whatever it means to be Italian. Particularly today, for with the fall of the blocs, we no longer have the USSR, the USA, or the Church as references. We must now reconstruct a national identity.[11]

Exhausted by the abuses of fascism, Italians have followed a politics which minimized issues of national identity, led by elites who preferred to entrench themselves in a wider Europeanism and internationalism—themes treated in detail here by Gianenrico Rusconi.[12]

Having considered the breadth of the sectors involved in illicit activities, the magistrates of Milan sounded the alarm. The discovery that corruption was so generalized, however, endangered the survival of the democratic regime. Therefore, instead of the spectacle of interminable trials, a political solution had to be that granted freedom to the guilty in return for a confession of offenses, the names of their guilty partners, confiscation of their booty, and banishment from public office for their lifetimes. In the process, as Carlo Guarnieri indicates, the judicial system is becoming a sovereign as well as an independent power equal to parliament. It now has a lobby or pressure group, the National Magistrates' Association (Associazione Nazionale Magistrati),[13] and a "party of judges" is beginning to form supported by the postfascists of the Alleanza Nazionale and by the post-Communists of the Democratic Party of the Left, as well as by their fellow travelers like *La Repubblica* and *L'Espresso.* For various ideological reasons they have not tried to defeat their rivals in the electoral arena, but rather to put them out of the game entirely in isolation cells or in the inhuman inferno of ordinary ones. Indeed, the magistrates of Milan are still today using a medieval technique from the Inquisition.[14] In the name of a good cause, they extract confessions from the accused through detention pending trial. In effect, they make them serve time prior to trial or conviction—and waiting for a trial can take as long as nine years—thereby paying a penalty not imposed by any court of law.

The judges have rediscovered the primacy and effectiveness of criminal law, as well as its Jacobin origin. The attorney general of Milan, entrusted with the task of using criminal law to purify civil society of corruption, has become an Inquisitor. The *avviso di garanzia*, a form of protection for the citizen, has degenerated into a de facto indictment and therefore a guilty verdict. It was expected that Berlusconi would receive an avviso di garanzia, which would bring down his government and cast the country headlong into instability. However, it came after Umberto Bossi, leader of the Lega, had left the government coalition. As Gianni Baget Bozzo has noted:

> Berlusconi has broad popular support, all the more significant because he removed an entire political class and a mode of managing power: that of the party factions and constituents which produced Tangentopoli. His authority to govern is the political aspect of changes which Mani Pulite initiated. It would be a defeat for Mani Pulite if the judges' diligence resulted in the restoration of politicians in areas exempt from investigations.[15]

Baget Bozzo's reference is to the regions of central Italy, governed by ex-Communists, where the attorneys general have failed to conduct investigations of the illicit financing of the PCI by powerful "red" cooperatives. Tangentopoli thus became a Lombardy-Veneto phenomenon, a type of showdown among the pool of magistrates in Milan and the ex-leader of the Socialists, Bettino Craxi, and his old friend, Silvio Berlusconi.

Italy is a blocked democracy, and its pluralism, offered as a symbol of robustness, is largely rhetorical hyperbole. There is a power and political vacuum that the judges are compelled to fill. Many of the reasons lie in the Italian proportional electoral system, which until the March 1994 elections made almost impossible an alternation of the government between the central bloc led by the Christian Democrats and the left bloc guided by the Communists. The troubling images that communism traditionally evoked also undermined the opposition's hopes of gaining the majority. Therefore, it resigned itself to juxtapose the role of critic (exercised in a flexible and changeable manner, varying with its own participation in the spoils), with that of codirector of the system. Once the Communist Party had discarded the cards of revolt and social democracy (held only for a year and then only tortuously), the impossibility of overturning the majority of the Christian Democrats meant the Communists had only one choice: to join in with the Christian Democrats. Thus was born "consociation." This move was tempered by public rhetoric concerning burning parliamentary issues and large but uninfluential mass demonstrations and general strikes. The appearance of democratic pluralism was maintained; the structures existed. But there was no alternation of parties in power. It was, therefore, a fictitious pluralism.[16]

CONSOCIATION INSTEAD OF ALTERNATION

The crisis of the nation is also the crisis of the state and of democracy. The exceedingly large number of people who live not for politics, but by politics, thanks to a parliamentary regime with almost 1,000 elected members, has facilitated illegal activity.[17] At every level they have been able to maneuver public allocations into "a channel of violent corruption in which the public and private have been combined in the worst way and have formed a sort of massive sewer."[18] The areas infected by the virus have been enlarged by the limitless number of perquisites in public offices, the preferential vote, unlimited electoral expenses, unaudited party budgets, the privilege of parliamentary immunity, no requirement that politicians reveal their holdings, the exchange vote, etc.[19] The scale of the catastrophe for the Italian political elite and Italian democracy is evident in the numbers: on 15 August 1994, of 945 members of parliament, 345 had received an avviso di garanzia and 151 were being investigated.

The system of proportional representation effectively prevented the alternation of parties in power from 1861 (the initial liberal regime) to 1922 (the advent of fascism), and from 1945 (antifascism) to today. Moreover—perhaps most impressive from an historical point of view—since 1861 all the political regimes in Italy have arisen from civil wars which were disguised as ideological or class conflicts. Only recently have some historians (C. Pavone, G. Ranzato, E. Galli della Loggia, among others) begun to probe this long-neglected aspect of our national construction. This new scenario has created a problem of legitimization that traverses the entirety of Italian history.

Delegitimization first hit the Catholics, who were hostile to the formation of the initial unitary and liberal state, then the Socialists, who opposed Italian intervention in World War I. The fascists then took power by means of open sedition, the March on Rome. After World War II, the Communists were hard hit (and then the Socialists) because they were perceived as being in the service of a foreign power, dedicated to subversion, and on the front line in the civil war, which bloodied the country in 1943–45. Moreover, although they were certainly antifascist, they were dubious democrats; the PCI welcomed a parliamentary path to socialism only in the eighth party congress held in 1956.

The depth of civil war had a singular consequence. The victors (and their international allies) recognized the existence of the opposition, but denied the possibility of its governing. Consociation in Italy was preferred over alternation. This system was born in 1876, five years after national unification, with the rise to power of the parliamentary left guided by Agostino Depretis. In Italy, both the right and left of the Risorgimento dreamed of the "Westminster model"—that is, a bipartisan system with a strong executive able to lead parliament, and the automatic accession of the majority party leader to the role of premier.[20] They governed, however, in the French style—that is, on the basis of parliamentary majority, which is broader than and different from a party majority.[21] This system, with the devastating effect of a virus, has long been called transformism,[22] and it infected the governments of 1876–1914, from Depretis to Giolitti, and all the post-1945 regimes.

Luciano Cafagna and Giuliano Amato have advanced a hypothesis to explain this state of affairs.[23] According to them, in managing power, the parties virtually acted as a monoparty regime, even if from 1861 to 1924 and after 1943 there was apparent pluralism and conflict. Until now majority and minority have been distrustful of their respective democratic reliability. Under these conditions, the possibility of alternating parties in power melted like snow in the sun. Lacking what was necessary, the governments of these periods were "monopartisan" and only internally differentiated.

The rightist opposition (monarchist and fascist) and the leftist opposition (socialists and Communists prone toward Stalinism) were considered extra-constitutional and/or anti-constitutional and therefore not legitimate. Thus they could not govern, and Italian democracy could not achieve a genuine alternation of parties in power. It was a sort of democratic dictatorship. This anomaly has dominated Italian politics since 1861, through liberal, fascist, and democratic-republican regimes and has no counterpart in other Western countries.[24]

This long-standing inability to turn over the leadership in power has shaped Italians' way of being. It explains the lack of moral revolt against the inexhaustible flow of corruption coming to light every day. It can be compared to the former Soviet Union and Eastern Europe, but on the national scene one needs only to have read a single article by Emilio Gentile to realize that the Fascist Party was the model of party hegemony. In addition to providing a civic religion, material benefits, solutions, and provisions, it was a mediator between the people and the state, from which it had taken over numerous functions. It embodied and encouraged party supremacy, party-centrism, and a winning consensus thanks to its enormous financial resources—not from the market, but above all from the state.[25] Thus after the crisis of 1929, the Fascist Party had direct and indirect control of a notable part of the country's economy—for example, majority shares in a set of businesses which represented 42 percent of the capital of Italian joint stock companies.

The fascist one-party system and the advanced process of state-controlled economy survived the decline of fascism. But nationalism, which to Mussolini derived from the anticapitalism of the origins, did not end with the death of the dictator. It was taken up again in the Italian Social Republic (the puppet regime created by Mussolini, by then totally hostage to the Nazis) and by the postwar Italian Social Movement Party (MSI). Still today it remains an ideological obstacle impeding the Alleanza Nazionale from accepting a politics of privatization and the dismantling of the enormous power of the state over the economy:

> Fascism was generally repudiated as a phenomenon extraneous to the sensibility and culture of the country, but the state gave generous subsidies, distributed pensions, reimbursed medical expenses, managed banks and businesses, recruited officials, and conferred diplomas according to the rules that went back to fascism. Certainly the parties were accused of "cryptofascist" alternation, but only when a particular institution—specifically the Rocco Code—was useful to some and damaging to others. In fact, what one did not like, the other did, and as a whole the Italians,

without ever having been fascists, continued to live unperturbed in a fascist state that was modified only gradually, as new conditions in the country demanded new laws and structures.[26]

After 1943 the antifascist parties, in both government and the opposition, went after public resources. They did not even attack, but rather strengthened, the capacity of the party in control to plunder the central and peripheral powers. Thus thanks to the work of their representatives appointed to various governing bodies, part of the budgetary funds from banks, insurance companies, mines, transportation, telecommunications, electrical energy systems, oil, iron and steel, and mechanical and food industries poured into the parties' coffers. These are the practices that the Milan judges are currently assessing and quantifying.

The public sector represents 50 percent of the national income and economy—a breadth of control that can be compared only to that of the ex-Communist countries. No Western democratic state has expenditures comparable to those of Italy, currently more than 53.5 percent of the GNP. The public debt (approximately 2 million billion lire) is 50 percent larger than the GNP of half the European nations. Second place in this robbery of the state went to the minority parties, with the Communists always getting fewer appointments than the PSI and other allies. The PCI's portion was limited because of international ties with the USSR and its threatening program toward the middle and business classes. But having fought fascism, participated in the Resistance and the drafting of the constitution, with control of the principal union (the CGIL), and with a feared capacity that was able to set off a civil war or paralyze the country (until the fall of the Berlin Wall it had about 30 percent of the votes and stable control of the administrations of central Italy), the PCI retained an enormous veto power. As a result, coopting the left became the government's fundamental strategy, shattering into a thousand pieces only after the fall of the Berlin Wall.

In the last four legislatures, the PCI and PDS accounted for 88 percent of the appointments made by the governments of Premiers Craxi, Andreotti, and Forlani. They could be extremely critical in public statements and in the press, but they were dear allies in the division of state resources that brought public debt in fifteen years from 170 thousand to about 2 million billion lire. From 1979 to March

1994 parliament approved 3,080 laws. The left voted with the majority or abstained in 2,741 of them. It said "no" to only 19.3 percent of the legislative measures proposed by the governing majority.[27] Even if Norberto Bobbio did not agree, the left was part of the governing coalition.[28]

These indications of fictitious democracy begin to explain the electoral debacle of the progressive coalition. They also explain why the most popular judge in Milan, Antonio Di Pietro, shows a cold, analytical passion—not an ethical rebellion or the hot emotion of one who feels offended and betrayed, as happened on 25 July 1943. Thus the fall of fascism, which, along with the "adventure" of the war, had broken every sympathetic relationship with the people, flooded the streets and plazas with joy. Today the drama of the Italians is that of one who, called to be the executioner, admits to having been an accomplice in the crime. The parties shaped the national politics, society, and culture and were generous with the nation's resources. For more than forty years the voters clung to them in a net of mutually implicating exchanges.

OLD AND NEW BOURGEOISIE

The electoral coalition formed by Silvio Berlusconi was not, as Adrian Lyttelton wrote, "The Triumph of TV."[29] Berlusconi owes his victory to the fact that unlike the left (which controlled the three state television channels, TV news, and the programs—led by Costanzo and Funari—with a larger audience of Berlusconi's private television), he knew how to denounce effectively the perverse linkages described above, in the name of a Second Republic to be led by a liberal, federalist, innovative bloc. Thanks to Berlusconi, for the first time in an Italian political competition, concrete problems and solutions were discussed (which does not, of course, mean the discussions were always realistic). In fact, his Polo della Libertà placed unemployment, excessive taxes, free education, etc. at the center of the electoral battle. The Progressisti (headed by the former Communist Party, now called the PDS) appeared uncertain and not very credible in view of their past record of unproductive public spending, stemming from party consociation, oppressive statism, and the traps and snares of state-union control of employment. They looked more like conservatives than innovators in the existing order.

At the same time, although the PCI and PDS have together ruled the Socialist Party since 1946 in many thousands of municipalities, they have not once "proven capable of uncovering and denouncing any of the facts that have been brought to light by the magistrates in the past two years"—not even in Milan.[30] Initially the PDS believed it would emerge unscathed from the crisis of the First Republic. The members of the PCI-PDS accused of corruption retained such a reserve of faith that they did not hesitate to attribute to themselves, and not to the party, all the offenses uncovered. And in the elections the PDS did relatively well. Nevertheless, the convictions of numerous officers and the opening of enquiries in Italy and abroad into the PCI-PDS financing by "red" cooperatives cracked the myth of honesty and impunity regarding the principal party of the left.

Part of the success of the left came from the fact that for the first time in the electoral history of Italy, the left enjoyed unhoped for and unrepeatable support from the press (*Corriere della sera, La Stampa, La Repubblica, Il Messaggero*); the most notable intellectuals; the three union confederations and Confindustria (whose daily paper, *Il Sole—24 Ore*, defined the best program as that of the Progressisti); and the academic lobby of ex-Christian Democrat and Communist opposition economists, which is very influential with financial markets and among foreign investors. Once again the electorate supported the left in the direct election of mayors, but it still expressed fear, not assuaged by time, about the idea of entrusting the PDS with the ministry of industry or defense. There was also a great public diffidence toward the leadership of the left, first of Occhetto and then of D'Alema. As Gianfranco Pasquino explains in this volume, they sought to recycle their old identity into a social democratic reformism. But the party still put forward too many recognized Communist officials (experts at sales talk and in consent with the internal party regime), along with movements (like the Alleanza Democratica) invented for particular parliamentary seats; a sample collection of journalists, magistrates, university teachers (updated and polished to look like new); and a squad of high-profile capitalists (Bruno Visentini, Franco De Benedetti, Ernesto Gismondi, etc.). It raised the banner of the market on the condition that the state and party control of the public television system and the economy not be touched. It was done in the name of social solidarity, a classic fig leaf.[31] According to the traditional Communist idea, conceived during the governments of Amato and Ciampi, many hoped that the attorneys general would open the way to Palazzo Chigi to the left, arresting or investigating their political opponents.[32]

The elections of 27–28 March and June 1994 demonstrated that the PDS was no longer in tune with its old electorate and, lacking a social reference group, without certainties. In the most industrialized northern areas, where they were traditionally very strong, the Progressisti were downsized or almost swept away. In Lombardy, the Polo won seventy-four of seventy-five electoral seats, in Piedmont thirty of thirty-six, and forty-six of forty-seven in the Veneto and the Friuli (strongholds of the DC). In terms of social or class composition the verdict was unambiguous. The working class, the small business owners, and the middle classes of central Italy (Tuscany, Umbria, Emilia Romagna), which traditionally voted for the left, shifted to the right. "Poorer" voters made the same choice: 48.2 percent voted for the Polo. The youth, aged 18–35, voted 44.3 percent for Berlusconi, Bossi, and Fini.[33] In Gianni Agnelli's daily paper an editorial rightly pointed it out:

> A left that won the bourgeois votes of the hills of Turin, losing instead the workers of Mirafiori, represents a slap in the face to the memory of Antonio Gramsci; a left that gets more votes in Basilicata than in Lombardy has by now been completely torn from its reformist roots. Rather than its natural function as representative of the working world, in the perception of the country, the tie of the left to the First Republic has survived, as well as its continuity of machinery, languages, and faces (beginning with those of Occhetto and D'Alema).[34]

At the beginning and in the course of the election campaign, still a victim of Leninist ideas, according to which every country is controlled by a handful of great families, PDS Secretary Achille Occhetto sought legitimization in the "good drawing rooms" of dynastic and familiaristic capitalism. De Benedetti, Agnelli, Pirelli, Marzotto, Falck, George Soros in New York, London, and NATO headquarters in Brussels (these last two were the first to be visited by Occhetto) were reassured of the nonsubversive, nonpunitive policy of the PDS in the case of a victory by the left in Italy.

Although the party could count on historically consolidated alliances with small business owners and cooperatives, in the "red" areas of Emilia Romagna, Tuscany, and Umbria, Occhetto did not know how to exploit a strategic role in the electoral program.[35] According to an industrial manager (and member of the PDS),

> Industrial politics of the left, like that of the large union confederations, was . . . identified and perceived as linked to the old "smokestacks," with scarce attention to the small businesses that were already present, but especially to new initiatives that could arise. . . . In this way it killed through neglect what was emerging as the novelty of the country's social system, the new backbone of the productive structure.[36]

For the Progressisti this was a sharp defeat, and its results will probably extend in time. In fact, the debacle of the left can be identified with the failure of the social project (the so-called "alliance with producers" against those living on unearned income) that was proposed by Enrico Berlinguer, secretary of the PCI in the 1970s, together with the younger and more advanced sectors of the Confindustria directed by Alberto Pirelli and the labor unions (which Claudio Baglioni discusses in this volume). This design was, in fact, the great dream of two young revolutionaries of prefascist Turin, the liberal Piero Gobetti and the Communist Antonio Gramsci.[37] It took the form of an alliance between dirigiste capitalism (large private and state enterprises) and factory proletariat (represented by the union and the Communist Party) in the name of the supremacy of profit over parasitism, unproductivity, budgets without revenue, etc. This "social pact" was a sort of triangular economic consociation under the protection of the state.

After the elections of March 1994, big business was no longer interested in these discussions. The protectionist measures of the pre-Berlusconi governments had, for example, assured the survival of Fiat. In a regime of free competition, it would have been destroyed by the Japanese automotive industry. After the year 2000, when foreign concerns will have free access to the Italian market, Fiat will probably be overcome by its continuing strategy and product quality crises. More generally, big business, as part of an oligarchic capitalism, is very traditional, with a few large families and groups, as Alain Friedman has demonstrated in his book on Fiat. Therefore industries have tens of thousands of employees and sales topping 10 thousand billion lire. Thus the search for agreements and exchanges with the state was inevitable, and Confindustria has always supported government. In exchange, it has received concessions and privileges—constant protection, the discouragement of unwelcome competition, facilitated access to bank credit, tax breaks, research financing, and the like.

Small and mid-sized businesses, with sales between 100 billion and 1,000 billion lire, have been held at a distance from this hothouse of incentives and favors. For example, the banks do not give them easy credit when they are in trouble, but grant it at discriminatory high rates compared to those for the big business clientele.[38] They also feel unfairly pressed by taxes and have been seeking greater laissez-faire in the labor market—that is, they want greater hiring freedom, more flexibility, a different salary structure, more tax relief to companies, fewer transfers (subsidies, distributions, etc.) to families and businesses, tax reductions on benefits, and reinvested capital gains. Working increasingly with foreign countries, they want to be free to negotiate salaries and services outside integrative company contracts and national agreements aimed at rendering labor costs compatible with programmed national development and inflation objectives. In recent years, large manufacturers have entrusted the presidency of their association, Confindustria, to leaders of the intermediate sectors (Merloni, Lucchini, Abete). But it has not placated the middle class manufacturers' dissatisfaction, resentment, and desire to count for more.[39]

It was Berlusconi, as Umberto Bossi had done, who realized the scope of the phenomenon that was affecting large and important parts of the country. In ten years (1981–91) small and mid-sized businesses had grown to 3,330,000, a 15 percent increase. From Lombardy they spread to the northeast, along the ridge of the Adriatic and into the central regions. They profited from the devaluation of the lira in the fall of 1992. They were no longer the poor relatives of capitalism, but one of the principal sources of national wealth and the most solid structures in the economic system.

There has always been little communication and integration between the world of big business and finance, on one hand, and small and mid-sized business, professionals, and service industries, on the other. Instead of a unity of interests, cultural and political objectives, and organization, there has been internal fracturing, a contradiction or antimony between the two segments of the bourgeoisie. This became obvious on 10 March 1994 (two weeks before the elections), when Berlusconi publicly attacked Confindustria, the principal association of the business world, even though he himself was on the board of directors, albeit an absentee.

The reasons for Berlusconi's unusual and unexpected polemic were both rightist and leftist. On one hand, they echoed the exorcisms of the Comintern against big business, the capital inherited by the great families and stashed in the sacred precincts of Mediobanca, the ties with conservative parties (from which sprang the contemptuous term "industry of the First Republic"), etc. On the other hand, he sang the praises of self-made capitalists, fighting on the labor front (Confindustria would be far from this), pressed by the treasury, discriminated against by banks and not represented, or represented rather poorly, by Confindustria.

Berlusconi's colleagues (particularly the economist Antonio Martino, appointed minister of foreign affairs) knew how to offer these classes what the Progressisti were incapable of offering: a commitment against exorbitant taxes (when they pay taxes, craftsmen and small businessmen pay the state approximately 60 percent of earnings), loosened labor laws, reductions in the cost of money, and against the oppressive state bureaucracy that "makes policy." They also denounced the practice of First Republic governments of entering into corporate agreements with the unions, entrusting them with the protection of social peace and dispossessing parliament. Berlusconi confessed to not frequenting the big business association:

> I cannot abide sitting with certain people. In Confindustria there is a rarified air; I do not breathe fresh air. I have always had the impression that those who go to Confindustria meetings are those whom it is better to not keep in the firm; the good ones usually have other things to do. They stay in the firm.[40]

Berlusconi probably intended to send a message to the president of Confindustria, Luigi Abete. As a small entrepreneur, he was also excluded from the "good drawing rooms" of Italian capitalism. Berlusconi was interested in lining up the union of Italian manufacturers in his favor—Barilla, Merloni, Lavazza, Boroli, Mentasti, Luigino

Rossi, Ferrero, and Gazzoni Frascara. Clearly the leader of Forza Italia aimed to widen the gap between big and small business.

An effective and astute editorialist in *La Stampa,* Mario Deaglio, understood the danger of his design.[41] He was quick to remind readers, with refined malevolence, that Berlusconi could not have truly set himself up as the *homo novus.* First, Fininvest was a large industrial group, and therefore its head could not legitimately represent microentrepreneurial capitalism. Second, "his enterprises not only came into being during the First Republic, but they were actually lovingly drawn out by eminent politicians of the period" (the reference is to Berlusconi's relationship with the Socialist premier, Bettino Craxi).

But this still did not dull the force of the Cavaliere's observations regarding the marginalization of small business. It is a crucial class in a period of rapid change, and it was undeniable that it was getting no help from the political world (nor from Confindustria) in resolving the essential problems of its growth.

Berlusconi, together with the political-entrepreneurial class that supported him, was not well liked by the big manufacturers. The conclusion of Deaglio's article shows that Fiat, like Confindustria, did not intend to give Berlusconi a hand. Certainly the Cavaliere "was one of them, but very different from them. One who played the piano and sang at parties, who opposed that wrinkled and airy vanity of the lawyer (Mr. Agnelli) with his own physical and elastic vanity" (Manzolini). In the eyes of his colleagues of an older and nobler lineage, he was not even an industrialist in the strict sense; he had a mercantile and nonproductive way of thinking. He was, in short, a great artisan, a tradesman. He sold publicity and consumer goods; he did not produce value added.[42] Confindustria was suspicious of his program to reduce taxes to 30 percent.

In the March 1994 elections seventy-two members of parliament were elected who claimed to have come from the entrepreneurial world (forty-seven to the House and twenty-five to the Senate). Never had so many captains of industry been seen at Montecitorio and Palazzo Madama. They were aligned essentially as follows: thirty-two in Forza Italia, twenty-three in the Lega, six in Alleanza Nazionale, five among the Progressisti, two in the PPI, one of the Pannella radicals, and one on the Segni slate.[43] Their number was almost equal to that of the members of Confindustria, Confagricoltura, and the Confederation of Small Businesses. According to the leader of the young industrialists of Syracuse, Stefania Prestigiacomo, elected in the ranks of Forza Italia,

> [In] the past it was Confindustria that pushed toward renewal. It was Confindustria that politically represented the entrepreneurs, a role that pushed other tasks to second place. But now "the new" has entered Parliament. Entrepreneurs are engaged in the first person. Political representation has passed directly to the House.[44]

It was *Corriere della sera*, the principal organ of the great entrepreneurial families of Lombardy and of Italy in general, that outlined precisely, in Marxist terms, the intercapitalistic contradiction which sprang from the elections:

> To one social class, the large industrial and financial bourgeoisie, which is realizing the highest concentration of economic power of all time in its own hands, there corresponds a parliamentary majority that has in the productive lower and middle middle classes, both commercial and professional, the font of its own electoral success and of it own political legitimization.[45]

According to Piero Ostellino, "The situation that has been created is potentially revolutionary." Other critics think that it could lead to civil war or an authoritarian degeneration of the political system.

The Berlusconi government granted the demands of this industrial world. To demonstrate that it had passed from the phase of delegation to that of direct representation, it named a small manufacturer of gun stocks, Vito Gnutti, minister of industry. The minister of public works, Roberto Radice, and the minister of the budget, Giancarlo Pagliarini, also came from the small business world. Confindustria took note of this convergence of government and small and mid-sized business. Before the general strike of the unions against the financial law (12 October 1994), Agnelli and De Benedetti, together with their principal colleagues, decided to invite Berlusconi to dinner (despite the violent criticism by the press of these two entrepreneurs) to discuss reconciliation and issue a warning not to weaken the politics of financial reform. But it remained a dinner, not a treaty of peace nor an alliance.

THE POSTELECTION PERIOD

It was easy for the Cavaliere to win the elections. But he did not survive the postelection period. The problem was not the danger of fascism, but the habit of the left to seek revenge for its own election defeats via the ideological criminalization of the winners. Moreover, anyone who accused the new majority of Peronism had to take note of Berlusconi's willingness to risk alienating public approval (as did happen) by drawing up a law that cut 50,000 billion lire in health care and pensions, affecting the largest and most sensitive reservoir of voters in the country.[46] Berlusconi also talked with the unions and yielded to some of their requests, and therefore the requests of the left. Apart from the folklore and eccentricities of some postfascists, the Italian right is rather similar to that of other European countries, as even Confindustria admitted, though it did not enjoy doing so.[47]

What was startling about Berlusconi's majority was its paucity of theoretical and cultural density and the scanty (or complete lack of) competence of most of the ministers and state commissioners. With few exceptions, they were chosen from among the lawyers and collaborators of Fininvest or members and vote bosses of the three coalition parties filling the thousands of pigeonholes in the state organization charts with faces familiar to the Milanese or Roman drawing rooms. Once more political contiguity, faithfulness to the new winners, was rewarded, just as the predecessors of Berlusconi, Fini, and Bossi had done.

A table published in the weekly *Il Mondo* showed that the bureaucrats appointed up to September 1994 were the same as those in office at the time of the DC and its allies. The extreme vulnerability and the weak decision-making ability of the premier was unexpected. The business culture of Forza Italia (modeled on Fininvest), the plebiscitary and rancorous culture of the Lega, and the totalitarian descent of Alleanza Nazionale have still to come to terms with the theory of the division of power and an elementary and essential principle of liberal democracy. The new president of the House, Irene Pivetti, noted that the new members of parliament

> are bearers of a certain business culture, which only cares about the private, and do not assimilate the institutional culture, which cares about the public. Thus, parliament is the victim of a new

consociation that among the old parties has been substituted by that of businessmen.[48]

The authoritarian paternalism of a large industrial group, the monocratic spirit of the old fascism (even if Fini is sincere in wishing for the conversion of the MSI ruling class—here examined by Piero Ignazi—to the moderate positions of men like Giscard or Chirac), and the democracy of applause of the Lega, united with the dilettantism and arrogance of the new majority, could be an explosive mixture. The new political forces are nonparties, nonideological, and without membership, organization, or rites (participation, the vote, "collective" decisions, internal democracy, etc.). They are tied together in some measure by the proportional system that normally demands the presence of a socially, ideologically, and organizationally rooted party.[49]

In elections with a single-member constituency, in which the electorate is approximately 100,000 people, an electoral committee suffices. It is not by chance that Forza Italia resembles a patrimonial system more than a party, or at most a set of electoral committees distributed throughout the national territory. The elected representatives and parliamentary groups should be the ones that count, but at present their function is to echo and be a footstool of the leader.[50] In a "party of the president," which Forza Italia is, plebiscitary democracy founded on the charisma of the leader is in force. As long as Berlusconi wins, he embodies the Weberian "dictator of the electoral battlefield." He alone counts. After his disappearance or weakening, the internal battle will take place, the in-fighting among members of parliament, organizing into groups or factions to fight for the leadership and/or reelection. It is easy to predict that with Berlusconi's crisis or exit from the scene, Forza Italia (entrusted by Malthusian democracy to the care of the former minister of defense, Cesare Previti) will dissolve.

The plebiscitary democracy of the Berlusconi business party is changing Italian democracy by means of the absolute importance it attributes to surveys and referenda. (The First Republic lengthened its agony with the latter.)[51] Combined with the will of the people expressed in the parliamentary majority, the results of the surveys are used as a further instrument of legitimization. Further, as happened in the case of Berlusconi's closest collaborators, it induces a turning back to a monist, absolutist conception of power. Their idea that the vote is the will of the people and that from it descends the right to subordinate all powers to the majority and to dispense them is Jacobin. It was taken up again by the Italian Communists during the drafting of the constitution:

> But the majority principle does not mean quite this. Within the democratic framework it expresses the right of the majority to not be subject to the minority, but is limited by the guarantee to the minority of the power to become the majority of tomorrow; it expresses the right of the majority to adopt the decisions it wishes, but is limited by the controls and balances that guarantee the respect on its part of the limits in which it must remain.[52]

The tendency that is emerging from the first months of government is that of substituting the consociation of the First Republic with the principle of not only giving all power (and consequent political responsibility) to the majority, but of the majority dividing it up (as Amato called it) and itself determining the rules of the game. When this balance was overturned and blown to the wind, it quickly produced the current raging storm of an inter-institutional war, of everyone against everyone. The rules of the game—that is, of the scope of authority—are now missing. The majority, with the pretext of vanquishing consociationism, "proceeds like a tank on all the battlefields that it encounters," while the minority is "driven by the instinct to overturn this government of usurpers by all means, even at the cost of entering into alliances with the most treacherous and adventurous factions of the enemy front"—that is, with Bossi.[53] This reflects the character of the current transition—that is, the limited time frame of this majority—as well as the vague and superficial ideological colorings of its components (federalism, postfascism, liberalism, etc.). They represent neither a "conservative revolution" nor assimilation into liberalism.[54]

Rather, we are in the presence of a greedy assault on the seat of power by those who fought the First Republic because they had been excluded from the dinner power and from the government party. Thanks to the fact that there remain only passive vestiges of a bizarre totalitarian mentality, I believe that Italians will be spared regime catastrophes. But they will not be able to escape serious damage. The public debt has shot to 2 million billion lire. The stock exchange lost

30 percent from May to October 1994. Foreign investors withdrew 30,000 billion lire. A climate of instability and uncertainty has isolated the country. It is like a microorganism under the microscope of the world, which rightly ignores and derides us, thanks also to our foreign policy of Pepe Le Moko (examined in this volume by Sergio Romano).

Because a country's international status is the extension of its internal politics and in general of its political system, Italy's international credibility and efficacy are similar to those of Greece and Portugal—i.e., rather feeble. This devaluation/marginalization from Europe and from the "club" of the more industrialized countries (the G7) is the result of the economic-financial problems (the deficit, inflation, high interest rates) stemming from traditional institutional problems. The principal problem among these is the state of executive power, which is increasingly impotent and at the mercy of a sovereign parliament. On top of this, there is a war of reciprocal delegitimation among the institutions of the state. Although Sabino Cassese dates the "government by assembly" in Italy to the 1970s,[55] the question remains whether the phenomenon (of Jacobin origin) of a parliament which legislates and governs has not been a constant in Italy's constitutional history since 1861.[56]

The prevalent thrust of the referenda voted for on 11 June—launched and supported by the liberal Marco Pannella— is toward repeal: they can cancel a law, but they cannot create a new one. Such a task remains reserved for parliament. Through the referenda, the populace responded to general issues like the right to divorce and abortion; the majority electoral system; and the rejection of life sentences and state funding for parties and for the nuclear industry, among others.[57]

On 11 June 1995, for the first time, the left tried to use the referendum for rather sophisticated questions such as the number of television networks that can be assigned to a private citizen, the ads and the grouping of ads therein, the payment of union dues, the schedule and liberalization of shops, etc. In reality, the television referendum had two objectives: to politically take Berlusconi out of the game (if he were defeated, Forza Italia would be dissolved) and to put back in operation on the state television system the monopoly of parties (in practice of the PDS, the DC and PSI having disappeared).

The post-Communists have made the media system a deadly center of power. It gives work, prestige, and image to the conspicuous class of intellectuals and journalists that are traditional electoral "hangers-on" of the left. They continue to be convinced that television is a type of occult persuader, even in politics. What counts, then, is not the quality and credibility of the messages, but the quantity.[58]

In Italy there is no pluralism of information. With RAI, as with Fininvest,

> the great majority of journalists completely ignore what is free and correct information. Rarely on the news (or in the papers) are the facts separate from opinion. Without a doubt Italian TV news shows are examples of biased "advocacy journalism," if not a journalism of propaganda pure and simple. On the basis of the axiom that it is not the arguments which are decisive, but the time from which a political leader can benefit on television, one can explain the victory of the Polo in the elections of 27 March 1994 and the recent referenda, not for political reasons, but because of the number of channels from which these were broadcast.[59]

In reality, this is the alibi used to explain the repeated defeats of the Progressisti. In the course of the electoral campaign the pool of judges opened a judicial inquest into Fininvest, examining its headquarters and files thoroughly and repeatedly. The manager of Publitalia, Marcello Dell'Utri, and other executives were arrested as a result of this investigation. The attorney general, Saverio Borrelli, threatened the administrator of the firm. This would be equivalent to causing it to fail, thereby lowering its market value at the very moment that Rupert Murdoch, Arab emirs, and others were discussing the acquisition of the Berlusconian asset.

The *giustizialismo* of the left uncovered a viscerally illiberal and anti-industrial vein. In the referendum campaign it sought not a chance to define new game rules and valid guarantees for all the players but rather a day of reckoning with its rival. It did not want to defeat it, but to demolish it once and for all, according to an ordeal principle or via pure repression.[60]

In April 1995 a second confrontation after the 27 March elections took place between the Polo and the Progressisti. It was on the local level and involved the election of mayors and presidents of the regions and provinces. It was the first time that the Polo participated in elections of this type, and, given the charismatic, centralist character of its leadership, it was not even minimally prepared. The left won in nine regions, capturing the absolute majority in none. It won the deep South (Puglie, Molise, Campania, Calabria, Abruzzo, Lazio) and the far North. However, these successes did not change the situation. Italy proved itself to be a nation divided, with two political lineups which are too equal and therefore too weak to express a majority.

The geographic distribution of the vote for the right has suddenly radically changed, and it will have notable political effects. The "northern wind" (anti-Stalinist, laissez-faire, federalist) has yielded to the "southern wind," which traditionally blows in favor of continuity. The southernization of the electoral consensus for the Polo means, first of all, the revival of the old Christian Democratic political class. But this phenomenon of putting the old elites back into circulation also involves the Progressisti. The mayoral and regional presidential candidates "gave an image of center-left, like a coalition fallen back on the past regime, like a sort of concentrate of the First Republic, in which the old enemies—Christian Democrats and Communists—supported each other in the face of the arrival of the barbarians" (that is, the right).[61]

Berlusconi has persisted in not resolving the dangerous conflict of interest between his role of entrepreneur and that of political leader of the rival lineup:

> Berlusconi's economic power was not a simple opportunity to contribute to the attainment of political power too. It was the determining cause of it. We do not find ourselves in front of a casual combination of economic power and politcal power. We find ourselves in front of the intentional and . . . well-calculated transformation of an economic power which . . . is itself fundamental in a democracy of the masses for winning political power.[62]

Few have asked themselves if referendum democracy is not merely a way of leaving things as they were—that is, a big show of gattopardismo.[63] Berlusconi, who won the referenda of 11 June, used them as a variation on his telecratic—that is, plebiscitary—conception of a true "dictatorship of the majority." The direct appeal to the people, through television, above and against the parties and the elective assemblies, is the Berlusconian form of *giustizialismo.*

Both of the two conceptions of giustizialismo are alien to the government presided over by Lamberto Dini, one of the top directors of Banca d'Italia. The former minister of the treasury in the Berlusconi cabinet is supported by the ex-Communists, the Lega, and other center-left forces. The Polo does not oppose him. Unlike his predecessors, Dini recognizes Italy's position: a nation with a peripheral economy strongly integrated into and dependent upon the international structure, especially Germany and the United States. A brilliant economist has described it as follows:

> In Italy there is an industrial structure completely inclined toward flexibility and short-term performance—strongly decentralized light industry, involvement of the work force, at the expense of business, with subcontracts and undersupplying. Heavy industry, when there is such, is entrusted to the state, which can risk the taxpayers' money during slumps. Ten years of a not easy-going politics of change could not but reinforce these tendencies, which have existed perhaps since time immemorial.[64]

Since the beginning of 1995, Dini and his experts have managed a phase of transition and slackening of the very harsh open political battle, with the glaring exit of the Lega from the majority after the dismissals of the Berlusconi government. He gives the pleasant sensation of being a premier who does not move on the basis of principle alone, unlike Berlusconi and all the premiers of the First Republic, according to whom Italy was at the center of the world. It is not now and never has been.

In order to win, Berlusconi's antagonist, Prodi, must be able to count on an alliance of the extreme left (such as the Communist Rifondazione) and the center (the Lega). But the Rifondazione, which has a classic Social Democratic party program, is a direct competitor of the PDS; they operate in the same social area. And the Lega is like Craxi's PSI—that is, a classic coalition party but less reliable. Like the fascists toward Mussolini, the Leghisti are not consenting victims of the social interests of their electorate of southern, antimonopolistic, and federalist small and mid-sized businesses.[65]

Between Bossi and his electors there is a Fuhrer-prinzip psychosis: total identification with the leader, who is forgiven his comings and goings from left to right to center, his operetta-like extremism, his worship of the ethnic principle, and his neopagan ideology of territory, language, and blood—that is, ancestry. It is true that Bossi is less extremist in his language.[66] But, if the transition of Italy toward a new politico-constitutional regime endures, Bossi will become a danger. His irresponsibility renders him a subversive. Only the political elections to be held in the fall of 1995 will give us an exact measure of this minority-rendered-majority by a mistaken postelectoral calculation by Berlusconi.[67]

As Italian political life continues to be dominated by the spirits of the past, the postfascists of Gianfranco Fini, and the post-Communists of Massimo D'Alema,[68] it is not clear what type of democracy Italy is destined for. Now the regime of the parties and the party government has been overturned but substituted with nothing.[69] Perhaps, as someone suggested, the Italians are only the fruit of an "invention of tradition" and that "there are none now, and there never were any."[70]

NOTES

I am grateful to the Ministero degli Affari Esteri, MURST, and CNR, which generously provided financial assistance toward the publication of this book.

1. Saverio Vertone, ed., *La cultura degli italiani* (Bologna: Il Mulino, 1994), p. 93; Silvio Lanaro, *L'Italia nuova* (Turin: Einaudi, 1988).

2. L. Ornaghi and V. E. Parsi, *La virtù dei migliori* (Bologna: Il Mulino, 1994), p. 63. Recently the diversity was analyzed in a positive light by Robert Putnam, *Making Democracy Work: Civic Traditions in Modern Italy* (Princeton: Princeton University Press, 1993).

3. Ernesto Galli della Loggia, "Capitalismo senza legge," *Corriere della sera,* 13 August 1993, p. 1; replies by Mario Pirani, "Il Ghino di Tacco della nostra economia," *La Repubblica,* 24 August 1993, p. 1, and Massimo Riva, "Le mani sporche del capitalismo italiano," *Micromega,* no. 1, 1994, pp. 78–85.

4. Giulio Sapelli, *Cleptocrazia* (Milan: Feltrinelli, 1994), and L. Barca and S. Trento, eds., *L'economia della corruzione* (Bari: Laterza, 1994).

5. Alberto Papuzzi, "Piccoli capitalisti crescono," *La Stampa,* 12 April 1994.

6. Cited by Eugenio Scalfari, "Il colpo di spugna su Mani Pulite," *La Repubblica,* 30 October 1994, p. 14.

7. *Ibid.*

8. Mauro Barberis, "La cultura giuridica degli italiani," *Il Mulino*, no. 4, 1992; now in Vertone, pp. 106–7.

9. Ornaghi and Parsi, p. 70.

10. Sergio Romano, "La crisi italiana: Traghetto senza pilota," *Rivista dei libri*, January 1994, p. 4.

11. See the interview by Marcello Veneziani, "Ho nostalgia di Palazzo Chigi," *L'Italia settimanale*, 26 October 1994, pp. 10–11.

12. See also the broader analysis in *Se cessiamo di essere una nazione* (Bologna: Il Mulino, 1993); the monograph of the magazine of geopolitics, *Limes*, dedicated to the theme "A che serve l'Italia: Perchè siamo una nazione" (1994); *Nazione e nazionalità in Italia*, ed. Giovanni Spadolini (Bari: Laterza, 1994); and the special issue (edited by Renzo De Felice) of the historical journal *Storia contemporanea*, no. 6, 1994, dedicated to the idea of a nation in the postwar Italian political parties.

13. See the rigorously documented studies of the expert Bolognese school: G. Freddi, *Tensione e conflitto nella magistratura* (Bari: Laterza, 1978); Francesca Zannotti, *La magistratura, un gruppo di pressione istituzionale* (Padua: Cedam, 1989); Carlo Guarnieri, *Magistratura e politica in Italia* (Bologna: Il Mulino, 1992); in addition, the numerous articles published by Giuseppe Di Federico in *Rivista trimestrale di diritto e procedura civile, Giustizia penale, Arel informazioni*, and *Quaderni costituzionali* (among others).

14. See among the many analyses by Italo Mereu: "Ma l'importante è riscoprire l' 'habeas corpus'," *Il Sole—24 Ore*, 20 July 1994; "Ritorna il vecchio metodo dell'Inquisizione," *Il Sole—24 Ore*, 8 September 1994, p. 18; "Al potere solo per concorso," *Il Sole—24 Ore*, 8 October 1994, p. 6. Of great balance, Giovanni Bognetti, "Magistrati senza politica" and "I rischi del corpo separato," in *Il Sole—24 Ore*, 21 and 22 July 1994, p. 6, respectively.

15. Gianni Baget Bozzo, "Nelle mani dei giudici-consoli," *Panorama*, 21 October 1994, p. 51.

16. See Donatella Della Porta, *Lo scambio occulto: Crisi e corruzione politica in Italia* (Bologna: Il Mulino, 1992; introduction by Alessandro Pizzorno) for the description (at apparently only the local level) and conceptualization of the phenomenology of corruption. The issue is subsequently developed by A. Pizzorno, *Le radici della politica assoluta ed altri saggi* (Milan: Feltrinelli, 1994). For a historic-descriptive character map and a broad reflection concerning political science, see Franco Cazzola: *Della corruzione: Fisiologia e patologia di un sistema politico* (Bologna: Il Mulino, 1988), and *Nodi e frammenti: Le radici lontane della crisi italiana* (Messina: Rubbettino, 1994); Sergio Turone, *Corrotti e corruttori: Dalla unità d'Italia alla P2* (Bari: Laterza, 1984).

17. See data in A. Mastropaolo: *Saggio sul professionismo politico* (Milan: Angeli, 1984), and *Il ceto politico: Teoria e pratiche* (Rome: Nuova Italia Scientifica, 1993), and Gianfranco Miglio, *Una repubblica migliore per gli italiani* (Milan: Giuffrè, 1990).

18. Paolo Sylos Labini, "Adamo Smith e l'etica," in *L'economia della corruzione,* ed. L. Barca and S. Trento (Bari: Laterza, 1993), p. 164.

19. See G. Amato, "Questione morale e sistema elettorale," *La Repubblica,* 16 December 1980, and Giorgio Ruffolo, "La questione morale come questione morale," *Micromega,* no. 3, 1987, pp. 9–10.

20. A. Lijphart, *Democrazie contemporanee* (Bologna: Il Mulino, 1988); Giuseppe Maranini, *Storia del potere in Italia 1848–1967* (Florence: Vallecchi, 1967); and Ernesto Bettinelli, *All'origine della democrazia dei partiti* (Milan: Edizioni di Comunità, 1982).

21. Domenico Zanichelli, "Introduzione storica allo studio del sistema politico italiano," in *Studi di storia costituzionale e politica del Risorgimento italiano* (Bologna: Zanichelli, 1900), and Francesco Bonini, "Problemi di storia costituzionale," *Rivista di storia contemporanea,* no. 2, 1987.

22. Virgilio Mura, "Il trasformismo: Fenomeno specifico o costante storica del sistema politico italiano?," *Teoria politica,* no. 1, 1987, and Giovanni Sabbatucci, "La soluzione trasformista," *Il Mulino,* no. 2, 1990, pp. 171–96.

23. See Luciano Cafagna, *La grande slavina* (Venice: Marsilio, 1993).

24. See Massimo L. Salvadori, *Storia d'Italia e crisi di regime* (Bologna: Il Mulino, 1994), p. 21; and E. Galli della Loggia, "Le radici storiche di una crisi," *Il Mulino,* no. 2, 1994, p. 229.

25. Among the many works, see Emilio Gentile, *La via italiana al totalitarismo: Il partito e lo stato nel regime fascista* (Florence: Nuova Italia Scientifica, 1995).

26. Sergio Romano, "Perchè gli italiani si disprezzano," *Limes,* no. 4, 1994, pp. 162–63. On the permanence of anticapitalism (and of antiliberalism) in the programs of the Movimento Sociale Italiano, see Salvatore Sechi, "Da Salò alla Repubblica presidenziale," *Mondo operaio,* no. 7, 1986, pp. 56–64.

27. This phenomenon was studied by Giuseppe Di Palma, *Sopravvivere senza governare* (Bologna: Il Mulino, 1978); Alberto Predieri, ed., *Il parlamento nel sistema politico italiano* (Milan: Comunità, 1975). For the most recent data, Adalberto Falletta, "PDS: l'opposizione-ombra," *Il Giornale,* 25 March 1994, p. 4, pointed out the results of a study (of which neither the title nor the editor was indicated) by the radical party representative Giuseppe Calderisi.

28. Norberto Bobbio, "La sinistra fa paura all'Italia," *La Stampa,* 30 March 1994, and the debate in the journal *Reset.*

29. Adrian Lyttelton, "Italy: The Triumph of TV," *New York Review of Books,* 11 August 1994, pp. 25–29.

30. See the editorial "I riflessi del PDS," *Il Sole—24 Ore,* 26 October 1994, p. 6.

31. Gianfranco Pasquino, "Ripartire dalla riforma dello Stato," *L'Unità,* 3 April 1994.

32. Mario Pirani, "La nuova Italia che ama il Cavaliere," *La Repubblica,* 1 October 1994.

33. Alberto Leiss, "Alleanze alla prova delle cifre," *L'Unità*, 1 May 1994.

34. Gad Lerner, "Chi ostacola una nuova sinistra," *La Stampa*, 20 April 1994.

35. Arturo Gismondi, "Lacrime amare nei salotti," *Il Giornale*, 5 April 1994.

36. Carlo Castellano, "La sinistra e i ceti medi," *La Repubblica*, 5 May 1994.

37. See the detailed analysis by Alberto Asor Rosa, *Storia d'Italia: Dall'Unità ad oggi* (Turin: Einaudi, 1975), pp. 1439–64.

38. See the statistics on how much it costs small businesses in "Banche dure coi Brambilla" and the comment "Brambilla chiede credito," *Il Sole—24 Ore*, 14 April 1994.

39. A. Pollio Salimbeni, "La destra vi porta fuori dall'Europa"; interview of Tana De Zulueta (Rome correspondent for *The Economist*), *L'Unità*, 10 March 1994; R. Armeni, "È in arrivo il liberismo feroce"; interview of Mario Deaglio, *L'Unità*, 29 April 1994.

40. Augusto Manzolini, "Berlusconi, guerra a Mani Pulite. Attacchi alla Confindustria: Gente incapace," *La Stampa*, 11 March 1994. The newspapers and friends of the industrial group of Carlo De Benedetti presented the middle classes siding with Berlusconi as not very productive, speculators, for the most part merchants. See Eugenio Scalfari, "Meditazioni sul tramonto della borghesia," *Micromega*, no. 4, 1994, pp. 23–32; Pirani, p. 1; Riva; and the numerous articles in *Micromega* by Paolo Flores d'Arcais, in which he paints Berlusconi and his electors as the Siamese twins of Craxism.

41. Mario Deaglio, "Capitalista contro capitalisti," *La Stampa*, 11 March 1994.

42. Alberto Statera, "Silvio e gli industriali: Così vicini, così lontani," *La Stampa*, 11 March 1994.

43. Marco Panara, "L'industria plaude: La 'sua' finanziaria," *La Repubblica*, 29 September 1994, and Roberto Roscani, "L'azzardo di Berlusconi: Dal piano bar alla post-politica," *L'Unità*, 29 April 1994, p. 4.

44. Cited in Roberto Seghetti, "Scossa all'Abete," *Panorama*, 4 June 1994.

45. See Piero Ostellino, "La Lega e le due borghesie," *Corriere della sera*, 26 April 1994.

46. Cited by Filippo Cavazzuti, "Più Peron che Thatcher," *Reset*, no. 8, 1994, pp. 19–20.

47. See the editorial "Così cresce la destra europea," *Il Sole—24 Ore*, 11 October 1994, and the opinion of the syndicalist Bruno Manghi, "Spiacevole ma chiaro," *Micromega*, no. 2, 1994, p. 131, according to which a consistent proportion of Italians rewarded the novelty of a rather modern right. The philosopher Gianni Vattimo confessed that Berlusconi "generally persuaded me about almost everything" (*ibid.*, p. 38). See the recent synthesis by R. Chiarini, *Destra italiana* (Venice: Marsilio, 1995).

48. Interview of Federico Orlando, "Interessi privati nel governo," *La Voce*, 16 October 1994.

49. Angelo Panebianco, *Modelli di partito* (Bologna: Il Mulino, 1982); Giovanni Sartori, *Teoria dei partiti e caso italiano* (Milan: Sugarco, 1982).

50. Angelo Panebianco, "Addio vecchi partiti," *Corriere della sera,* 26 June 1994.

51. See the important reconstruction by Marcello Fedele, *Democrazia referendaria* (Rome: Donzelli, 1994).

52. See Giuliano Amato, "Tre principi contro l'urlio," *Panorama,* 21 October 1994, p. 35, and Norberto Bobbio, "Separazione come arte liberale," *La Stampa,* 10 February 1994, p. 1.

53. See the editorial by the director Paolo Mieli, "Silvio, il braccio e la trincea," *Corriere della sera,* 6 November 1994, p. 1. An appeal in the same direction, analogous to that cited by Giuliano Amato, was launched the day before by the speaker of the government and minister of relations with parliament, Giuliano Ferrara, "Caro Silvio, con le regole vinci," *Il Sole—24 Ore,* 5 November 1994.

54. The following tackle these different aspects: Marcello Veneziani, *La rivoluzione conservatrice* (Milan: Sugarco, 1994); Ernesto Galli della Loggia in *Intervista sulla destra,* ed. Lucio Caracciolo (Bari: Laterza, 1994); Piero Ignazi in his articles in *Il Sole—24 Ore*; the monograph *Destre* of the post-Communist journal *Democrazia e diritto,* no. 1, 1994, p. 482, with contributors like Roberto Chiarini, Dino Cofrancesco, Franco Ferraresi, Domenico Settembrini, Marco Tarchi, and Giovanni Tassani.

55. Sabino Cassese, *Maggioranza e minoranza* (Milan: Garzanti, 1995).

56. See Giorgio Rebuffa, *La Costituzione impossibile* (Bologna: Il Mulino, 1995), and the studies of Giuglielmo Negri.

57. See Fedele and also A. Chimenti, *Storia del referendum* (Bari: Laterza, 1993).

58. Wolfgang Achtner, "Cattive notizie sulla televisione," *Il Mulino,* no. 1, 1995, p. 122.

59. Angelo Panebianco, "Lezione a sinistra," *Corriere della sera,* 13 June 1995.

60. Ezio Mauro, "La coincidenza," *La Stampa,* 11 June 1995, and Ernesto Galli della Loggia, "I referendum senza equita," *Corriere della sera,* 31 May 1995.

61. Luigi Bobbio, "Il vento del Nord non soffia per loro," *Reset,* no. 17, May 1995, p. 32.

62. Norberto Bobbio: "Un confine tra politica e potere TV," *La Stampa,* 21 May 1995, and "La lezione dei dodici referendum," *La Stampa,* 13 June 1995.

63. Filippo Ceccarelli, "Ma quei voti popolari a che cosa sono serviti?," *La Stampa,* 12 June 1995.

64. Marcello De Cecco, "L'impossibilità di essere normali"; insert in "Affari e Finanza," *La Repubblica,* 5 June 1995.

65. See Ilio Diamanti, *La Lega* (Rome: Donzelli, 1993), and Arturo Parisi, "Leghe leghisti legami," *Polis,* no. 2, 1992.

66. See the interview by Giuliano Amato and Alberto Statera, "Sinistra, pentiti per vincere," *La Stampa,* 17 June 1995.

67. See Gianni Baget Bozzo, "La Lega non è di destra nè di sinistra ma è fedele solo a Bossi," *Il Giornale,* 14 June 1995.

68. Enzo Bettiza, "Destra in cerca di bussola," *La Stampa,* no. 278, 1994.

69. The following studies are dedicated to reflections on these themes, with a comparative perspective of experiences and the political science literature of other Western countries: Mauro Calise, *Dopo la partitocrazia: L'Italia tra modelli e realtà* (Turin: Einaudi, 1994); Sergio Fabbrini, *Quale democrazia: L'Italia e gli altri* (Bari: Laterza, 1994); Salvatore Vassallo, *Il governo di partito in Italia* (Bologna: Il Mulino, 1994).

70. Dino Messina, "Norberto Bobbio: Siamo sicuri che ci siano gli italiani?," *Corriere della sera,* 20 May 1994; Piero Ottone, *L'Italia è un paese civile?* (Milan: Mondadori, 1995).

Old and New Problems

TOWARD THE SECOND REPUBLIC? THE ITALIAN PARLIAMENTARY ELECTION OF MARCH 1994

Giacomo Sani

History will tell whether the recent Italian parliamentary election marked a transition between the First and Second Republics. It is clear, in any event, that the 27 March contest had a number of novel elements. It was held under vastly new rules; it saw the emergence of new actors at the elite level; it stimulated new behaviors on the part of voters. These three factors combined produced a verdict with far-reaching implications for the configuration of the party system and significant consequences for the political system. Though the change was drastic—dramatic for some of the old protagonists and exhilarating for the new ones—the outcome was not totally unexpected. Signs of an impending storm had been quite evident since the early 1990s.

The purpose of this contribution is to explore these dimensions of change. It starts with a brief description of the contrast between the pattern of electoral stability in previous decades and the cycle of instability that began in 1990. It then moves on to a brief review of the new electoral system introduced in 1993. This is followed by a description of the salient features of the campaign and an analysis of the verdict in terms of both votes and seats.

THE PATTERN OF STABILITY: 1946–87

For some forty years (1946–87), the Italian party system and the Italian electorate were characterized by remarkable stability. Though their strength varied somewhat from year to year, the parties which had emerged in the early postwar period managed to retain their shares of popular consensus through decades characterized by massive social change. Three political groups—the Christian Democrats (DC), the Communist Party (PCI), and the Socialist Party (PSI)—cornered large shares of the electoral market contest after contest. A spate of smaller political groups—ranging from the far right (Movimento Sociale Italiano—MSI) through the center (PLI, PRI, PSDI) to the left (PDUP, DP)—contributed to create a fragmented multiparty configuration which remained basically stable through the years. As I have shown elsewhere, the structured nature of the electoral market had several components:

(a) The persistence through time of the major social cleavages;
(b) A stable alignment between organized social groups and political parties;
(c) High levels of party identification and/or importance of subcultural voting (*voto di appartenenza*);
(d) A shared definition of the space of competition; and
(e) The transmission of political orientation across generational lines by various agencies of socialization and a modest impact of the turnover of the electorate on the distribution of the vote.

Over the years, the picture changed, but only gradually. Party strength from election to election varied by only modest amounts—generally one or two percentage points, often a fraction of a point. Resounding victories like those of the DC in 1948 and the PCI in 1976 were rare events. There were occasional splits and mergers of political groups; some small parties appeared on the scene while others disappeared, yet these developments did not alter the basic configuration of the party system. Volatility rates increased occasionally but remained basically in the low range; voters' shifts from one party to another generally benefited or penalized groups within the same political family. Modest and gradual variations in the territorial distribution of the vote occurred, but at the end of the 1980s the electoral map of Italy still showed a remarkable similarity to that of the 1950s.

THE ELECTORAL CYCLE OF THE EARLY 1990s

The picture changed considerably in the early 1990s, when four interrelated developments took place. First, some of the traditional parties underwent a process of transformation. In 1990 the PCI began a metamorphosis which eventually led to the formation of two groups: a larger, more moderate majority regrouped as the Democratic Party of the Left (Partito Democratico della Sinistra—PDS), while the more radical minority faction formed a group called Rifondazione Comunista (RC). The DC, heavily involved in the massive scandals that came to light in 1992–93, split into the Partito Popolare Italiano (PPI) and the Centro Cristiano Democratico (CCD). Some traditional groups also tainted by scandals literally disintegrated (Social Democrats and Liberals) or were on the verge of disappearing (Socialists and Republicans).

Second, the configuration of the party system was altered by the emergence of new protagonists. In 1990 some regionally based political groups—particularly the Lega Lombarda and the Liga Veneta, which until then had been minor actors, came to play a significant role in Italian politics. Another circumstance was the birth in 1992 of a movement led by former Christian Democrat Mario Segni (Il Patto). But the greatest change was the appearance in late 1993 of Forza Italia, the political movement built by and around media tycoon Silvio Berlusconi.

Third, these changes at the elite level were accompanied by unprecedented shifts in behavior at the mass level. Rates of electoral volatility increased slowly at first and then more and more rapidly in the contests of 1990 (nationwide regional elections), 1992 (parliamentary elections), and 1993 (municipal elections in a number of major cities).

Last, the rules of the electoral game, which had remained basically unchanged for half a century, were drastically changed. The series of reforms began in 1991 with a referendum on preference voting. It continued in 1993 with the adoption of a new system for the election of mayors and city councils and a referendum on the electoral law for the Senate. It culminated in the reform of the electoral system for both chambers which was approved in the summer of 1993. (The major events that constitute the cycle of the early 1990s are listed in chronological order in Table 1.)

Table 1

Major Events in Italian Electoral Cycle, 1990–93

1990

Returns of regional elections held nationwide record major advances of Lega Lombarda and other regional groups in the northern areas.

June: The referendum of preferential voting shows that the electorate favors change in the rules of the game.

1992

April: Parliamentary elections are held and Lega Nord scores a major victory in all northern regions. Support for governing parties declines. Fragmentation increases.

November: Local elections show continuing growth of Lega in a number of communities.

1993

March: Parliament approves a new law for the election of communal and provincial councils which provides for the direct election of mayors in two-round contests.

April: Passage of a referendum on the electoral law for the Senate modifies the old system and opens the door for the election of three-fourths of the 315 senators in single-member plurality districts.

June: Municipal elections are held in a number of communities on the basis of the new law approved in March. Major victories are scored by the Lega in several communities, including Milan. Leftist coalitions prevail in Turin and Catania.

August: Parliament approves new rules, according to which 75 percent of the seats of both houses will be assigned in single-member districts on the basis of plurality. The remaining seats will be awarded on the basis of proportional representation.

November: Municipal elections are held in several communities, including major cities. Candidates backed by the left are elected in Rome, Naples, Venice, Genoa, and Trieste. Lega Nord candidates prevail in smaller communities of the North. Old centrist parties are in disarray or on the brink of extinction.

December: Parliament approves the new electoral districts and passes legislation regulating the conduct of campaigns, spots, polls, and expenditures.

THE NEW RULES

To understand how political groups approached the campaign it is necessary to describe briefly the new electoral system approved in the summer of 1993. Though inspired by the same principle (a mixture of plurality and proportional representation), the electoral laws for the House and Senate differ noticeably in their mechanics. Thus they must be considered separately.

ELECTORAL LAW FOR THE SENATE

The 315 senators are elected on a regional basis. The number of seats assigned to each region is based on its population, but there are some exceptions to the demographic criterion. The Italian constitution prescribes that Val d'Aosta should have one seat, Molise two seats, and none of the other regions may have fewer than seven seats. The territory of each region is divided into a number of single-member districts equal to three-fourths of the total seats assigned to the region. This is the "plurality quota." The remainder of the seats is to be awarded on the basis of proportional representation (PR). Population data and senatorial seats subdivided into "plurality seats" (totaling 232) and "PR seats" (totaling 83) are displayed in Table 2.

Candidacies for the districts of a region can be presented by political groups using a common symbol and denomination or by single individuals who run as independents. Voters express their preference through the use of a single paper ballot, which contains the names of the candidates running in each of the districts. Each name is accompanied by a symbol. The procedure for awarding seats to the winners is as follows. In each single-member district the seat is awarded to the candidate that has obtained the highest number of valid votes. The rest of the seats are awarded to the competing groups on the basis of the votes received by their candidates (in the districts in which they have not won the seat) using the D'Hondt method. Once the number of seats attributed to each party has been established, its candidates are ranked in terms of the proportion of valid votes received in their districts. The seats won by a party are then awarded to the candidates receiving the highest proportion of votes in their district. Independent candidates do not participate in this second phase.

Table 2

Data Regulating Election to Senate

Region	Population	Total Seats	Districts	PR Quota
Val d'Aosta	115,938	1	1	- -
Piemonte	4,302,565	23	17	6
Lombardia	8,856,074	47	35	12
Trentino	890,360	7	6	1
Veneto	4,380,797	23	17	6
Friuli V.G.	1,197,666	7	5	2
Liguria	1,676,282	9	6	3
Emilia R.	3,909,512	21	15	6
Toscana	3,529,946	19	14	5
Umbria	811,831	7	5	2
Marche	1,429,205	8	6	2
Lazio	5,140,371	28	21	7
Abruzzi	1,249,054	7	5	2
Molise	330,900	2	2	- -
Campania	5,630,280	30	22	8
Puglia	4,031,885	22	16	6
Basilicata	610,528	7	5	2
Calabria	2,070,203	11	8	3
Sicilia	4,966,386	27	20	7
Sardegna	1,648,248	9	6	3
Total	56,778,031	315.	232	83

ELECTORAL LAW FOR THE CHAMBER OF DEPUTIES (HOUSE)

For elections to the House the peninsula is divided into twenty-six constituencies (*circoscrizioni*). In several cases the constituency corresponds to the territory of a region, while in others it corresponds to parts of a region. In no case, however, does the constituency cross over regional borders.

The law attributes to each constituency a number of seats proportional to its population. Each constituency is divided into a number of districts (*collegi*). The number of districts is equal to three-fourths of the total number of seats assigned to each constituency. This is the "plurality quota"; the rest of the seats are awarded on the basis of proportional representation. Population data and House seats, subdivided into plurality seats (475) and PR seats (155), are shown in Table 3.

Table 3

Data Regulating Election to Chamber of Deputies (House)

Constituency	Population	Total Seats	Districts	PR Quota
1. Piemonte-1	2,236,765	25	19	6
2. Piemonte-2	2,065,800	23	17	6
3. Lombardia-1	3,738,865	41	31	10
4. Lombardia-2	3,744,866	42	32	10
5. Lombardia-3	1,372,523	15	11	4
6. Trent.A.A.	890,360	10	8	2
7. Veneto-1	2,604,622	29	22	7
8. Veneto-2	1,776,175	20	15	5
9. Friuli V.G.	1,197,666	13	10	3
10. Liguria	1,676,282	19	14	5
11. Emilia R.	3,909,512	43	32	11
12. Toscana	3,529,946	39	29	10
13. Umbria	811,831	9	7	2
14. Marche	1,429,205	16	12	4
15. Lazio-1	3,761,067	42	32	10
16. Lazio-2	1,379,304	15	11	4
17. Abruzzi	1,249,054	14	11	3
18. Molise	330,900	4	3	1
19. Campania-1	3,016,026	33	25	8
20. Campania-2	2,614,254	29	22	7
21. Puglia	4,031,885	45	34	11
22. Basilicata	610,528	7	5	2
23. Calabria	2,070,203	23	17	6
24. Sicilia-1	2,405,921	27	20	7
25. Sicilia-2	2,560,465	28	21	7
26. Sardegna	1,648,248	18	14	4
Subtotal	56,662,093	629	474	155
27. Val d'Aosta	115,938	1	1	--
Total	56,778,031	630	475	155

There are two kinds of candidacies: individual district candidacies and constituency-wide lists of candidates. Candidates running in a district must declare their link (*collegamento*) with one or more of the lists of candidates presented by parties in the constituency. The name of a district candidate can also appear on a constituency-wide list (in up to three constituencies). Voters express their preferences using two separate ballots. The first contains the names of the candidates running in each district. The second contains a short list (up to four names) of constituency-wide candidates. The procedure for awarding the seats to the winners is as follows. In each single-member district the seat is awarded to the candidate who has obtained the highest number of valid votes. The remaining seats are awarded to the constituency lists on the basis of proportional representation. Two conditions apply. First, only the political groups which have received at least 4 percent of the votes at the national level are admitted to the distribution of these seats. Second, only part of the votes received by political groups is used to determine the number of seats awarded to them. The procedure is fairly complex, and it involves the calculation of a quotient at the national level.

THE LINEUP AND THE CAMPAIGN

At the beginning of 1994, the new institutional machinery for holding elections was ready. All that was needed was a formal dissolution of parliament by the President of the Republic. This came after a short debate on 16 January, and the election date was set for 27–28 March. Party symbols were to be presented by 21 February, and candidacies, supported by the required number of signatures, were due by 24 February. The formal beginning of the campaign was set for 25 February.

After the dissolution of parliament, there were a number of contacts and negotiations among parties for the formation of electoral alliances and the choice of candidates. In the process, tensions surfaced among prospective allies as well as within parties. At issue were the number of candidates that each group would secure for itself and the assignment of safe or at least promising districts. At several points in this process it seemed as if an alliance in the making was about to collapse. When the deadline expired, the lineup of political groups running for the two chambers was as indicated in Table 4.

Table 4

Electoral Alliances in Single-Member Districts

Left (Progessisti)

Partito Democratico della Sinistra (PDS)
Partito della Rifondazione Comunista (RC)
Verdi
La Rete
Partito Socialista
Cristiano Sociali

Center

Partito Popolare Italiano (PPI)
Patto Segni

Right

A. Polo della Libertà
- Forza Italia
- Lega Nord
- Centro Cristiano Democratico (CCD)
- Unione di Centro

B. Polo del Buon Governo
- Forza Italia
- Alleanza Nazionale (AN)
- Centro Cristiano Democratico (CCD)
- Unione di Centro

In the House and Senate races for the seats to be awarded in the single-member districts three major blocs emerged. The first included candidates representing several groups of the left running in practically all 475 districts under the common label of Progressisti. Within this bloc the largest group of candidates were from the PDS, followed at a distance by RC, but other minor parties (Greens [Verdi],

La Rete, Cristiano Sociali, and Socialists) were represented as well. The second bloc, the center, was made up of politicians drawn from the Partito Popolare Italiano and Patto Segni. In addition to former DC personnel, candidates of the center included some moderates from the center-left. A candidate of the center was present in 461 districts. The third, the rightist bloc, was made up of two separate alliances: one between Forza Italia and Lega Nord, which presented its candidates in 278 districts of the northern regions under the label of Polo della Libertà, and one between Forza Italia and Alleanza Nazionale, with candidates in 188 districts in the central and southern regions with the denomination of Polo del Buon Governo. Since Alleanza Nazionale also ran its own people in 280 districts, mostly in the northern areas, the map of rightist candidacies resembled more a patchwork than a homogeneous cartel. This effect was compounded by the presence on the ballot of a number of independent candidates, generally local personalities without party backing.

In the competition for the House seats to be awarded on the basis of proportional representation the various political groups attempted to present separate constituency lists of candidates. However, not all of them succeeded in collecting the necessary number of signatures required by law. After the deadline passed, it turned out that only four groups had lists in all twenty-six constituencies (PDS, PPI, AN, PS), while Forza Italia was present in twenty-five and Rifondazione in twenty-four. The territorial coverage of smaller groups was spottier.

If the separate list strategy made sense for the parties likely to stay well above the 4 percent threshold level, it was a risky decision for the smaller political groups, particularly for those that did not manage to be present in all constituencies. Poor organization, personal rivalries, and unrealistic expectations as to the likely level of popular support led several of these groups to make what turned out to be a disastrous choice.

New legislation for the conduct of the campaign had been passed shortly before the election (December 1993), and it caused a certain amount of confusion. The new elements included a ceiling on campaign expenditures by individual candidates and groups, as well as limits on campaign donations and procedures for the collection of funds. The law also set down detailed rules concerning candidates' use of the media, appearances on radio and television programs, and "equal time" opportunities. Perhaps the most significant innovation was the prohibition of campaign advertising in the press and through radio and television "spots." Public opinion polls were regulated as well, and the publication of survey results was prohibited during the last fifteen days of the campaign.

The regulations were supposed to be in effect during the thirty days of the official campaign, but there is no way to determine to what extent they were applied. It is clear, however, that in the period preceeding the start of the campaign there was a heavy use of television by some political groups. From late January to late February, Forza Italia launched a massive wave of political commercials featuring Berlusconi through the three channels controlled by Fininvest. Use of the media, particularly of television, became a campaign issue. The left accused the Berlusconi camp of unfair practices and biased news coverage. The right responded by arguing that the programs of the three channels of RAI-TV, the public network, leaned heavily to the left. The center complained that its candidates were not given adequate coverage in the programs of either network.

To study the flow of political communication several observation points for the campaign were set up at academic institutions: the University of Rome, the Catholic University and the Institute of Modern Languages of Milan, the University of Perugia, and the University of Pavia. The project set up at the last institution covered the broadcasts of the seven most important television channels transmitting nationwide. All broadcasts containing materials pertinent to the contest were covered and classified. The project had a dual purpose. The first was to record materials for future studies of political communication. The second was more immediate: to feed back into the campaign the results of the study so that the public would be able to have some information as to the impartiality of the media.

A full report on the results of the project will be published in the next few months. The preliminary findings indicate that all channels devoted considerable time to the campaign, both during regular newscasts and in special programs such as debates and talk shows. Overall, it appears that leaders and candidates of the center were given less exposure than those of the other two electoral blocs. RAI programs were somewhat more balanced than those of Fininvest, though among the three private channels there were significant differences in terms of exposure, treatment given to candidates, and slant. The bias was particularly visible in the case of one news program whose editor and anchorman openly declared his sympathy for Forza Italia and behaved accordingly.

Throughout the period but prior to the prohibition deadline, voting intentions were explored by public opinion polls conducted by various institutes. Though the samples and the interviewing techniques varied somewhat from study to study, most surveys showed convergent results. In the early polls prior to the announcement of candidacies, the parties of the left appeared to be slightly ahead of the right, with the center running third and well behind. Judging from the data released periodically by the CIRM institute, by early February the right had overtaken the left as the leading bloc (Figure 1). It seems likely that the swing reflected the entry into the arena of Berlusconi, who announced his intention of running on 26 January. In the following weeks, voting intentions for the three blocs remained fairly stable. However, the data showed that within the rightist bloc Forza Italia was gradually gaining ground, while its ally in the northern areas suffered a slight decline (Figure 2). Polls taken after mid-March and not published at the time but released later show that little apparently changed during the last two weeks of the campaign. Indeed, the 10 March data anticipated the actual results quite closely.

THE ELECTORATE: TURNOVER AND PARTICIPATION

In Italy voting age requirements are eighteen years for elections to the House and twenty-five for the Senate. Electoral registration procedures are automatic. The names of people who turn eighteen years of age in the interval between two elections are transferred from the population registry of the community in which they have legal residence to the electoral registry. Voting certificates are issued and delivered by local administrative bodies. Undelivered certificates can be picked up by citizens even on election day.

Since the previous parliamentary election (1992), the number of Italians included in the electoral registry has increased from 47.4 to 48.2 million (the latter figure includes some 42 million citizens entitled to vote for the Senate). The net growth (0.8 million) reflects the

Figure 1

Voting Intentions, 1994

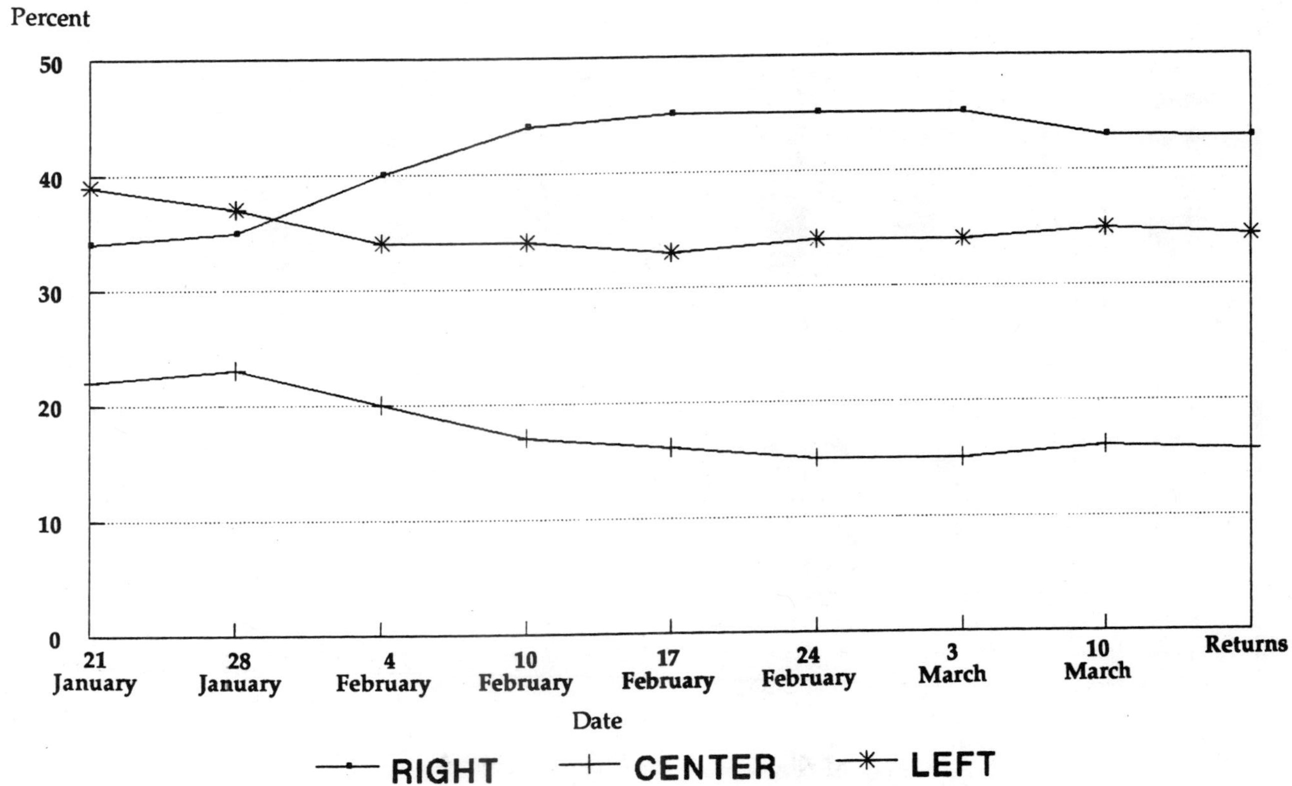

Source: CIRM.

Figure 2

Voting Intentions for Lega Nord and Forza Italia, 1994

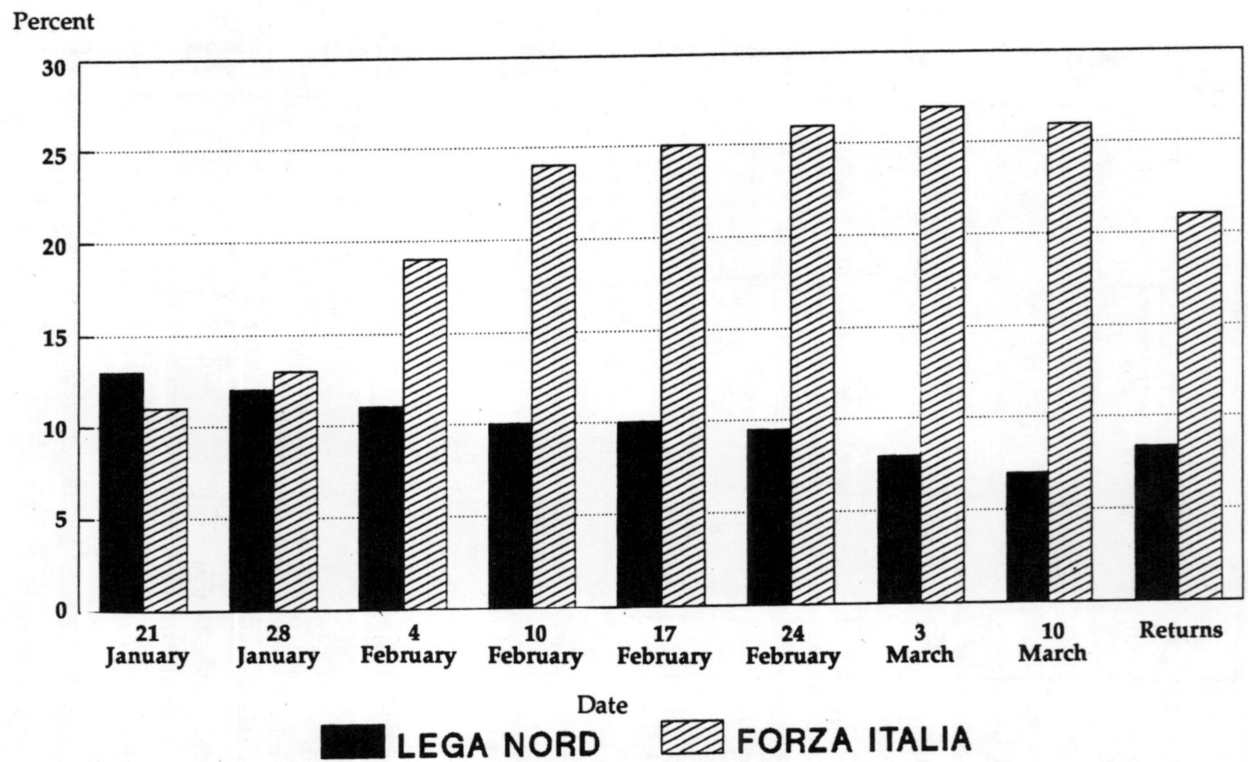

Source: CIRM.

entry into the electoral arena of 1.7 million people who had reached voting age since 1992 and the deletion from the registry (due mostly to death) of approximately 0.9 million. Thus in the short interval between the two elections turnover involved a total of 2.6 million individuals.

For a variety of technical reasons—registration procedures, home delivery of voting certificates, polling stations set up in hospitals, discounts on transportation, extended period of voting, formal administrative penalties for nonvoters—turnout rates in Italy have been consistently high throughout the postwar period. High participation was also likely because of the existence in the law and in the political culture of the nation of the idea that the act of voting is both a right and a civic duty. These favorable conditions notwithstanding, from the mid-1970s on participation rates began to decline and the number of invalid and blank ballots increased. By 1992, approximately 17 percent of the registered voters either stayed home or failed to cast a valid ballot.

In 1994 two contradictory forces affected turnout. On the one hand, voting hours were extended to cover Sunday, 27 March, and all of Monday, 29 March. This was done to accommodate the Jewish community, which did not want the election to coincide with the celebration of a holiday (Jewish Easter). On the other hand, the electoral reform passed in 1993 redefined the act of voting as a right and eliminated the mild penalties associated with nonvoting.

Initially the monitoring of turnout at the end of the first day indicated that there might be a sharp drop in the rate of participation. However, when the polling stations closed on 28 March, turnout was only marginally lower than it had been in 1992. Over 86 percent of the citizenry cast a ballot for the House and 85.5 percent for the Senate. Compared with 1992, valid votes dropped by about 3 percentage points to a new low of 80.1 percent (Figure 3).

As in preceeding elections, turnout was heavier in the northern and central regions. Piedmont, Lombardy, Veneto, and Emilia had participation rates above 90 percent. In Sicily and other regions of the South turnout was some 20 percentage points lower. The stability is demonstrated at a lower level of aggregation (the 475 districts) by a sizable coefficient of linear correlation between turnout rates in 1992 and 1994 (0.97). In the general turmoil of 1994, participation represented an element of continuity.

Figure 3

Voter Turnout Rates, 1948–94

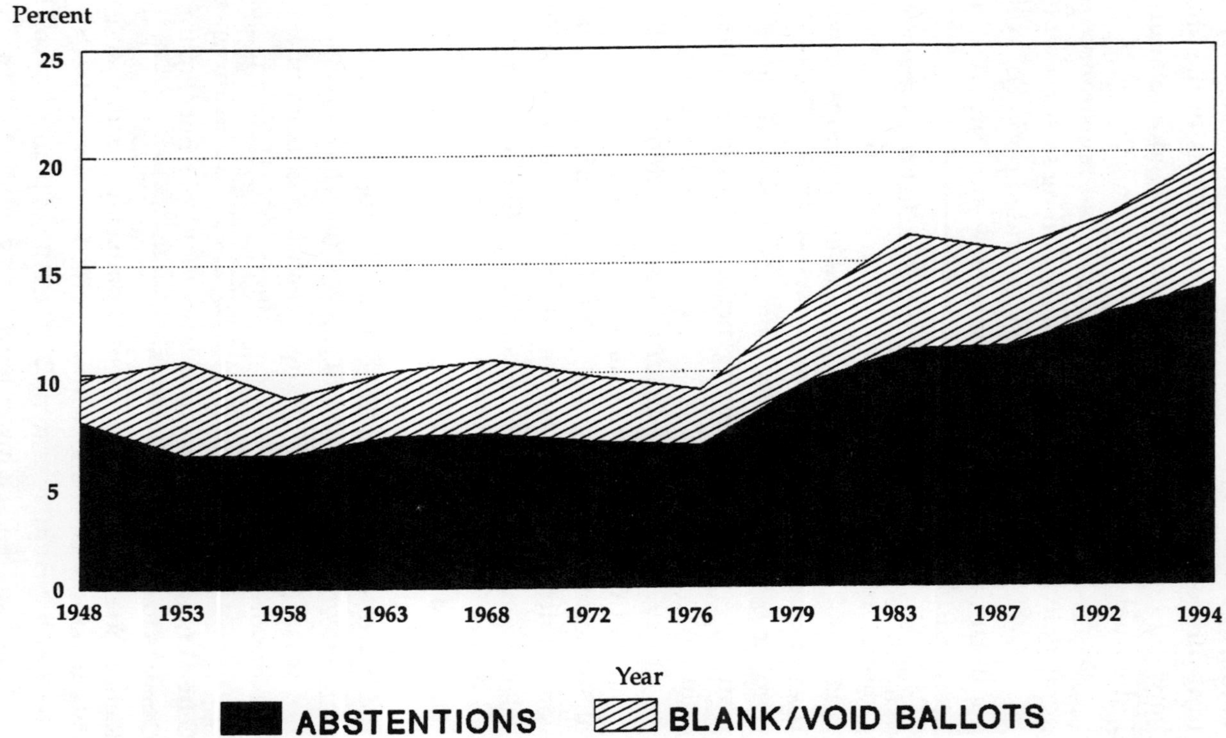

THE VERDICT: THE PROPORTIONAL REPRESENTATION QUOTA

Exit polls were conducted during the two voting days and were released immediately after the closing of the voting stations. The results suggested that the two alliances of the center-right would score a resounding victory. The prediction was fully confirmed by the vote count and even more by the projection of the number of seats obtained by the various competitors. Although the strength of political groups in parliament is obviously the more significant aspect of the verdict, it is useful to start from an analysis of the shares of the vote cast for the PR quota of seats. The data and the comments that follow refer mostly to the election for the House.

As Table 5 shows, the votes for the three major partners of the right outnumbered those received by the progressive alliance by a considerable margin. The center came in third, well behind the two major formations. The returns for the two chambers differed somewhat: the margin of victory for the right was smaller in the race for the Senate (7.2 percent) than in that for the House (8.5 percent). This is not too surprising considering the different composition of the two electorates and the presence of a number of independent candidacies in the contest for the upper house. But the difference had some significant political implications, as we shall see below.

Table 5

Results of 27 March Election

	House[a]		Senate	
	Votes	Percent	Votes	Percent
Left	13,244,673	34.4%	10,999,404	33.2%
Center	6,046,210	15.7	5,518,615	16.7
Right	16,561,657	42.9	13,345,134	40.4
Others	2,723,937	7.0	3,215,246	9.7
Total	38,594,477	100	33,078,399	100

[a]Vote cast in the constituencies for the proportional representation quota.

The verdict left no doubt as to who had won, and the three leaders of the alliance (Berlusconi, Fini, and Bossi), had good reason to celebrate. However, it was immediately clear that some of the partners in the winning camp had more reason to be satisfied than others. Forza Italia, with 21 percent of the vote, emerged as the strongest of the three, a remarkable feat considering that the movement had been born only a few months before the election. Never in Italian electoral history had a new political group managed to surge suddenly to such a high level of consensus. Quite remarkable also was the performance of Alleanza Nazionale—13.5 percent of the votes cast—considering that its backbone, the MSI, only two years earlier had barely been above the 5 percent level. Secretary Fini could rejoice in the fact that the growing strength of this movement, signaled in the municipal elections held in 1993, had been confirmed by the returns of the parliamentary elections. As to the third partner, Lega Nord, there was little reason to celebrate since it had posted a minor loss (from 8.6 to 8.4 percent). But Bossi could point out that in a difficult campaign Lega Nord had held its own, and indeed it had managed through a shrewd deal to reap a considerable reward in terms of seats.

Though the left and the center were both defeated, the two outcomes were rather different. The center literally collapsed. The legitimate heir of the old DC (the PPI) lost two-thirds of its electoral base; the movement led by Mario Segni (Patto) barely made it above the 4 percent threshold; the other smaller groups of the center—Social Democrats, Liberals, and Republicans—were wiped out. The disaster is highlighted by a comparison with the preceeding parliamentary election (Table 6). In less than two years, the center declined from 40 to 16 percent of the vote. If one includes the fate suffered by the Socialist Party, the picture for the old governing forces looks even gloomier.

The defeat of the left was rather bitter in light of the expectations that had been built up in some quarters. The returns showed clearly that the Progressisti were unable to attract more than one-third of the electorate and thus had no credible claim to being a governing majority. Judged by other criteria, the performance of the left was not that bad. The PDS increased its share by 4 points, and RC and the other minor partners held on to what they had had two years before. In previous contests this would have been interpreted

Table 6

Parliamentary Votes by Party Coalition, 1992 and 1994
(Percent)

Party Coalition	1992	1994
Right		
MSI	5.6%	13.5%
Lega Nord	8.6	8.4
Forza Italia	- -	21.0
Total	14.2	42.9
Center-Left		
PSI	13.6	2.2
PSDI	2.7	- -
PRI	4.4	- -
DC	29.7	15.7
PLI	2.8	- -
Total	53.3	17.9
Left		
PDS	16.1	20.4
RC	5.6	6.0
Verdi	2.8	2.7
La Rete	1.9	1.9
Total	26.4	31.0

as a significant victory. In 1994, after the illusion created by the returns of municipal elections in the big cities, it was a sound defeat. Yet those very figures provide evidence of continuing strength on the part of the leftist groups.

Analysis of the returns at the constituency level provides some further evidence on the nature of the popular verdict. The two major groups of the left (PDS and RC) have broadened their support bases in all areas, with some noticeable advances in the South, and continue to be the dominant force in the traditional "Red Belt" of Emilia, Tuscany, and Umbria. However, they remain quite weak in the old industrial areas of the North. The distribution of strength for the two partners of the center is fairly flat, perhaps with the exception of Sardinia (home of Patto leader Segni). The losses, measured against the benchmark of the DC vote in 1992, have been staggering. In most areas more than half of the support base of the DC is gone. Alleanza Nazionale posted gains nationwide. It increased its thin base of support in the North. It reached higher levels in the areas of the Center and of the South in which it was already relatively stronger. In Latium and Apulia it captured one-fourth of the vote, an unthinkable goal only a few years ago. Forza Italia did well in all constituencies, particularly at the two extremes of the peninsula. It had the largest share of the market in twelve constituencies, and it ran second (mostly by a few points) in nine others. Finally, the performance of the Lega Nord was mixed—stable in comparison with the previous parliamentary election but far below the level of expectations that had been built by the victories obtained in municipal elections throughout 1993. Its basis of support remains limited to the northern areas, particularly upper Lombardy and Veneto.

THE VERDICT: THE RACES IN SINGLE-MEMBER DISTRICTS

The returns for the PR quota are a good starting point because they provide evidence about the strength of the various political groups in the country. However, from the political point of view the most important races were those fought in the single-member districts (475 for the House and 232 for the Senate). With three-fourths of the seats at stake in either chamber, this was clearly the most important battleground. Moreover, the district races were one of the novel aspects of the election, and it is interesting to see how parties and voters reacted to it.

Our analysis, which is limited to the contests for the seats in the House, can be summarized as follows. In most districts the number of candidates was fairly limited (on average, 4.5 candidates per district). Only in about 10 percent of the cases was the race limited to two or three persons. Relatively infrequent also were the districts with more than five candidates. All together 2,146 men and women competed, a much smaller figure than in earlier elections and not a very large number considering that three electoral blocs were running nationwide and that Alleanza Nazionale ran independently in the northern areas. One factor keeping the number of candidates reasonably low had to do with the difficulties encountered by some groups in securing the necessary signatures to put up their candidates.

The mean margin of victory of the winner over the runner-up candidate was about 18 percentage points (slightly more for the candidates of the right, slightly less for those of the left), but the figure hides a considerable amount of variation. In one-third of the districts the winner received a sizable majority—well above 50 percent—while in others victory was secured by a relatively narrow gap over the runner-up. In 10 percent of the districts the winner made it by less than 3 percentage points, and in 15 percent of the districts by less than 5 percentage points.

Three major patterns of competition can be identified in the data. The most common is the "one candidate dominant pattern," a situation characterized by the clear prevalence of one candidate over all his opponents. This occurred in over half of the districts, where the winner defeated his opponent by at least 15 percentage points and often by more. A second configuration of competition was the "two-way close race." Here the winning candidate had only one serious competitor and eventually won by less than 5 percentage points (53 districts) or by less than 10 points (134 cases). In a handful of cases a third pattern was evident which would be called a "three-way close race." In these districts the race turned out to be a very close contest among three or even four candidates, and eventually the winner won by less than 5 percent (17 cases) or by less then 10 percent (13 cases). Situations of this sort were rare, and they occurred only in those districts where for one reason or another one of the electoral blocs running nationwide failed to reach agreement on common candidates.

Looking at the party labels of the competitors, we find that in a large number of cases the contest involved a candidate of the right and a candidate of the left. Centrists and other candidates generally came in third or fourth. Overall, the two cartels of the right scored a major victory. By pooling their forces, the two alternate sets of partners easily overcame the competition in many districts. The common candidates of Forza Italia and Lega Nord swept most of the northern districts. In Lombardy, Veneto, and Friuli Venezia Giulia they gained almost every single district. The alliance between Forza Italia and Alleanza Nazionale had a good showing in the rest of the country. As expected, candidates sponsored by the Progressisti did quite well in the old Red Belt regions, practically eliminating the opposition. But they were no match for the Forza Italia–Lega Nord candidates in the North. In other races the left did well only in districts in which the right failed to coalesce. The center was penalized by the flat configuration of its vote. In district after district, centrist candidates received only a few percentage points more (or less) than the national average; as a consequence they came in third in most districts and posed a creditable challenge in only a few others. In the end, they won only four seats.

SHIFTS IN VOTING CHOICE

Even a cursory glance at the returns is enough to establish that unprecedented and massive voting shifts occurred in 1994. Forza Italia alone, an alternative not present in 1992, attracted over 8 million votes. A significant number of other citizens shifted away from prior choices and expressed their preference for Alleanza Nazionale. Thus the question: where did the votes that contributed to the victory of the right come from?

Prior to the election, the hypothesis generally shared by observers was that the collapse of the old centrist bloc would benefit the electoral alliance of the right rather than the progressive front. Survey data collected at the beginning of the campaign on past voting behavior and voting intentions in March suggested that this was indeed the case. Using data of this type collected by the SWG institute in mid-March, I presented some estimates on the likely flows of votes from 1992 to 1994. As Table 7 shows, the predictions for 1994 are very close to the actual outcome of the election. Also, the values of the internal cells of the table coincide to a large extent with data derived from exit polls carried out during the election. In brief, the story was this: as the parties of the old center (DC, PSI, PSDI, PRI, PLI) disintegrated, a massive transfer of votes took place. It mostly benefited the right. In other words, it was the inability of the leftist coalition to attract these "voters on the move" that decided the contest of 1994.

Table 7

Projected Vote Transfers from 1992 to 1994
(Percent)

Vote in 1992	Left	Center	Right	Others	Total
PDS	16.1%				16.1%
Rifondazione Comunista	5.6				5.6
La Rete	2.8				2.8
Verdi	1.9				1.9
PSI	3.1	2.0%	7.8%	0.7%	13.6
PRI/PSDI/PLI	2.0	3.3	3.7	0.9	9.9
DC	1.5	13.2	14.5	0.5	29.7
Lega Nord			8.7		8.7
MSI			5.4		5.4
Others	0.5		2.0	3.8	6.3
Total 1994	33.5	18.5	42.1	5.9	100.0

In spite of the unprecedented rate of change, some continuities in electoral behavior are apparent in the data, particularly with respect to the votes cast for the left in the upper half of the peninsula. As Figure 4 shows, the geographical structure of the support bases of the parties that formed the progressive front has changed little since 1992. Indeed the scatterplot of the vote percentages received in the north-central regions by the parties of this bloc in 1992 and 1994 has a remarkably linear structure. The same holds, but to a somewhat lesser extent, for the data about the central-southern districts. This geographical asymmetry is in line with previous findings on rates of electoral stability in various areas of the country. In short, the earthquake hit North and South alike, but in the North the phenomenon occurred with a certain degree of orderliness.

FROM VOTES TO SEATS

In previous Italian elections the number of seats obtained by the various political groups could be estimated with great accuracy

Figure 4

Vote for Left in Five Northern Regions, 1992 and 1994

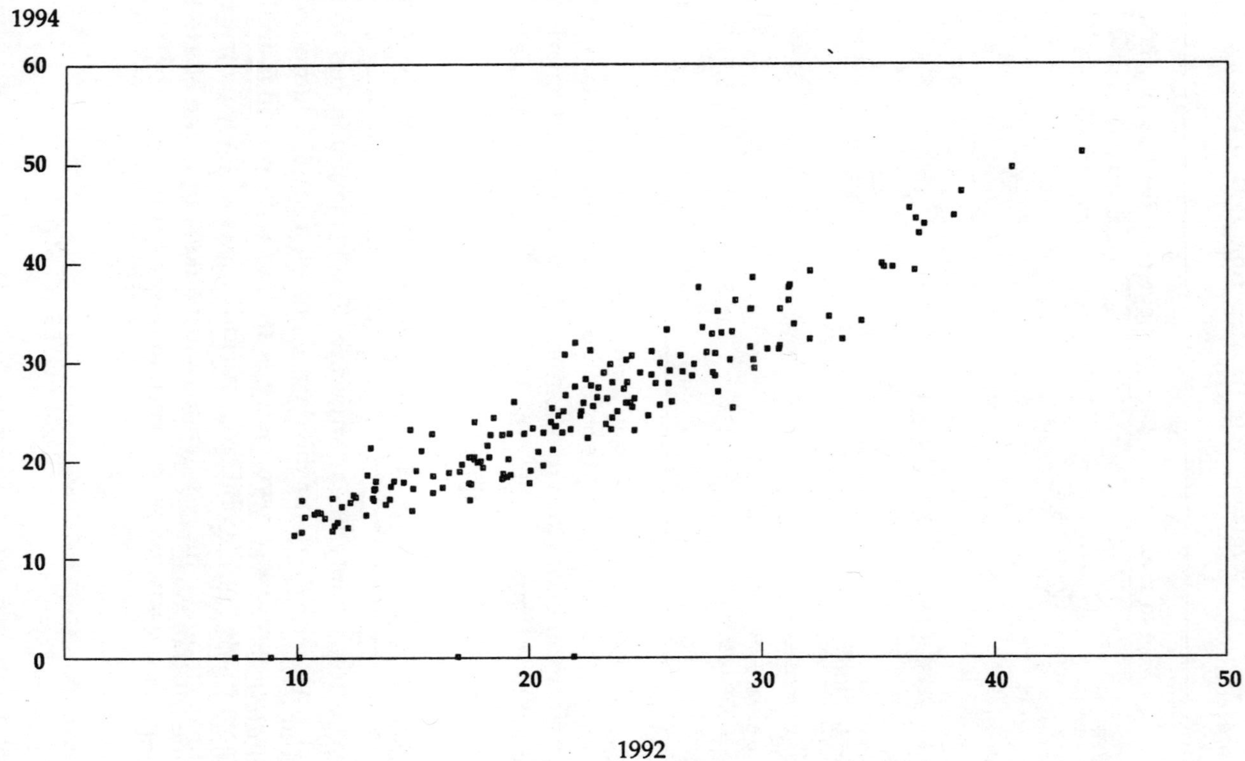

on the basis of the percent of the vote they received. Indeed when we look at the scatterplot of the two variables "percent of vote" and "percent of seats" for the series of elections from 1948 to 1992, we find an almost perfect straight line (Figure 5).

Proportionality had a number of consequences for the strategies of parties and the behavior of voters. Political leaders knew that they could get a few seats in parliament even if they received only a fairly small share of the vote. In some cases they had little incentive to coalesce; in others, they were not discouraged from seceding from larger political groups. For their part, electors knew that they could pick their most preferred party—even a small one—without wasting their votes. The adoption of new rules changed all that. It introduced new constraints—opportunities as well as risks—for both politicians and voters. Thus the ground was set for the emergence of a new type of electoral logic. But to what extent did it take hold? A preliminary analysis of the data, summarized in Table 8, suggests the following answer:

1. The attribution of three-fourths of the seats in single-member districts forced political leaders to seek cooperative strategies that led to the presentation of common candidates in the single-member districts. These, however, were temporary rather than permanent alliances since, once elected, candidates maintained their partisan identities.

2. The existence of a quota of seats to be attributed on the basis of PR encouraged the leaders of all parties to present separate lists of constituency candidates. For small groups this was a risky choice since the failure to reach the 4 percent level would have meant exclusion from the distribution of the PR quota. When the votes were counted, it turned out that several of these groups were indeed excluded.

3. The existence of two separate ballots (one for the district and one for the constituency) would have allowed electors to split their vote. They could have made their choice "strategically" in the district (i.e., for a candidate with a fair chance of winning even if not a preferred choice) and "sincerely" in the constituency (i.e., picking the preferred list). Preliminary findings indicate that ticket splitting was relatively rare. Most electors cast their ballots in a consistent way.

4. As expected, in 1994 the relation between votes and seats was no longer linear as it had been in the past. The outcome dispropor-

Figure 5

Votes and Seats in House, 1948–94

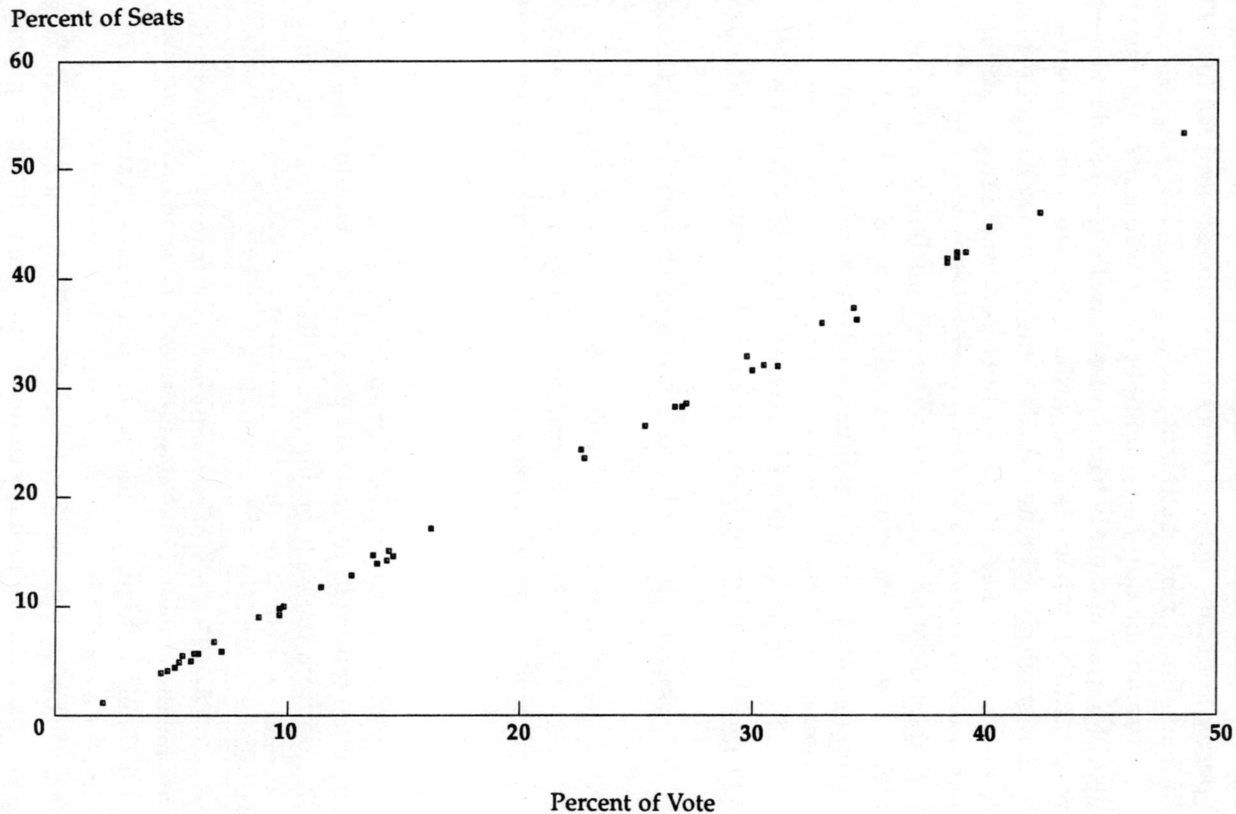

Table 8

Seats Obtained in Single-Member Districts and in Constituencies

Political Group/ Coalition	Single-Member Districts		PR		Total		Percent of Vote
	N	Percent	N	Percent	N	Percent	
House							
Left	164	34.5%	49	31.6%	213	33.8%	34.4%
Center	4	0.8	42	27.1	46	7.3	15.7
Right	302	63.6	64	41.3	366	58.1	42.9
Others	5	1.1			5	0.8	7.0
Total	475	100	155	100	630	100	100
Senate							
Left	96	41.4	26	31.3	122	38.8	33.2
Center	3	1.3	28	33.7	31	9.8	16.7
Right	128	55.2	27	32.5	155	49.2	40.4
Others	5	2.1	2	2.5	7	2.2	9.7
Total	232	100	83	100	315	100	100

tionately rewarded the political groups whose candidates placed at the top in the districts (the right and to a lesser extent the left), and conversely it seriously penalized the losers (the center). The center was handicapped by both the modest share of the vote and its uniform distribution in the various areas of the country.

5. The distribution of seats on the basis of a PR quota somewhat reduced the distortion between votes and seats. The center, punished in the districts, recovered some strength in the constituencies. Conversely, the advantage of the right in the districts was reduced somewhat by the distribution of seats in the constituencies. The different mechanics of the rules for the two houses of parliament concerning the linkage between the single-member districts and PR quota produced two rather different outcomes. The right won a comfortable majority of seats in the House but failed to reach the 50 percent level in the Senate.

VOLATILITY AND FRAGMENTATION

The contest of 1994 set a new record in terms of both the volatility and fragmentation of the vote. In the preceding twenty years, variations in party strength between pairs of consecutive elections had been rather modest. This had occurred in 1976, when the PCI reached its peak. In 1992, the split of the former Communists and the surge of the Lega Nord pushed the index upward. At the time, that seemed quite a change from the past, but as Figure 6 shows, the real electoral earthquake happened in 1994, when the index of volatility more than doubled. The collapse of some of the old protagonists and the emergence of new forces pushed volatility rates to an unprecedented high level.

If an increase in volatility was in the cards, few would have expected a similar trend as far as fragmentation is concerned. Indeed the new electoral system contained elements that were supposed to "recompact" the party system, reducing the number of political groups on the ballots and in parliament. This did not occur; in fact, the index of fragmentation went up another notch or two in 1994 (Figure 7). Critics of the electoral law passed in 1993 can correctly point out that the new system did not do enough to discourage

Figure 6

Volatility Rates, 1972–94

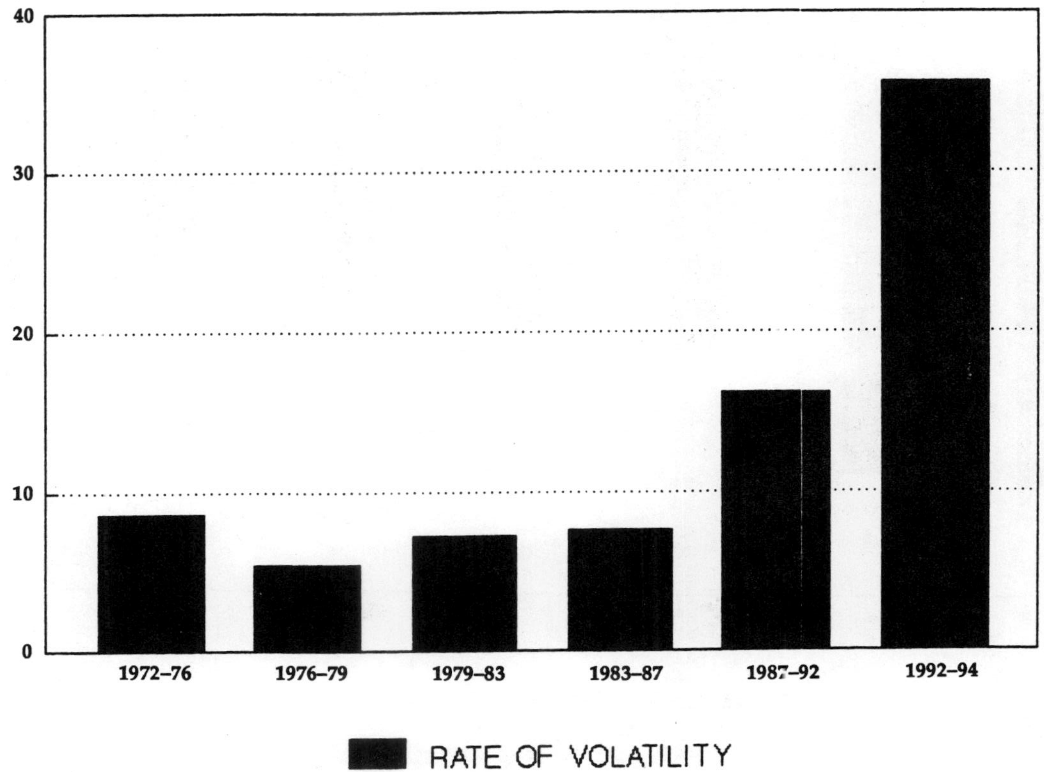

Figure 7

Vote Fragmentation, 1972–94

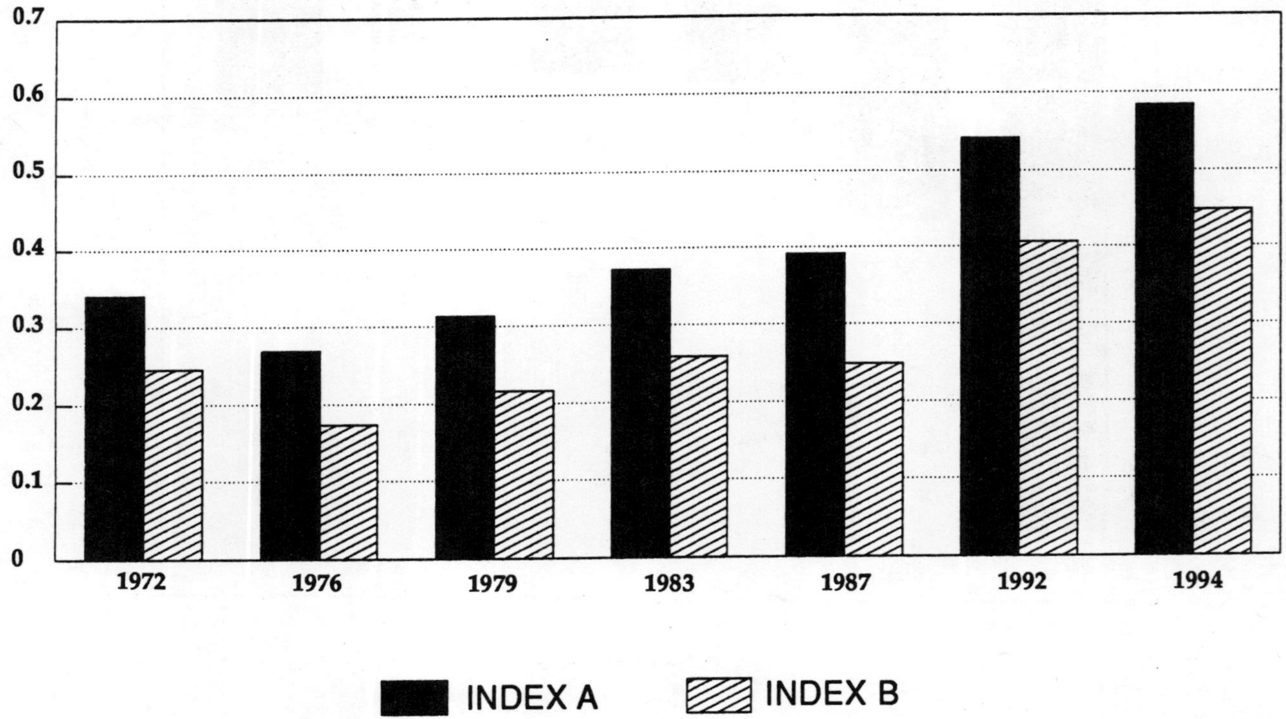

fragmentation. It may also be that, at least in the short run, institutional factors are effective only within the limits imposed by the features of the political culture of a country. For almost half a century, Italians have operated under a proportional representation system, and it was perhaps unrealistic to expect them to suddenly learn majoritarian logic.

CATEGORIES FOR A CRISIS

Alessandro Pizzorno

Great was the goodness of the knights of old!
Here they were rivals, of different faiths,
still, off they went together in mutual trust, through the
dark woods and crooked paths.
—L. Ariosto, *Orlando Furioso*, 1, 22

OVERT POLITICS AND COVERT POLITICS

For decades, anyone who observed the protagonists on the Italian political scene could not have *not* thought that the destiny of the first Italian republic was to be torn apart by a clash among irreconcilable enemy parties. Only now do we realize that all its evils spring from the strange (but as we shall see very explainable) circumstance that those parties for some time—actually almost from the beginning—were not in fact enemies. Rather they were very friendly to each other and quite capable of agreeing without too many hindrances. Even the rather well-constructed analytic models, like those of Sartori, which presented the Italian political system as polarized among extremely ideologically distant parties, fell into the trap of considering the political players as what they said they were and not by what they did. They presented imagined polarization where instead there was consociationalism, haughty antagonism where instead the players were hand in glove—or thereabouts.[1]

One could respond that in the eyes of the population that chooses the political players, when it intends to participate in their activities or to elect its representatives, these players are none other than what they say and appear to be. This is also true, but it is not the only thing that counts; actually at times it counts very little. A simple rule applies in these matters: studying politics always requires distinguishing two levels on which the players act. One level is that of ideological discourse, declarations of principle, propaganda, and various forms of self-presentation. It serves, at least for the players themselves, to identify them and distinguish them from each other in the eyes of those who want to choose and follow them. Therefore, we will call this the level of *overt identifiability*—that is, overt distinguishability. This includes not only discourse, but also demonstrative actions, votes in parliament, and therefore legal choices. More than mere ideology, then, all public political action is included.

Even given all this, it is well known that there is more to political activity. Often it is this "more" that is the most important part. Above all, at least in many cases, it counts more for the players themselves because it is more directly tied to their interests. It deals with the daily activity of political personnel or those tied to them who enter into exchanges, agreements, and various transactions with each other. Favors are offered (which one individual can grant thanks to his position in the system) in exchange for other favors or votes or money for the individual or his group, ward, party, or movement. The nature of these relationships is such that the identity of those who participate in them is not immediately or easily discernible. The majority are relationships that remain largely hidden. The fewer people who know about them, the better. Often they are, for one reason or another, prosecutable by law, even if at times standard political morality takes them for granted. It may be that individuals enter into such relationships only one time, or, if repeatedly, not in their institutional roles. It is as if they unfold in an uncertain and changing light, in which it is difficult to distinguish who is who and at what one is aiming. Only the "initiates" know how to do it well, those who understand the language and signs and recognize in whose name they are truly speaking. We can call this level that of secret or *covert identifiability.* We shall see below how these categories and others that derive from them can illuminate the case of the Italian crisis.

HOW COVERT POLITICAL ACTING DEVELOPED DURING THE FIRST TWO DECADES OF THE REPUBLIC

Covert political acting is not constituted only of illicit activities. Perfectly legitimate forms of covert acting can be beneficial to the collective and made in good faith. One thinks of the paradox of the identifiability of the Italian political players at the liberation from fascism. The ideological distinctions among the six parties which made up the so-called exarch could not be sharper. From right to left they represented the widest ideological spectrum that could have been put together in the postfascist world—the widest spectrum, that is, of possible conceptions of political reconstruction of postwar society. At least their self-representations made it appear so. But if we look instead at what they did and not what they said, the distinctions blur. They were allied in a government—one could say just owing to the battle against fascism. This held them together; they could not have acted differently. It was not only this. There was already a divergence between self-representation and discretionary power—i.e., covert acting—which the Uomo Qualunque movement grasped and from which it briefly reaped its successes—and that would have been represented and developed in the following years of history.

Then the antifascist alliance shattered and two opposing political lineups formed. Could it be said that at least at this point the disparities in representation were beginning to correspond to behavioral reality? There are two possible interpretations. Some say that the two parts were ideologically polarized. One embodied and defended the regime; the other denied its legitimacy. Others think that the opposition of the two parts was limited to reflecting in Italy the opposition of the two dominant global lineups. The two interpretations could seem compatible and directly cumulative. But it is not so.

First, it must be noted that the opposition did not contest the Republican regime, but instead declared great loyalty to the constitution. Someone will argue that this was only propaganda. But in saying so, he will abandon the criterion of distinguishing the players only by what they claimed to be, and the task of demonstrating what their true identity was remains.

We concede that from the declared self-representations, an outside observer, using some contrived measure, could draw the conclusion that there existed much ideological disparity and polarization. It will forever remain to be explained how this could be reconciled with so much happening covertly—that is, in parliamentary commissions and communal councils (officially public environments but which in fact remain in the shadows and are not used by the political players in self-representation), and—still more undercover—the exchanges of illicit favors and the collaborations and connivances necessary to this end. This was the area in which, sheltered from the attention of the electorate—and especially the "true believers" of one ideology or another (or at least their consciences, given that many true believers were participants)—the first consociational micro-pacts were formed. From there Italian society had a hand in governing de facto. It suffices to note that in the 1950s more than 90 percent of the laws issued by parliament were unanimously approved. In the same years the first big scandals involving the appropriation of parasitic incomes with the collaboration of all parties came to light and went practically unpunished (the most relevant example being that of the INGIC).

The two interpretations, therefore, cannot merely be combined. If one chooses the first and imagines Italy polarized by opposing ideologies into two militant camps, the real behavior of the political class would appear abnormal. By definition, ideology prescribes non-negotiable ends to action and cannot allow consociational compromises.[2] It was not for nothing, however, that very much later, when the consociational "way" was overtly chosen, the compromise was called "historic." The unwitting irony of the announcement was twofold. It was said that openly conducting the practices that had before remained covert raised them to the level of history. In fact ideology affirmed that history was only that which developed on the overt level. In addition, it was claimed that the declaration of a historic turning point was necessary to render overt to all an identity that actually continued the preceding identity.

If the second interpretation is chosen, which sees the polarization as derivative of support, though biased, of the global lineups, the consociational behavior begun in these years in areas that did not involve international ties acquires quite a different sense. It acquires the sense of an obligatory action for whoever wanted to make a social system function, somehow or other, for quotidian tasks—a system which (to believe those who fiercely opposed it, some in the West, some in the East) appeared daily at the point of splitting like an amoeba.

In other words, it is thanks to the consociational practices set in motion, in spite of the ideological declaration, that the Italian political system did not go the Greek route of civil war. (It is known that the Greek case was the negative model to which Togliatti continually referred.) The motivation to avoid disruptive conflicts was not all. It could explain some position of the summits of the lineups. The system, nevertheless, could function only if the players at various levels obtained benefits from it. And benefits were not lacking, from the exchanges of favors to the collaboration in initiatives, which would not have succeeded had they been promoted by only one side. Generally, on the part of the government, the interest lay in getting around an impasse which threatened to put it in a bad light in the eyes of the populace, and also an "underground" interest in not winning hands down (through the secular experience of peasant societies one knows that if someone wins hands down, one never knows). For the opposition, the interest was that of not heightening a dispute in which it would have been the loser, and instead using the resources it had—parliamentary obstruction power, local power in broad zones, and the ability to control conflicts—in exchange for recognition of its legitimacy to coexist.[3]

As for gladiatorial acting on an overt level,[4] it could justify itself simply with the interest in flaunting support and loyalty to the international patrons on whom the two Italian lineups depended and then obtaining support from them. But there was more. In defining the parties as bearers of ideological positions, political activity acquired a "high" quality.[5] By this I mean that quality thanks to which political choice is seen as determinant of the ethical positions of the people, the political vocation as ethically superior to other professional vocations, political responsibility as taking precedent over other forms of responsibility, and not choosing politically as a shameful sin. Sin came from such a "high" idea of permanent politics and the prestige of the parties, from such a "high" idea of the exalted. It was then in the interest of these, and then of every single militant and directing politician, to sustain a political culture that depended on such a hierarchy of values. This is not due only or primarily to motivations of prestige and personal reward and recognition, but also to the position of control of the consociational life, first, and then the economic one, as the parties called it.

Consider as illustrations the events associated with the development of interest groups. From the beginning, in the postwar period the interest groups presented themselves with clear politico-ideological labels. The parties were not yet well organized, and the interest groups allied with one or another lineup. With the Western-capitalistic victory assured in our country and any danger of a violent surge of social conflicts wiped out, an autonomous development of interest groups could have been expected. Instead, the opposite happened. The opposition of the political lineups, on the overt level, continued to dress itself again in global ideology, and consequently it remained practically impossible to not cross a party if it wanted to organize some associative activity. Interest groups then had to take sides and subordinate their activity to the strategic needs of this or that lineup. When associative resources—constituted of the capacity of individuals to engage in collective causes, or generally in activities that involve at least temporary sacrifice of individual interests for collective ends—are totally (or almost totally) diverted through political channels, one has in fact a paralysis of pluralism, even if appearances may differ.

Even before being at the origin of corruption of political life, which exploded in the 1980s, covert consociationalism, which put down roots in the 1950s, was blamed for the unsuccessful development of civil society in Italy. It was blamed for the widespread inability of autonomous initiatives in the name of collective causes, the mortification of social, nonpolitical vocations, and (not last) the absence or near absence of political analytical ability conducted according to nonideologized disciplinary canons able to reflect on the parts in conflict, instead of submitting its conclusions to them. It is on this last point that we shall now reflect.

It is true that in the most difficult situation, that of the abduction of Aldo Moro, the high office of the state was reaffirmed politically by representatives of the two cultures. But there were good reasons for both to act as they did. The Communists had to confirm the widest distance from their own terrorist cousins. As for the Christian Democrats, there were probably reasons that are still difficult to plumb today (and that did not present themselves again—for example, at the time of the Cirillo case).

HOW SOCIAL CONFLICTS SERVE TO REINFORCE CONSOCIATIONALISM AMONG THE PARTIES

We indicated above how the two levels of relationships among the political players added to the supremacy of politics, established the premises for the unsuccessful development of autonomous associative initiatives among the members of civil society, and how from this a delay ensued in the process of institutionalization of the conflicts. In fact, in Italy social conflict was used by political parties. If social factions had been able to act autonomously and the conflict had been institutionalized, its political use would have had to cease, and thus the monopoly of associative initiatives on the part of the parties would have fallen.

Instead the political use lasted for quite a while, and the effects were not insignificant. In order to realize how the process developed it is necessary to remember the conditions of social conflict in Italy in the 1950s. The labor market, after having been compromised in the postwar period by political means (the firing freeze) became unfavorable in terms of job openings—that is, for the working classes. On the one hand, within these classes persisted a type of surplus of militancy (residue of the partisan struggle and postwar enthusiasm) that led to struggles that were almost always destined to fail. Added to this there was strong American pressure to expel the Communist representatives in at least some factories. Thus the situation was unbalanced. On the other hand, the opposition enjoyed parliamentary obstruction power, which rendered the passage of a legislative program extremely difficult without some negotiation between the majority and minority. Beyond this it enjoyed a legitimacy in political society derived from its role in the antifascist struggle, on which the legitimacy of the regime as a whole was founded.

Therefore two different strategies were advanced by the opposition. One was to set free the representatives of the social forces in conflict (in effect, the labor unions) and then let market forces determine the outcome of the conflicts. Then, acting as parliamentary opposition, it would aim to become the majority by winning constituents of the center with proposals for realizable programs. In this way it would not give up so much of its own programmatic identity because this was already potentially reformist and not much more. It took the identity of representatives of a new world that was forming in the East, and that, though not well known or defined—or precisely for this reason—spoke to the imagination of many. As for the social conflict, it was wrongly imagined; we will see that the conditions of a hostile labor market would endure, that the claimed weakness of the working classes was inherent to capitalist relationships, and that it could be sustained thanks only to the opposition parties.

Due to faith in the efficacy of identification with that "new world" (as exploitable as it was indefinite) and distrust in altering the relationships of force on the labor market, a different strategy was chosen. The conflict was provoked also where it was known that it was losing contractually, by exploiting the potential of disturbing order. It was transferred to parliament, or other political seats, offering to contain it or extinguish it in exchange for political benefits. These could have been either relative to the same factions in conflict—essentially protection from the use of force on the part of the police and from private punitive measures like dismissals—or dense in benefits for the social ranks to which the constituents of the opposition generally belonged. Or they could have been relative to the political class of the opposition that was part of the negotiations. In the first case, the authority of the state was spent—which, however, had already been inflated in the beginning by the government in order to negotiate its restriction. In the second case, the taxpayers' money was spent and, by spending in deficit, so was the wealth of future generations. In the third case, a hand was given to the tacit collaboration of the political class of the government and the political class of the opposition in being essentially joined in institutions and generally in the consociational disposability of both.

Nevertheless, it can happen that social conflict escapes the hand of whoever controls and uses it, thereby threatening the consociational strategy. The political parties in fact see themselves restricted to supporting one or another social faction. This seemed to happen in Italy precisely when new conflicts emerged in very unforeseen forms—first the industrial conflict of 1962, then the student conflict, followed by a larger resurgence of the industrial conflict in 1968–69. Together the conflicts were presented as principally anticonsociational. The industrial conflict appeared at least in the beginning as anti-union. When the unions reabsorbed it, generalizing and expanding it, the claim of union autonomy from the parties emerged. Due to the truly multigenerational relevance that the student conflict ended up assuming, it can be called "cultural conflict." It moved against goals that are typically an expression of consociationalism and separation of the covert and overt levels in political activity. The "delegation," as it was called in contemporary jargon, became attached, and the deputation proceedings reached an agreement as much as they served to constitute a separate political class. The falsity of the overt identifications that the parties proposed (though not honoring them) and which they used to cover the absence of real distinctions was denounced. New basic identities were favored which were depicted, though vaguely, as reflecting new social divisions.

In these conflicts plausible political projects were not expressed—only obscure cultural intolerances. Time will clear them up. However, they very soon gave rise to the true and proper political divisions that the ideologico-consociational control of civil society had maintained as latent, like those involving divorce and abortion. The distinguishable traits present "in costume" came to be used to force a road between very immobile politicians.

The threat of armed conflict with terrorism was then superimposed on that of social conflicts and removed it. Unfortunately, we are still not in the position to say how much was manipulated by international forces and/or internal forces in armed disputes and attacks. However, we can say with certainty that that which I call the covert level was by then solidly rooted in the Italian political system, intertwining with the secret activities of the state or its organs. Accompanying the activity which was, all things considered, a bit squalid and directed at the control of parasitic income (perhaps not completely separated from it, at least at the high levels) were the operations of subjects whose references remained in illegal international markets more than in the country. The parallels thus drawn between covert activities of the political class and organized crime are striking. For both, in local spheres, the appropriation of income took place through the control of contract allocation and extortion (and for politicians with the equivalent activity—that is, misappropriation). In international spheres it was through participation in drug and arms trafficking. The parallels were probably not determined by the attitudes of the people involved, but by the structure of the clandestine situation that is alike for both organized crime and covert political activities.

Beyond this new and not easily investigable level of power relations, social conflicts plus terrorism created a circumstance which frightened the political class, with the effect, paradoxical only in appearance, of breathing new life into consociationalism. And this was transferred from the covert to the overt level. Strong gladiatorial valence was given to the political elections of 1976. Electoral enthusiasm replaced worker or student enthusiasm. A notable collective mobilization began, thus rekindling the approval of the political class and its functions. The "distinguishability" of the programs of the opposing lineups was less clear than ever—but this mattered little. The conflict had been symbolic and served to demonstrate that political disputes could still happen. The result was that those who were so sharply torn began now to govern together. Great was the goodness of modern politicians!

HOW THE COLLECTION OF FINANCIAL RESOURCES SHAPED THE POLITICAL SYSTEM

It can be said that the road taken by the parties in the Italian postwar and postfascist periods passed from the accumulation of enthusiasm to the accumulation of money. In the beginning the norms of custom were so inspired by the primacy of politics that everything seemed justifiable in the name of a "cause"; in the face of a "cause," speaking of corruption had to be considered petty. In addition, the flow of money to the parties had an almost institutional appearance—a percentage of commercial exchange with Eastern countries for the former, a percentage on the balance sheets of government agencies. The returns, save for individual cases, were of a general sort, coinciding, that is, with the political orientation of a faction. The money, even if collected through legal channels, financed as much as was necessary to "make politics."

Even on this small scale it was necessary that the parties pass from the offices of government—central and local—to society—that is, the offices of those able to control parasitic income. In the beginning placing men of the governing parties at the head of economic units could also have had some justification because from these positions they could have carried out general economic politics in a coordinated manner. But this intent revealed itself early on as illusory and remained only a false aim. The party occupation of society served essentially to enable the flow of income to the parties. It was politics now in the service of collecting money, no longer vice-versa. Therefore, the nature of politics changed.

The electoral fixedness, and in any case the *ad escludendum* rule that impeded the opposition from entering government, rendered still more illusory (at least at the central level) the electoral function of controlling government activity without weakening the dispute on the scene. To this was added a flourishing symbolic activity specific to the pet political style of the intellectual class. Radical—or in any case omnicomprehensive—reforms were made which were much discussed in ideological arguments in terms of probably unrealizable plans. While this offered a certain symbolic fulfillment of the desire for reforms, it made this desire slowly dry up, as the reforms were shelved or realized in ways very different from those which had been discussed. The subjects admitted to the market of parasitic income became increasingly mixed and united in disparate ways, abandoning the original associations made along party lines.

Because of this, reference to a party increasingly lost the sole characteristic of reference from which one draws credit to enter into secret exchanges. Not only did factions, subfactions, and personal alliances begin to fragment single parties, but also associations became transversal, from party to party, and included figures from the worlds of business, publishing, and journalism. Politicians became businessmen investing their political credit and were followed not by party members, but by "meddlers." External associations became important for ensuring credit on such a market. Secret or semi-secret societies were able to utilize their experience in clandestine activities and above all allowed the outlining of credit relationships that were less visible (and therefore more useful) than others. Frequently, in cases in which there existed liaisons with organized crime—as judicial enquiries seem to be revealing—this type of relationship had the advantage of advancing sanctions that were more severe for those who broke the rules of *omertà* (the conspiracy of silence associated with the Mafia).

If everything noted to this point is true, it could be concluded that the term "partyocracy" (*partitocrazia*) is not appropriate for such a system. The term "party" (*partito*), however, is a term of covert political discourse. It remains to be asked how much it was actually used in the language of covert transactions. Certainly it is too indistinct a term for analytical language. There are not many acts easily imputed to the party subject as such. The term partyocracy comes from a season in which the parties acted as collective subjects guided by powerful secretaries, at least in part responsible, if not to the members as such, at least to the elite internal circles formed by members. The secretaries were able to answer for their members, for their parliamentary groups, for their mass associations, and to other subjects of the political system, represented, however, by other parties. The selection of political personnel, and above all the personnel of the "underground government," was made for the most part by the party secretaries, also according to fairly preestablished rules.[6] The term partyocracy was thus able to depict the situation fairly faithfully.

The system I have outlined above is different. The parties can be considered subjects of action only during the election period—that is, when overt political activity dominates. Acting as intermediaries between the covert and overt levels is in fact their most powerful function. Subjects of different types then have access to the overt level. The agreement of some of them with whoever has the power of unitary decision in a party is generally due to the presence of a single player in whom the party temporarily identifies.

I have noted that a condition that must be maintained for a system is that certain external ties are in some way zeroed out or weakened. I will now try to show how this happened in Italy.

HOW CONTROL OF THE ENVIRONMENT WAS REALIZED

We noted above that the degree of discretionary power of a political class in changing, in the pursuit of private interests, the proxy that it receives from the population is in large part a function of its capacity to control the environment in which it works. Without being able to be systematic (because a great deal of knowledge is missing or is imprecise and not assessable), I will limit myself here to examining briefly four aspects of the Italian case that are of particular interest: the expansion of the political class as such, connivances with the bureaucracy, connivances with the business world, and the dispute with the magistracy.

I have repeatedly used the term "political class," taking it for granted that what I intended was clear. Probably for what I had to say, it was sufficiently clear. But some clarifications will be useful at this point. Elected political personnel certainly make up a part of the political class. If elected members of communal, provincial, and regional councils are included, the number of elected political personnel in Italy approaches 160,000—a very high number and a very much higher percentage of the population than in other European countries except France.[7] The importance of this fact can be understood if we think of circumstances in Italy, where municipalities are never consolidated, even when it would seem obvious to do so, and when new things instead can be created of them, and thus new provinces and regions are created. All this serves to increase the number of elected political personnel. The same can be said about district councils. The advantages of increasing the numbers are obvious. The number of people that have a part, or think they have a part, in the exercise of political power is increased. The population base of potential career politicians is enlarged. At the same time, those chosen are given the chance to prove themselves at successive levels of commitment and complexity. The borders of the political market are extended—that is, the borders of the politically and administratively controlled exchanges of favors and benefits—for example, between the political class and the population. The breadth of the potential political market can be assessed in a fairly plausible manner from recent quantitative data. It can be estimated that at least 20–25 million Italians had some personal relationship with an elected politician (using the definition given above).

The breadth of these relationships between the political class and the population is an important element for explaining the stability of a system of covert political activity.[8] The nature of these widespread relationships would suggest also that this is a precarious stability. They are, in fact, for the most part characterized by demands of one of the two parties against promises of the other, with an inevitable low rate of satisfactory return on the promises and a consequent accumulation of delusions and grudges.

Another consequence of this expansion of the market of political factors is the weakening of "decision centers" and the multiplication and prolongation of negotiations every time decisions are necessary. This also means that it is never clear "where the buck stops," as the Americans say. That is, it is unclear at what point someone will take responsibility or someone will pay for making a mistake or refusing to make a decision. Further, two methods of governing can be distinguished here. One specifies levels of responsibility, and there is no way to shift burdens to other levels. The other is one in which the shift from one level to another is always possible and negotiable, in a manner that frequently lays the burdens on the system as a whole, obliging its members to unwittingly be in agreement.

It is clear that the second method, that of transferable and negotiable responsibility, reinforces the acquisition of consensus through favors rather than through the realization of programs. In the Italian situation a typical case that favored the leveling of responsibilities and "pluri-negotiablity" was the loss of financial autonomy of local agencies. The administration lost expenditure responsibility, and the decision-award relationship or electoral penalization was replaced with the web of exchanges with political authorities at other levels.

The control of bureaucracy is generally obtained by politicizing it. In order to limit this politicization as much as necessary, the bureaucracy is divided into two parts; the collusion of one is necessary, and of the other it is less so. This is how the so-called reform of state management (which divided government personnel into managers and staff) was implemented. The shared interest of the two strata was thus ruptured, and any possible esprit de corps internal to an administration was weakened, as was any consequent capacity for overt resistance to the demands of politicians. Instead the possibility of organized relations between political personnel and state management personnel was reinforced.

It was noted above that a constraint on the discretionary power of the political class is formed through access to the decisions of private interest delegations. When such access is very open and institutionalized, collusion becomes more difficult. In Italy, three circumstances above all characterized relations between the business world and political power: the large extension of the public economy and of the direct power of the political class on the economy; family property and scant institutionalization of business structures; and the relation of direct pressure from entrepreneurial class to political power (instead of through the delegation). To all this was then probably added the persistent effects of the original division between Catholic and Masonic finances. Even though the web of these elements was not studied in detail, it can be said that it originally involved the extensive collusion of economic and political power, as has begun to emerge in recent judiciary inquests. The hypothesis is that it was not simply misappropriation (that is, extortion) on the part of those able to collect private money in exchange for public government decisions, but rather that a stratum formed in which public and private power colluded to appropriate both public and private wealth.

HOW THE STATE CAN LAWFULLY BE OPPOSED TO THE PRINCIPLE OF DELEGATION

As noted, if a political class wants to enjoy discretionary power in order to divert government resources for its own ends, it must either have a consenting magistracy or be in the position to neutralize it. Phrased in these terms, the issue risks neglecting the general historic picture within which the relationship between judiciary and representative power developed. While in the formation of Western liberal democracies judiciary power was seen rather as an expression of the old regimes and an obstacle to the passage of complete power to the sovereign people, its position has changed almost everywhere in the last decades, due to both the enlargement of the area of intervention of judiciary power and the progressive and popular aura attributed to it. The reasons for this are all connected to the process of emptying out and fossilization of the representative mechanisms in contemporary liberal democracies. We can summarize, bearing in mind two points discussed above—the reduction of the control of those represented over representatives and the reduction of government program power. To this is added the development of what could be called the capacity for self-delegation. This includes not only delegations organized by the interests which have been present in some measure from the beginning of the construction of representative regimes, but also the expansion of access to the law and consequent substitution of private delegations, in many cases by those who first appealed to the political delegation.[9]

In the Italian case the expansion of power of judges was marked by a very specific constitutional history, in which the autonomy of the magistracy was perfected from the late 1950s to the late 1970s. Further, it was accompanied by a generational renewal and the development of a true ideology of judiciary power, seen as temporary power in a situation in which the opposition was impotent or collusive and representative power was distorted to the ends of private power.[10] This provoked open disputes between the magistracy and the political class which lasted for more than a decade.[11] In the distinction of overt and covert levels proposed above, the magistracy took the position of guardian of the rules of the overt level. The attacks of the political class on the magistracy were to protect personal interests. But they were also the expression of a traditional concept of politics in representative regimes, according to which being elected by the people is the only legitimization (the institution of parliamentary immunity being a typical expression of this conception of legitimacy). Any disruption of delegation power is extremely limiting. The causal sequence that leads to the particular projection of the magistracy in representative democracies would be the following. The impasse of representative power leads to consociational agreements internal to the political class. These agreements render citizen control useless. The development of a level of covert activity is thus generated which in turn justifies the intervention of the magistracy.

HOW POLITICAL STYLE KEPT CHANGING

The political life of a country is not made up solely of decisions, exchanges, use of power, enrichments, and even solidarities and sacrifices. It is also made up of criteria of recognition and reward and judgments of how people conduct themselves in these activities. These criteria accompany and reinforce different modes and styles of practicing politics. Also in the general experience, according to which power must be considered a common criterion for measuring success in political activity, it is possible to discern, in different political styles, different expressions under which success is recognized and rewarded and power enjoyed.

In contemporary political life three principal political styles can be distinguished: ideological, civil, and consumer. To go to the heart of what distinguishes them, the circles from which the politicians aim to attain recognition and reward and the ways in which recognition and reward are expressed must be considered. It can be said that ideological style thirsts for recognition and reward on the part of a community of the faithful—party, movement, church, or sect.

Recognition and reward are bestowed by judging the suitability of a certain conduct or discourse according to ideological dictates. Success frequently has a content more intellectual than specifically political—that is, measurable in institutional power. Those who work in this style aim more toward the mastery of discourse and persuasion than of administration.

Civil style is specific to the politician who aims for recognition and reward reflecting the values of good institutional order. This recognition is sought from the abstract majority of citizens. Being recognized by them is not as much an end in itself as an end of a good process of collaboration in political duties. In this sense, civil style, which can also be called "service style," does not manifest itself only in political activity in the strict sense, but also in tasks of developing inside other institutions and organizations. It consists, in fact, of having as a goal the successful running of a collective enterprise.

Consumer style could be called a closed, self-referential system. The criterion for political success is not in seeking ends dictated by ideology (as in ideological style), nor in service useful to a given collective (as in civil style). Rather this criterion is found simply in the external signs of success itself—those which demonstrate how political power is acquired to permit the appropriation of nonpolitical means of success. While for both ideological style and civil style political success consists of demonstrated capacity to achieve collective ends, for consumer style political success applies solely to the single person.

Since the quest for recognition is characteristic of the ambition for every type of success, who recognizes consumer success? Since in these cases one of the effects of success consists of personal enrichment, it could be observed that it is not necessary to define some specific circle of recognition and reward. Monetary enrichment seems to need simply the recognition of all those who recognize the value of money and are forced to accept it when it is spent. In other words, the circle of recognition here would seem to coincide with the market. In reality, this type of recognition and reward is anonymous and broken up—like the use of money—and it does not permit the construction of the identity of a successful person. (Who will be satisfied with the recognition and rewards of waiters in grand hotels?) It is also necessary that monetarily measurable success have as a referent one or more verifiable circles.

It is useful at this point to introduce the concept of "court." It serves to indicate cases in which the successful politician needs to surround him or herself with a court, a tangible sign that someone appreciates his or her success. The presence of a court is only one of the ways in which such a showy consumer style can be expressed. In a general manner, this can be described as acting on a stage in a continual play in front of some public. The ultimate measure of power seems to be the power of being seen, of becoming the object of mass consumption. This explains the otherwise inexplicable importance that politicians attribute to the media. Narcissism is only an exaggerated example of the general rule for the successful politician: some marginal figures pretend to always be on television in order to complain that television does not dedicate enough time to them. The rule is to appear as frequently as possible in front of the public, not to communicate things, but simply to be seen. Political power manifests itself essentially as "appearance power" because frequently for those in politics appearance is the only remaining mode of recognition and reward.

It can be said that in Italy the ideological style exhausted itself during the 1970s. With the dramatic moments over, room was left for the consumer style. Shrewd investigations would be necessary to ascertain in which out-of-the-way recesses of Italian society the civil style survived temptations and attacks.

NOTES

This is an occasional article and is not furnished with the references that would allow for checking certain assertions I make. Rather I supply a list of people through whom I sought to inform myself on certain phenomena, or from whose works, though not finding a suitable point in which to cite them, I learned a great deal: Marcello De Cecco, Donatella Della Porta, Bruno Calise, Antonio La Spina, Leonardo Morlino, Massimo Morisi, Gianfranco Pasquino, Giulio Sappelli, Alberto Vannucci, and, last but not least, even if unfortunately through conversations which took place when he knew less than what he certainly knows now, Giuliano Amato. In addition, I wish to thank all those who discussed earlier versions of this manuscript at the Meridiana conference in Palermo, May 1993, and the Associazione Italiana di Scienza Politica conference, June 1993, in Pisa.

1. The term "consociationalism" (*consociativismo)* risks misunderstandings that were manifested in journalistic polemics in an earlier version of this text. It is a mode of governing in which party representatives who are presented as irreconcilable reconcile in order to govern together instead of letting a majority rule. This generally occurs when opposing parties distinguish themselves as cultural identities (ethnic, linguistic, religious, and the like) that are in the position of demanding from their members a loyalty superior to that owed the state. At times the opposing identities are of an ideological nature (as in the case of Austria, where the opposition is nevertheless reinforced by the matching clerical/anticlerical distinction, and in the case of Italy). In these cases, letting the majority principle function could lead to a civil war. L. Cafagna, in *La grande slavina,* clearly sees the inherently consociational nature of the Italian political system. But he does not succeed in reconciling it with the polarization that seems present and even decisive to him as well. Thus he makes the mistake of resurrecting the present crisis of polarization. This is paradoxical because polarization leads to breaches and splits, not to corruption and collusion. It leads to raising guns, not raising glasses. It suffices to turn one's mind to the distinction that I discuss between the overtly acting politician and the covertly acting politician.

2. This is the point at which consociationalism by ideology and consociationalism by cultural identity (ethnic, linguistic, religious) diverge. The identities which the latter is prone to render compatible are strong and irreconcilable. There will not be arbitration, contractual or concordant conduct which will affect it to the point of putting its identity at risk. The compromises, then, are not dangerous. This is not so in the case of ideological identities. Exposing them to negotiations and compromises means eroding them and ultimately reabsorbing them into daily objectives. The theory of ideological polarization, then, faces a dilemma. Too many empirical facts prove it wrong, and it denies that there was daily compromise. Alternatively, too many empirical facts prove it wrong, and it considers that it dealt with compromises made according to "ideologies"—which, not for this reason, shortened ideological distances—and so is unable to recognize the distinction between ideological and cultural identity.

3. In interviews conducted after the publication of part of this text I was repeatedly asked if I judged the consociationalism of these years to be good or evil—as if the judgment of an analyst counts. But given that such curiosity seems inevitable, I will simply say that it was good because it put off the threats of civil war, and it was evil because it put in place the foundation for a regime of corruption.

4. By "gladiatorial acting" in politics, I mean conflictual action that is very aggressively expressed and is depicted, so to speak, as "to the death," without the two parties proposing to do very different things—that is, without presenting substantial programmatic differences.

5. "High" and absolute politics are discussed elsewhere in this volume.

6. On this point see Calise and Mannheimer, *I governi misurati.*

7. For this and other information that follows, I refer to the indispensable research directed by Gianfranco Bettin in G. Bettin and A. Magnier, *Chi governa la città* (Padua: CEDAM, 1991), and numerous articles, among which the most important are those appearing in *Polis* 5, 2 (1991) on local administrators in Italy.

8. It is necessary at this point to stress that "covert political activity" does not mean illegal activity, but simply activity that is not included in the criteria of programmatic "recognizability" or distinguishing factors with which political subjects present themselves to the public.

9. On this last point, with reference to the United States but with evident predictive value for other liberal democracies as well, see L. Friedman, *The Republic of Choice: Law, Authority and Culture* (Cambridge: Harvard University Press, 1990). On the expansion of the power of judges in various contemporary juridical systems, see M. Cappelletti, ed., *The Judicial Process in Comparative Perspective* (Oxford: Clarendon Press, 1989). The literature on the draining of delegation power is limited. In Italy this theme was recently treated by D. Zolo, *Il principato democratico* (Feltrinelli, 1991).

10. The most up-to-date and comprehensive text on the recent history of the magistracy in Italy is C. Guarnieri, *Magistratura e politica in Italia* (Il Mulino, 1993). See also my introduction in D. Della Porta, *Lo scambio occulto* (Il Mulino, 1992).

11. Well illustrated in M. DeLuca and F. Giustolisi, "Gli anni ottanta tra giudici e insabbiatori," *Micromega* 2, 93: 101–17. For a good comparison with what happened elsewhere, see "Tangenti in salsa francese," pp. 67–76 in the same issue.

THE POLITICAL ROLE OF THE ITALIAN JUDICIARY

Carlo Guarnieri

The recent waves of arrests and indictments of politicians and civil servants on various charges of corruption and bribery have put the Italian judiciary in the media spotlight, both in Italy and abroad. Of course in any developed country the fight against corruption is one of the main tasks (but not the exclusive one) of the judicial system. In Italy, however, the meaning of the recent cases of political corruption, as well as the dramatic impact of judicial actions on the political system, cannot be fully understood without some knowledge of the institutional setup in which the Italian judiciary operates. In fact, since the end of World War II, the institutional setting of the Italian judiciary has been radically transformed in an attempt to make it as independent as possible from the political environment. As a result, the position of the judiciary in the Italian political system seems to be rather peculiar on many counts. In order to assess the extent of this peculiarity, its origins, and its implications, we must first briefly look at the role of the judiciary in democratic systems and then compare the present institutional setting of the Italian judiciary with those in other democratic countries.

THE JUDICIARY IN DEMOCRATIC REGIMES

The judiciaries of major democratic regimes—England, the United States, France, and Germany—have a number of common features:[1]

1) The process through which judges are recruited is always more or less directly influenced by the political environment. This influence is exercised in different ways. The greatest difference lies

between countries of civil law and common law. In the former, the process is normally run, through some kind of public competition, by the Ministry of Justice, and therefore by officers or magistrates more or less answerable to the executive branch. In the latter, the political branches of government are directly involved in the appointment process. This is the case in England, where the Lord Chancellor plays a prominent role, and in the United States, where appointments at the federal level are made by the president with the advice and consent of the Senate, while in a number of states judges are elected by local voters, often for limited terms of office.

2) Prosecution is entrusted to magistrates or officers directly or indirectly responsible to other governmental bodies, if not to the voters themselves. Existing prosecution systems range from the classic ministerial structure, in either its centralized (France) or federalized (Germany) version, to semi-autonomous governmental organizations (the Crown Prosecution Service in England), to the U.S. federal prosecution system, which is more or less under executive control (Eisenstein 1979), to the direct election of the chief prosecutor, as is the case in many American states. Only in France do prosecutors and judges belong to the same corps, even though French prosecutors are directly responsible to the Minister of Justice. Elsewhere judges and prosecutors belong to separate organizations, although they may under certain conditions cross over from one branch to the other.[2]

In all these countries, despite some significant variations, these institutional traits (among others) act as checks on judicial power—that is, they are institutional means through which the other branches of government—or in some cases the voters themselves—can *indirectly* influence the behavior of judges and the political significance of the judicial system. The influence on the process of recruitment, even when only indirect, assures at least to a certain extent that the values of the individuals who perform judicial functions will not be too out of step with those prevailing in the political system. The position of the prosecuting branch guarantees the passivity of the judicial system—that is, it lacks a self-starter—and allows the political environment to some extent to regulate the demands for action placed upon the judicial system.[3]

The cases analyzed involve systems with different levels of institutional independence, however. In common law countries, judicial guarantees of independence from the political system seem to be stronger. Moreover, in civil law countries judges tend to have less *internal* independence—that is, vis-à-vis other judges. In fact, the organizational setting within which the judges operate is different in these countries. Unlike common law judicial organizations, in the judiciary of civil law countries the following is true (Di Federico 1976; Freddi 1978):

1) Judicial personnel are selected by examinations, which the candidates take at an early age—usually right after university studies—and no consideration is given to the candidates' previous professional nonjudicial experience;
2) The professional training of a judge takes place in large part within the judicial body;
3) Organizational roles are ordered according to a hierarchy. Advancement up the career ladder is competitive, and promotions are granted according to formal criteria combining seniority and merit, merit being assessed with great discretionary judgment by hierarchical superiors.

Generally speaking, in both civil and common law judicial organizations a need is felt for checks designed to ensure that the institutional goals are pursued by their members. Anglo-Saxon judiciaries, which tend to employ individuals trained outside the organization (usually with a lengthy apprenticeship), rely less upon internal controls. On the other hand, in continental Europe, where personnel are recruited without significant professional experience, young judges are placed at the bottom of the pyramid-like structure, and their organizational socialization is constantly monitored through a career based on a hierarchical ladder (Freddi 1978).[4]

THE PECULIARITY OF THE ITALIAN CASE

Traditionally the Italian judiciary has been structurally very similar to other continental European judiciaries; during Unification (1859–70) the influence of Napoleonic models of governmental organization was especially strong. Even later, notwithstanding some minor adjustments, the basic structure did not change very much, at least until the end of World War II. Therefore, the Italian judiciary exemplified the traditional characteristics of the civil law judicial bureaucracies outlined above: applicants for the judiciary were—and still are—selected on the basis of their general institutional knowledge of several branches of the law as tested by written and oral exams and guaranteed by a university degree in law; professional training and experience was—and is—to be acquired inside the judicial organization, starting from the bottom of the pyramid-like hierarchy since candidates for the judiciary were—and are—encouraged to enter the competition soon after graduation; the organizational units of the judiciary, as well as the organizational roles, were ordered according to the principle of hierarchy; promotions to higher positions (there were nine hierarchically ordered ranks) were granted according to traditional criteria, seniority and merit, by hierarchical superiors enjoying substantial discretion, with the government playing an important role in the appointments to higher positions; the approach to work performance and role assignment was—and is—"generalistic," where members of the judiciary were—and are—supposed to be able to perform equally well all organizational roles formally associated with their rank.[5]

Immediately after the war, in 1946, as a reaction to past abuses—occurring to a different degree during both the liberal and fascist regimes—the guarantees of judges and public prosecutors vis-à-vis the executive branch were somewhat reinforced, although the hierarchical character of the judiciary was left untouched. The constitution of 1948 envisaged the institution of a self-governing body of the judiciary—the Higher Council of the Judiciary, composed two-thirds of magistrates elected by their colleagues and one-third of lawyers or law professors elected by parliament, to which all decisions concerning the status of magistrates would be assigned—and also foresaw special guarantees for public prosecutors. Furthermore, the principle of compulsory prosecution of criminal offenses by the public prosecutor was written into the constitution.

At first, the constitutional design for the administration of justice was not implemented. Only after 1959 did things begin to change, leading to a great increase in both internal and external independence of Italian judges. In that year, the Higher Council of the Judiciary was instituted, progressively taking away the powers of the executive in the administration of judicial personnel—i.e., of both judges and public prosecutors. At present, this unit is composed of thirty-three members: three *ex officio* members (the President of the Republic and the president and attorney general of the Court of Cassation); ten elected by parliament (the electoral quorum is such that representation has been assured to parties of the left—i.e., Socialist and Communist); and twenty elected by all the magistrates. Its main function is to make all decisions concerning judicial personnel (recruitment, promotions, transfers, disciplinary sanctions, and so on). Note that even a summary indication of the functions and composition of the Higher Council indicates a breach in the traditional bureaucratic structure of the judiciary, insofar as lower- and middle-ranking magistrates could for the first time participate in decisional processes regarding the distribution of organizational rewards and sanctions, not only with respect to their peers, but also with regard to higher-level magistrates.[6]

A second major modification in the organizational setup of the judiciary concerned the system of promotions. Under pressure from the majority of lower-ranking magistrates, strongly organized in their professional association (Freddi 1978; Guarnieri 1992), parliament passed a series of laws between 1963 and 1973 which dismantled step by step the traditional system of promotions. Those supporting such laws in parliament hoped that

> the changes would, among other things, promote a greater efficiency in the judicial machinery, and meet the growing expectations in society for a "less formalistic" and "more substantive" rendering of justice which would be more attentive to the socio-political implications of the adjudicative function (Di Federico and Guarnieri 1988: 168).

The outcome of this policy has been that candidates having the seniority requirements to compete for promotion at different levels of the judicial hierarchy are no longer evaluated (as they were until the 1960s) on either written/oral exams or their written works, but rather on a "global" assessment of their judicial performance. In fact, as a result of this global assessment, all candidates who fulfill the seniority requirements are promoted to the highest ranks. It is a phenomenon that can be explained by the composition of the Higher Council: its members are elected by the very colleagues they have to evaluate. In sum,

Nowadays the young graduates in law, by simply passing an entrance examination where her or his general scholastic knowledge of some basic principles is tested, often in a rather benevolent, unsystematic fashion, can more or less rest assured that the mere passing of time will ensure that in 28 years she or he will reach the peak of the judicial career, until recently reserved for only a little over 1 per cent of the magistrates. [Therefore] in a rather short time interval, while the other traditional characteristics of the judicial machinery and of the judicial workflow have remained substantially unchanged, judges have in many respects been relieved of their traditional anxious dependence on the higher echelons of the judicial hierarchy, and of the need of anticipating in their behavior and performance the expectations of the judicial elite in order to attain organisational gratifications. As for the hoped for consequences we mentioned, one can certainly say that the partial dismantling of the traditional means of organisational control over judicial performance has further accentuated the already lax work habits of the majority of the mag istrates (Di Federico and Guarnieri 1988: 169–70).

As a general result of these processes, in Italy a peculiar judicial setting has emerged in comparison with other democratic regimes. First of all, Italian magistrates today enjoy guarantees of both internal and external independence broader than those found in any other democratic country. The traditional hierarchy has been completely dismantled. Both in the process of recruitment and professional socialization and in administering the guarantees of their status, Italian judges and public prosecutors are subject to limits which are unquestionably less restrictive than elsewhere. All decisions relating to them are taken by only one body, the Higher Council of the Judiciary, two-thirds of whose members are magistrates elected by the entire judicial corps. The Italian judiciary is thus not subject to the external controls often criticized but still prevalent in France—which remains most faithful to the hierarchical traditions typical of a bureaucratic setting, with a judiciary strongly conditioned by the executive branch. The Italian judiciary is less restricted even than its German counterpart, which is influenced to a certain extent by both the executive and legislative branches. In addition, the recruitment of Italian magistrates, unlike recruitment in common law countries, is completely removed from intervention from the political environment.

On the other hand, little has changed in the bureaucratic setting of the Italian judiciary except for the aforementioned dismantling of judicial hierarchy. The mode of recruitment—exclusively from the bottom, with the categorical exclusion of any lateral entry, allowing into the corps young graduates without any professional experience—as well as the generalistic approach to work performance and role assignment has not changed substantially. Training, therefore, is handled internally, even though the instruments that once allowed the judicial elite to control and influence this process are no longer working. At present, unlike in other civil law countries, after a short and casual apprenticeship of more or less one year, a young magistrate is entrusted with judicial (or prosecutorial) duties, and her or his professional competence is not subject to later evaluations.[7] From this point of view, it could be said that the Italian judiciary combines *in an original way* features typical of continental systems with elements found in Anglo-Saxon judiciaries.

The uniqueness of the institutional setting of the Italian judiciary becomes even more clear if we consider the position of public prosecutors. In all the main democratic countries institutional ties exist between prosecuting officers and the political system.[8] Even with some variation from country to country, specific mechanisms always allow the prosecution to be influenced by the political environment, at least along general lines. In contrast, in Italy the institutional means at the disposal of the political system are few and at any rate scantily used. The status of public prosecutors is identical to that of judges. In fact, prosecuting magistrates and judges are part of the same body that governs itself through the Higher Council of the Judiciary.

Therefore, Italy stands out for the unusual relationships that exist between the judiciary and the other governmental branches since the latter are almost completely without *institutional* means to influence the former. In fact, as we have seen, within democratic regimes, there are, broadly speaking, two types of judges. On one hand, there is the common law judge—usually an established professional, recruited at a mature age, who is granted extensive guarantees of independence. On the other stands the civil law judge, who enters the judiciary through public competitive examinations right after graduating from university, usually spending her or his entire working life there, going through the stages of a long career but subject to continuous evaluations from higher-ranking colleagues and, in certain cases, the minister of justice. In the common law case, the political branches intervene only at the time of the judge's recruitment or in the rare case of serious breach of conduct. There is not a judicial career as such: the judges are called to fill specific positions, and promotions to higher levels are not foreseen, at least institutionally. A civil law judge, however, perhaps because the initial examination is not believed to be sufficiently reliable, remains subject to various forms of control that limit her or his independence. Thus, at least from these points of view, the Italian setting is radically different from both traditions.

THE ROOTS OF THE PECULIARITY . . .

In order to understand the reasons behind the Italian peculiarity, th, we have to emphasize, first, that the radical transformation of the institutional setting of the judiciary has been, generally speaking, warmly welcomed by the Italian legal culture (Guarnieri 1992: 118–28). Traditionally in Italy, not unlike other civil law countries (Freddi 1978; Merryman 1985),

> [The role of the judge] has been defined as limited to the mere interpretation of existing law, a role definition which excluded any sort of "creativity" on the part of the judge for the solution of the concrete cases brought before him, apart from that arising from his technical ability to find in the existing law the correct legal answer. Actually, one can say that such a role definition has been the fundamental myth or value in reference to which the very legitimation of the judicial function has been based (Di Federico and Guarnieri 1988: 153).

Therefore, in order to assure an effective and impartial performance of the judge's institutional functions, it was enough to strengthen as much as possible her or his guarantees of independence, protecting her or him from the pressures of "politics." As we have seen, such an argument found widespread support among the drafters of the constitution. Even later, not much effort was devoted to considering all the implications of the new role the Italian judiciary was beginning to play. To be sure, in the 1960s the traditional assumptions of Italian judicial folklore (Cappelletti, Merryman, and Perillo 1967) came under strong attack from a new generation of "progressive" scholars—those proposing a "democratic" reform of the traditional setting, leading (among other things) to a dismantling of the judicial career—and found a good reception among an increasing number of judges. As was pointed out, due to the enormous number of legal norms, often the byproducts of hurried parliamentary compromises, it was completely unrealistic to depict the judicial role as a purely technical, executory activity. In fact, judges enjoy wide discretionary powers due to the intrinsic nature of legislation. Thus judges make policy, even though—the progressives maintained—they should and can make it according to the values embodied in the constitution.[9] But even then scarce attention was devoted to the problem of the political legitimation of policymaking judges:

> [F]ew observers, inside and outside the judiciary, have confronted the problem of justifying the presence of independent and policy making judges in a democracy. Very often, the problem is "solved," even through sophisticated argumentations, by claiming that "at the end" judges do not "really" make policy, because they limit themselves to passively interpret the law, or because they act only according to the prescriptions of the Constitution (Di Federico and Guarnieri 1988: 156).[10]

In any case, it has been maintained (Pizzorusso 1990), the composition of the Higher Council of the Judiciary, one-third of whose members are elected by parliament, assures an institutional connection between the political branches and the judiciary, therefore guaranteeing its democratic legitimacy.

On the other hand, the transformations that have characterized the Italian judiciary in the postwar period have been accompanied and supported by the growing conflict which developed inside the judicial corps through the 1950s and 1960s. The reasons for such conflict lie for the most part in the structure of the judicial career, which did not seem to allow a balanced distribution of professional rewards, and in the political and unionization liberties guaranteed by the new democratic regime, as well as in the emergence after 1959 of a new institutional player such as the Higher Council of the Judiciary (Freddi 1972, 1978). Of course in the postwar era many of the bureaucratic judiciaries of continental Europe have experienced a certain level of internal conflict. The case of the Italian judiciary stands out, if at all, for the particular harshness of its conflict and, as we shall see below, for the reactions of the political system (Mancini 1980; Guarnieri 1992).

The conflict within the judicial body drove the progressive magistrates to seek allies elsewhere, in the face of opposition from higher-ranking magistrates and the initial lack of sensitivity on the part of the government. Such a search was directed to public opinion—where on the whole they found support, albeit without concrete consequences—and, more strategically, to political parties. At this point, an important change occurred in the relationship between the judiciary and politics. Broadly speaking, at least until the end of the 1950s the Italian judiciary was governed mainly by the higher-ranking magistrates, acting very often in full agreement with the minister of justice .[11] Thus direct interventions by the executive in judicial affairs were rare since the hierarchical setting allowed more discrete intervention through senior magistrates. Beginning in the 1960s, new and increasingly more important relationships evolved between the political parties and the representatives of the magistrates' association. The parties of the opposition, like the Communist Party, or those that were slowly moving from the opposition to government roles, like the socialist, were obviously interested in developing contacts with a strategic body like the judiciary and above all in strengthening its guarantees of independence from an executive branch they did not expect to fully control. In this situation, the party traditionally in government, the Christian Democrats, found itself confronted by a group of new and dangerous competitors. Its internal fragmentation, with the growing competition among the various factions, gave to the judiciary enough opportunities to find allies even there. Finally, these new relationships between the judiciary and politics, together with the growth of socialist and above all Communist influence on the decisionmaking of the parliament in the 1960s and the 1970s (Di Palma 1977), resulted in the approval of reforms that satisfied the demands of the magistrates' association and created an attitude of general acquiescence toward the initiatives of the judiciary (Di Federico 1989).

Even if other elements—such as involving the judiciary in the fight against terrorism in the 1970s—could have supported such an evolution, the new relationships between the judiciary and its political environment and, moreover, the strong proportionalist trend emerging in the Italian political system in the 1960s and the 1970s (Cotta 1991), with its drift toward "sharing, dispersing, and limiting power" (Lijphart 1989: 34), seem to be the most relevant factors. This statement is supported by the cases of France and even more so Spain, with their different outcomes. In these cases, not only have different parties alternated in power, but also the legislative process has been (at least until today) solidly in the hands of the government, and the demands of the judiciary for a reform of its institutional setup and an increase of its independence have been, at least so far, resisted.[12]

. . . AND ITS CONSEQUENCES

The main result of this process of change has been the creation of a unique institutional relationship between the judiciary and the political system, at least in comparison with that prevailing in other democratic countries. As a consequence, the actions of Italian magistrates can greatly affect the political environment, as well as the other structures of government.[13] Such political significance is remarkable in the criminal field. Unlike what happens in all other democratic countries—with the possible partial exception of Germany—in Italy criminal initiative is mandatory. In other words, the Italian criminal process is governed by the principle of compulsory prosecution, as required under the constitution: "The public prosecutor has the duty to institute criminal proceedings" (Art. 112).

The concrete meaning of the principle of compulsory prosecution is far from clear:

> [It] is currently interpreted in Italy as denying to the public prosecutor any discretion in deciding whether or not to start a criminal prosecution. It is maintained, at least by the great majority of Italian jurists, that in every case where a suspicion arises that a crime has been committed the public prosecutor must request a decision from the judge, even if he is convinced of the innocence of the accused (Di Federico and Guarnieri 1988: 172).

By requiring prosecutors to start a prosecution and ask for a judicial decision every time there is *some* evidence that a crime has been committed, it assigns to the prosecuting authorities a task impossible to perform.[14] Actually, the principle has very often been interpreted in a formal way—that is, when the prosecutor finds some evidence of a crime, she or he must open a file. Nothing more is required, and often criminal initiatives lag behind until the statute of limitations has to be applied. This situation, together with the lack of substantial controls on prosecutorial activity, has made the prosecution virtually unaccountable for the policy choices it inevitably has to make. Unlike what happens in most continental European countries, Italian prosecutors are not responsible for their actions, or inactions, to the minister of justice or to anyone else. In addition, according to Italian procedural law, a person under investigation has to be notified by the prosecution. The prosecutor has some discretion over when to send the notification: at the beginning of the investigation or just before the first court appearance. This discretion, which in ordinary cases can have only a limited impact, can have a tremendous effect in politically significant cases, especially in connection with the media. Notwithstanding the fact that the notification should not be made public, the media are invariably able to find out about it. Given the strong inquisitorial tendencies of Italian political culture, a notification—which per se does not signal any criminal responsibility—is often interpreted as a guilty verdict and in any case cannot but damage the public image of politicians. It has to be appreciated that the principle of compulsory prosecution together with the notification that an investigation is being carried out makes this very likely to occur.

A related factor which accounts for the significance of the Italian judiciary is the structure of public prosecution. As pointed out, in nearly all democratic countries institutional ties exist between the prosecuting officers and the political system. The case in Italy is different. Italian public prosecutors enjoy a very high degree of independence from the political environment: prosecuting magistrates and judges are part of the same body, which governs itself through the Higher Council of the Judiciary.[15] Therefore, the chief prosecutors, as well as all magistrates, are nominated by a body where the representatives of the political environment are only a minority. Moreover, the general structure of the prosecution is characterized by a high level of decentralization. Every prosecutorial office is autonomous from the others. Only in the field of organized crime has the disappointment with the lack of coordination in the fight against the Mafia led to the recent establishment of a special structure—the Anti-Mafia District Directions, at the regional level, with a national office (the National Anti-Mafia Direction) at the top—in charge of dealing with all the investigations against the Mafia and organized crime. But the power of the chief prosecutor even inside these offices cannot be overemphasized. The career of his assistants—*sostituti*—has been made by the Higher Council, like that of all magistrates, de facto coinciding with seniority. The result is a system which is fairly fragmented but which allows the prosecution a wide margin of action. Beyond the elements just mentioned, we have to consider another important factor—i.e., that the same corps is performing both prosecutorial and judicial functions. The fact that prosecutors and judges belong to the same organization, together with the widespread practice that many magistrates switch from one function to another during their careers, has not failed to encourage structural collusion between prosecutors and judges.

At another level, however, it has to be underlined that politically more incisive interventions by the judiciary are more likely to occur today than in the past, not only because of the pressure of interested political actors, but also because, beyond the general transformations that have occurred in the judicial role in democratic regimes (Cappelletti 1989; Pederzoli 1990), the present-day judicial organization no longer seems capable of upholding the traditional definition of judicial role. As we have seen, the traditional conception viewed the judge as a technical, passive executor of options previously processed by the legislature and expounded by academic doctrine. But the controls once exercised by higher-ranking judges have been radically reduced. The influence of academic doctrine has also lessened, not only because it appears much more diversified today than before—and many are advocating a more activist posture by the judges anyway—but also because the organizational mechanisms that once supported its importance—that is, the evaluation of judicial rulings (and therefore the judges' conforming to the trends of the doctrine) as a base for career advancement—are no longer working (Di Federico 1976, 1985; Rebuffa 1993; Damaska 1986).

Moreover, two other important phenomena seem to be related to such an institutional setting. First is the development of organized factions (*correnti*) inside the judiciary. At least since the early 1960s, the professional association of Italian magistrates (Associazione Nazionale Magistrati) has been officially divided into ideologically differentiated factions, each with a stable (albeit small) organizational structure. Today, after a history of splits and reunifications, the main factions are, from left to right, Magistratura Democratica, Movimenti Riuniti, Unità per la Costituzione, and Magistratura Indipendente (Guarnieri 1992: 97–108). The growth of judicial associations is a phenomenon that can also be found elsewhere—for example, in France and Spain—but in Italy it has acquired more importance because of the role (unheard of in other countries) that the correnti play in crucial decisionmaking bodies like the Higher Council of the Judiciary. As we have seen, these factions resulted from conflicts that developed within the judiciary over a specific theme: the career. They have become the instruments through which the magistrates very effectively articulate their demands to parliament and to the government, even though the strength of the correnti is due mainly to the influence they exert on the Higher Council. The changes in that body's electoral rules—especially the introduction in 1975 of a proportional system with competing lists of candidates—have contributed to make the correnti stronger; since 1976 all magistrates elected to the Higher Council have belonged to one or another *corrente* (see Table 1). In this way, the possibility of being represented in the council has been offered to all the main groups.

The role of the correnti cannot be understood without taking into account that the dismantling of the hierarchical structure, by de facto associating rank exclusively with length of service, has deprived the council of criteria with which to evaluate magistrates in the cases when, for example, appointments are to be made to higher positions or transfers have to be decided and several applicants compete for the same position. In these cases (Di Federico 1985; Rebuffa 1993: 91–98), since the council must choose among candidates of the same rank who are therefore all (at least formally) equally qualified, a candidate's tie to a faction or party could be very important. In other words, when a transfer or promotion occurs which is not on the basis of simple seniority, it is very likely the result of a deal among the factions and parties, which often support one another in

Table 1

ELECTIONS TO HIGHER COUNCIL BY CORRENTE, 1976–90

Year	Right ← Magistratura Indipendente (MI)	Terzo Potere (TP)[a]	Unità per la Costituzione (UC)	Movimenti Riuniti (MR)[b]	→ Left Magistratura Democratica (MD)	Other[c]	Votes
1976	2,156	1,190	1,336		755	506	5,943
	36%	20%	22%		13%	9%	
	[8][d]	[4]	[5]		[2]	[1]	
1981	2,263		2,557		803	297	5,990
	38%		43%		14%	5%	
	[8]		[9]		[3]		
1986	2,078		2,517		1,107	402	6,159
	34%		41%		19%	6%	
	[7]		[9]		[3]	[1]	
1990	1,828		2,236	714	1,337		6,115
	30%		36%	12%	22%		
	[5]		[8]	[3]	[4]		

Source: Guarnieri (1992: 102).

[a] TP was a center-left faction which in 1979 fused with UC.

[b] MR was formed by splinter groups from MI and UC.

[c] Includes some short-lived moderate or conservative factions.

[d] Figures in brackets represent number of seats.

reciprocal exchanges.[16] In this way, the magistrates—at least those (not a few) in some degree "interested" in decisions to be made by the Higher Council—cannot fail to take into account the logic of its decisionmaking, being therefore aware of the complex configuration of factional *and* party forces that play a role in it.

Thus in this context, one cannot be surprised that a strong tendency has emerged toward the development of connections between the judiciary and the political environment. As we have seen, the origin of these connections can be located in the period in which the lower-ranking magistrates tried to reform—actually to abolish—the career system. At that time, they successfully tried to influence the political parties in order to achieve their goals. But the growing political significance of the Italian judiciary in the last twenty years has also given a strong incentive to the political class to carefully cultivate the judiciary. Personal ties are difficult to document in full, but they have often been reported and are based above all on the flourishing of extrajudicial duties assigned with remarkable frequency to many magistrates by the political—and social—environment.[17] Another sign of the development of such connections and of their ramifications in other institutions is without doubt the growing number of magistrates elected to parliament and the not-so-rare cases of rapidly rising political careers.[18] Personal ties often support more complex relationships among groups or factions of magistrates and parties (Zannotti 1989). In the latter case, there are naturally some connections of an ideological nature—the most visible, but not the only one, being that between Magistratura Democratica and the parties of the left (Pappalardo 1987). But there are also different ties we may call "opportunistic." In any case, such connections, which from time to time have not excluded tensions and conflicts, tend to produce as the main (if not the only) outcome the exchange of reciprocal favors between magistrates and parties.[19] Such exchanges have found a useful institutional seat in the Higher Council, where representatives of the magistrates' factions continuously interact with the representatives of both government and opposition political parties (Rebuffa 1993). It is difficult to conceive of politicians and magistrates as two distinct and opposing groups because of the strong ties that in some ways bind them. This phenomenon is exemplified by the conflict that erupted, especially between 1990 and 1992, on the powers of the Higher Council. The alignments which emerged inside the council at that time—in which President of the Republic Cossiga was confronted by the vice president, a former Christian Democrat politician and a lay member of the council, and by the majority of both magistrates and lay members, all advocating a larger role for the council—can be taken as evidence of the fact that the conflict was not simply between magistrates and politicians. However, the consequences of these connections have acted, at least until recently, as a sort of check on the power of the judiciary since they have been affecting its actions, even though they were not institutionally foreseen.

POLITICS AND JUSTICE IN THE ITALIAN CASE

Not surprisingly, the growth of judicial power in Italy has triggered strong responses from the political environment. The cooptation of magistrates by political forces, even though not always successful, has been made easier by their low institutional identification due to the mode of recruitment: still bureaucratic but not followed by subsequent checks (Di Federico 1981). Another consequence has been the increasing political significance of the Higher Council. In more general terms, the Italian case can be interpreted as an exemplification of the rather obvious statement that power systems are complex. It is impossible to completely conceal the influence of the political environment on the judiciary. In every democratic regime the judiciary and politics are in some way connected:

> The "disconnectedness" of the judicial process from the political system . . . is only relative. . . . What distinguishes judicial from other kinds of political actors is not that the judges are outside the system but that they are related to it in a different fashion than are other decision makers (Peltason 1968: 287).

If this connection is not achieved at least mainly through institutional means, it will be achieved through noninstitutional ones (i.e., extrajudicial duties) or through an overemphasis of the few that are institutional—for example, through the role played by the Higher Council.[20]

In Italy the exchanges between politics and the judiciary do not follow the patterns found in other democratic regimes. In civil law countries, the political branches exercise influence on a judiciary organized along bureaucratic, hierarchical lines through the powers they have on higher-ranking judges. In contrast, in Anglo-Saxon countries the influence of the political system is channeled mainly through the recruitment process. In Italy, even though the selection of judicial personnel is still made through public examinations at a youthful age, the internal hierarchy has been dismantled. The power of the higher-ranking judges, as well as that of the government, has been dramatically reduced, notwithstanding the fact that the political system is able to exercise some influence through its representatives in the Higher Council. In this context some magistrates have been able and willing to pursue unorthodox policies, even though not being in any way held democratically accountable for their decisions. The shortcomings of this setting are clear: the low guarantees of professional qualification of the judiciary and the spreading throughout the judicial corps of political considerations, as demonstrated in the decisionmaking inside the Higher Council. Thus, notwithstanding their strong guarantees of independence, Italian judges and magistrates can be said to have become highly politicized, with their behavior highly conditioned by political considerations both internal and external to the corps.

The election of April 1992 marked a new phase in the evolution of the Italian political system. The decline of the electoral fortunes of all main parties, as well as the rise of new parties—a trend that has been reinforced by following administrative by-elections—has shown the emergence of a new attitude in public opinion, at least in central and northern Italy. This attitude has had an immediate impact—for example, on the recent willingness of many businessmen to give evidence to prosecutors investigating the corruption of public officials. In this new situation, with spreading popular dissatisfaction in the performance of the political system, as well as an abrupt weakening of the old political class, the judiciary, or at least a part of it, has decided to take its chance. At first, only a few prosecutorial offices decided to follow the example of Milan, where the most relevant corruption investigation has been carried out. The offices in the South have shown (at least so far) a remarkable degree of caution. For example, only recently have the prosecutors in Naples started to investigate the many scandals that have notoriously plagued that area. Even the placing of former Prime Minister

Andreotti under investigation on charges of organized crime connections was decided only after a new chief prosecutor, a magistrate from Turin, was appointed by the Higher Council to the Palermo office. Actually, only part of the judiciary—that less connected with the traditional political class—is resolutely moving to fight corruption. The rest have taken a wait and see attitude. But it is likely that these new developments will have a distinct impact on the internal dynamics of the judiciary. The breaking down of old political arrangements cannot be without consequences. As we have seen, in the last thirty years at least parts of the judiciary—and especially those in key positions—have been in intimate relationships with the political class. Therefore, the changes occurring in the political system will certainly affect even the power structure of the judiciary, resulting in growing internal tensions and conflict.[21]

As a general evaluation based on a comparative analysis of the institutional setting of the judiciary in the main democratic countries, we can say that the powers in the hands of the Italian judiciary are without doubt very strong. Yet whether these powers will be effectively used and in what directions depends primarily on the judiciary's willingness to act, or more specifically on its sensitivity to pressures from various social and political forces. Therefore, these powers can be employed to attain different goals, some of which are desirable and others of which might not be.[22] All in all, the strong powers presently enjoyed by the Italian judiciary are the product not only of the present weakness of the national political class, but also, as we have pointed out, of the judiciary's peculiar institutional setting. Therefore, even though "government by the judiciary" in the Italian version is likely to endure until the political system finds a new equilibrium, even then Italy will stand out among democratic regimes as a special case of judicial power.

NOTES

1. For details on the differences among systems, see (among others) Guarnieri (1981, 1984, and 1992); Dechênes and Shetreet, eds. (1985); and Waltman and Holland, eds. (1988).

2. Only in France and in Italy does the same term—Magistrature or Magistratura respectively—refer to personnel who could perform both prosecutorial and judicial roles.

3. As already underlined by Hamilton in *The Federalist,* no. 78. According to Cappelletti (1989), the respect for procedural rules is essential to the democratic legitimation of an independent judiciary.

4. For detailed analyses of the recruitment process in France and Germany, see Mestitz (1990) and Pederzoli (1992).

5. For a more detailed account of the characteristics of Italian judicial personnel, see Di Federico and Guarnieri (1988: 161ff.).

6. As Di Federico and Guarnieri note, "[The Council] has drastically curtailed the previous formal and informal systems of information gathering on the official and private behaviour of the members of the judiciary," resulting in a dramatic reduction of the hierarchical controls on magistrates' behavior (1988: 167–68).

7. In other civil law countries, before or after the recruitment a training period of at least two years—and even more—is always foreseen. In common law countries the situation is, as we have noted, rather different.

8. This statement also applies to cases other than those considered here. For example, see Baar (for Canada) and Board (for Sweden) in Waltman and Holland, eds. (1988); for the Netherlands, Austria, Switzerland, and Norway, see Jenscheck and Leibinger, eds. (1979); for Spain, Grenados (1989).

9. In this process an important role was played by the introduction of the judicial review of legislation in 1956, as well as by the increasing role of EC norms and regulations (Cappelletti 1989).

10. For an authoritative example, see Pizzorusso (1990: 64ff.).

11. This was true thanks also to the fact that magistrates were—and are—in charge of all important positions inside the Ministry of Justice (Di Federico 1976).

12. For an attempt at comparison of Italian and Spanish political development in the field of the administration of justice, see Guarnieri (1993). Even though a recent reform has somewhat reinforced the guarantees of independence of French magistrates, France has remained the democratic country most faithful to the traditional, bureaucratic, executive-dominated model of judicial setting.

13. For some examples, see Di Federico (1981 and 1989) and Zannotti (1989).

14. See Di Federico (1989 and 1991). For the general problems involved in the implementation of this principle, see Guarnieri (1984: esp. 125–52).

15. For a long time and to a certain extent even today, the principle of compulsory prosecution has been interpreted in such a way as to imply a "judicialization" of the role of the public prosecutor (Guarnieri 1984: esp. ch. 1).

16. Recall that in addition to the twenty magistrates elected by the corps the Higher Council is presently composed of ten lawyers or law professors chosen by parliament, usually along strict party lines.

17. The range of extrajudicial duties of Italian magistrates is extremely wide. Among them an important role is played by well-paid appointments as arbitrators in disputes between state-owned companies or as consultants for various governmental departments. For more details see Di Federico (1981) and Zannotti (1981).

18. In the present parliament there are thirteen magistrates. There have also been some cases of magistrate ministers or deputy ministers. Magistrates elected to parliament or performing governmental functions are on leave from the corps but maintain the right to be reinstalled after leaving their political or administrative jobs. However, their career—i.e., their promotion by seniority to higher ranks—is not affected by the time spent on leave outside the corps.

19. This could explain, for example, the long and often ineffective investigations (at least recently) into political corruption, as well as parliamentary generosity in setting judicial salaries, now on the average from two to three times higher than those of higher civil servants. For some data on the connections among politicians and magistrates at the local level, see della Porta (1992).

20. In recent years, the significance of this body has steadily increased, de facto progressively eroding the traditional position enjoyed by the Court of Cassation as the apex of the judicial system. Even though the Court of Cassation remains the court of last resort—at least in the ordinary jurisdiction—the Higher Council exercises, at least potentially, a strong influence on judges' behavior through the role it plays in administering their status.

21. In the summer of 1993 the Italian newspapers reported the arrest of the senior vice president of the Milan tribunal on charges of corruption related to the big political scandal of the Enimont. The arrest has led to a heated debate among the different judicial factions in which the appointment policy of the Higher Council has been sharply criticized. In the following months the cases of magistrates under investigation, or even arrested, on charges of corruption or association with organized crime have multiplied, expecially in the South.

22. As an example of a desirable goal, in addition to what we have already noted about the investigations on political corruption, we can mention the recent successes in the fight against organized crime. Even though these developments have to some extent to be credited to some organizational reforms of the police force and prosecution, as well as to a weakening of the traditional ties between organized crime and at least a part of the political class, they show a new attitude in some sectors of the judiciary. On the other hand, one cannot fail to notice that in this situation the rights of the citizens in the criminal process are not well safeguarded. Even though the process has assumed, at least since 1989, an "accusatorial," American-style look (Amodio and Selvaggi 1989), the wide powers enjoyed by the prosecution and the organizational connection between the prosecutor and the judge, both belonging to the same corps, strike an uneven balance between the two conflicting parties, to the disadvantage of the defendant.

REFERENCES

Amodio, E., and Selvaggi, E. 1989. "An Accusatorial System in a Civil Law Country: The 1988 Italian Code of Criminal Procedure." *Temple Law Review* 62: 1211–24.

Cappelletti, M. 1989. *The Judicial Process in Comparative Perspective*. Oxford: Clarendon Press.

Cappelletti, M.; Merryman, J. H.; and Perillo, J. M. 1967. *The Italian Legal System: An Introduction*. Stanford: Stanford University Press.

Cotta, M. 1991. "Il Parlamento nel sistema politico italiano: Mutamenti istituzionali e cicli politici." *Quaderni costituzionali* 11: 201–23.

Damaska, M. R. 1986. *The Faces of Justice and State Authority*. New Haven: Yale University Press.

Dechênes, J., and Shetreet, S., eds. 1985. *Judicial Independence: The Contemporary Debate*. Dordrecht: Nijhoff.

della Porta, D. 1992. *La corruzione politica in Italia: Tre casi di governo locale*. Bologna: Il Mulino.

Di Federico, G. 1976. "The Italian Judicial Profession and Its Bureaucratic Setting." *Juridical Review* 1: 40–57.

———. 1981. "Gli incarichi extragiudiziari dei magistrati." Introduction to Zannotti (1981).

———. 1985. "Le qualificazioni professionali del corpo giudiziario: Carenze attuali, possibili riforme e difficoltà di attuarle." *Rivista trimestrale di scienza dell'amministrazione* 32, 4: 21–60.

———. 1989. "The Crisis of the Justice System and the Referendum on the Judiciary." In *Italian Politics: A Review*, ed. R. Leonardi and P. G. Corbetta, vol. 3, pp. 25–49. London: Pinter.

———. 1991. "Obbligatorietà dell'azione penale, coordinamento delle attività del pubblico ministero e loro rispondenza alle aspettative della communità." In *Accusa e ruolo del p.m. nell'evoluzione del sistema italiano*. Naples: Jovene.

Di Federico, G., and Guarnieri, C. 1988. "The Courts in Italy." In Waltman and Holland, eds., pp. 153–80.

Di Palma, G. 1977. *Surviving without Governing*. Berkeley: University of California Press.

Eisenstein, J. 1979. *Counsel for the United States: U.S. Attorneys in the Political and Legal Systems*. Baltimore: Johns Hopkins University Press.

Freddi, G. 1972. "La magistratura come organizzazione burocratica." *Politica del diritto* 3: 325–39.

———. 1978. *Tensioni e conflitto nella magistratura*. Bari: Laterza.

Grenados, F. 1989. *El Ministerio Fiscal (del presente al futuro)*. Madrid: Tecnos.

Guarnieri, C. 1981. *L'indipendenza della magistratura.* Padua: CEDAM.

———. 1984. *Pubblico ministero e sistema politico.* Padua: CEDAM.

———. 1992. *Magistratura e politica in Italia.* Bologna: Il Mulino.

———. 1993. "The Judiciary in the Transition from Authoritarianism to Democracy: The Case of Italy and Spain." Paper presented at the IPSA Research Committee on Comparative Judicial Studies, Santa Fe, New Mexico.

Jenscheck, H. H., and Leibinger, R., eds. 1979. *Funktion und Tätigkeit der Anklagebehörde im ausländischen Recht.* Baden-Baden: Nomos.

Lijphart, A. 1989. "Democratic Political Systems: Types, Cases, Causes, and Consequences." *Journal of Theoretical Politics* 1: 33–48.

Mancini, G. F. 1980. "Politics and the Judges: The European Perspective." *Modern Law Review* 43: 1–17.

Merryman, J. H. 1985. *The Civil Law Tradition,* 2d ed. Stanford: Stanford University Press.

Mestitz, A. 1990. *Selezione e formazione professionale dei magistrati e degli avvocati in Francia.* Padua: CEDAM.

Pappalardo, S. 1987. *Gli iconoclasti Magistratura Democratica nel quadro della Associazione Nazionale Magistrati.* Milan: Franco Angeli.

Pederzoli, P. 1990. "Il giudice nei regimi democratici." *Rivista italiana di scienza politica* 20: 293–329.

———. 1992. *Selezione e formazione delle professioni legali in Germania.* Padua: CEDAM.

Peltason, J. W. 1968. "Judicial Process: Introduction." In *International Encyclopedia of the Social Sciences,* vol. 8, pp. 283–91. New York: Macmillan.

Pizzorusso, A. 1990. *L'organizzazione della giustizia in Italia.* Turin: Einaudi.

Rebuffa. G. 1993. *La funzione giudiziaria.* Turin: Giappichelli.

Waltman, J. L., and Holland, K. M., eds. 1988. *The Political Role of Law Courts in Modern Democracies.* London: Macmillan.

Zannotti, F. 1981. *Le attività extragiudiziarie dei magistrati ordinari.* Padua: CEDAM.

———. 1989. *La magistratura, un gruppo di pressione istituzionale: L'autodeterminazione delle retribuzioni.* Padua: CEDAM.

RECONSTRUCTING ITALY: THE ECONOMY

Pippo Ranci

A QUESTION FOR FUTURE HISTORIANS: IS THIS A TURNING POINT?

Only at a distance in time can one examine a period of turbulence and decide whether it represents a mere disturbance around a trend or a change in the direction of the trend itself. Yet contemporaries, who are not in an ideal position to know, are the most interested in understanding what is happening around them.

My initial purpose in writing this essay was to gather evidence for and against the hypothesis that the Italian economy and economic policy are now taking a sharp turn away from established trends. I soon realized that I had put the issue in too broad terms. Broad questions present a greater appeal but usually have no unique answer. Instead the general question can be split into many individual questions dealing with specific issues, such as inflation, employment, the public debt, and industrial growth. For some of these, the evidence of a sharp turn is rather clear—at least in my view—while for others I shall conclude that the established trend, be it positive or negative, has not been reversed.

Clear evidence of a turnaround, where there has been one, surfaces mainly around the first cabinet following the general election of spring 1992, led by law professor and experienced politician Giuliano Amato, and the following cabinet, the last one before the general election of March 1994, led by central bank governor Carlo Azeglio Ciampi. Much of the work for determining the turnaround had been done before, but the contribution of the two mentioned cabinets has been decisive.

Five main elements can be distinguished in the 1992–93 turnaround: the end of inflation, the balancing of external accounts, the taming of the public deficit, privatizations, and the end of the "extraordinary" policies for the Mezzogiorno (South). I shall briefly describe each of them. Since we are in the early stages of a radical process of change, the outlook for the future is very uncertain. I shall just present five main weaknesses which still affect the economic outlook for Italy, but in the process a few robust reasons for hope will emerge.

THE END OF INFLATION

Since the early 1970s Italy has been a relatively high-inflation country. The retail price index topped the highest rate of increase in the early 1980s, after the second oil shock, at 21 percent. For twenty years the inflation rate has been continuously and significantly higher than the European average. It now lies around 4 percent, in line with the rest of Europe, and is still declining.

Inflationary impulses from outside—the two oil shocks of 1973 and 1979—have been supplemented by internal wage shocks. The effect of each shock was magnified and extended by a strong wage–price spiral, whose main component was the indexation mechanism of wages established in 1947 and reinforced in 1975. Its inflationary impact was immediately evident to economists (Franco Modigliani wrote clearly and in timely fashion against the 1975 agreement.) A long eighteen-year period was devoted to a gradual dismantling, first by reducing the effect of indexation on retirement compensation, then by weakening and finally abolishing the indexation clause itself. This was agreed to in July 1992 with a historical and dramatic triangular deal among government, the main unions, and employers' organizations. It was followed by a further agreement in July 1993 which established the substance of collective negotiations at both the national and firm level, so that the usual overlapping of wage increases negotiated at the two levels was prevented. These last two rounds of negotiation were decisive and went far beyond most observers' expectations only a few years ago; in a sense there has been a turnaround, but I prefer to say that there has been a remarkable acceleration and completion of an action started fifteen years before. To achieve the result a patient buildup of union consensus has been necessary, along with the use of fiscal incentives, a compensatory crackdown on the fiscal treatment of incomes other than wages, and one open confrontation through a referendum in 1984, when the proposal to restore indexation, advanced by the Communist-led CGIL union, was defeated by the electorate.

Other policies helped. Since Italy joined the European Monetary System (EMS) in 1979, the Bank of Italy has kept monetary policy severely in line, making it clear that the excess of Italian over European inflation would not be fully compensated by realignments of the exchange rate—and it was not until the breakdown of the system in 1992. For twelve years employers and unions have known that the competitiveness of Italy's products was inversely related to the growth of labor costs set in lire, and they have learned wage restraint. The effect of such awareness was evident in the much lower rate of inflation in the sectors open to international trade (mainly manufacturing) compared to inflation in the sheltered sectors such as retail trade and professional and financial services.

Some help in restraining inflationary behavior outside manufacturing has been provided by the new climate set by the European Single Market. A gradual dismantling of nontariff barriers has exposed previously sheltered sectors to international competition; even where the change has not been completed, expectations have been effectively modified. Finally, the recession of the early 1990s has helped, clearly setting the alternative between higher wages for a diminishing number of employed and greater employment achievable via a general reduction of labor costs. The orientation toward solidarity prevailed in the unions, but this was made possible only by a clear and wide understanding of the alternative, while previously and for many years the alternative itself had been rejected, seen as a biased, deceptive way of laying down the issue.

To the general surprise and dismay of econometric model-builders and forecasters, the massive devaluation of the lira in October 1992 has had practically no impact on the internal rate of inflation. This is largely due to the deep recession under way, but also to a wider inflation awareness. The unions have stuck to the July 1992 agreement even after one of its main elements, exchange rate stability, waned. Someone insinuated that they had been deceived by the government. In fact, the government and central bank were taken aback by the international storm and sincerely—even naively—attempted to peg the lira, probably for too long. The ensuing price stability has confirmed that the unions were right not to react.

NO LONGER LIVING BEYOND OUR MEANS: THE BALANCING OF EXTERNAL ACCOUNTS

As a consequence of a high relative inflation rate, the lira has broken away from all currency agreements of which it has been a part, from the Smithsonian Agreement of 1972 until the breakdown of the EMS in 1992. Successive devaluations have singled out the lira as the weak currency in the EC. But until 1979 devaluations maintained the competitiveness of Italy's products. No longer so after it joined the EMS.

The Bank of Italy reluctantly devalued the lira several times between 1979 and 1992, taking care to keep the amount of devaluation lower than required to accommodate Italian inflation. The lira became an overvalued currency, and Italian products suffered a loss of competitiveness on the international markets. Many measures were proposed for such a loss; with respect to the German mark, it ranged from less than 10 percent if measured using production prices to over 20 percent using retail prices. As a consequence, Italy's external balance (current account) has been in the red every year since 1979, with exceptions only for 1983 and 1986. After a recession-induced surplus in 1983, the current account balance draws a regularly declining line: from a surplus of 0.5 percent of GDP to a deficit of 2.1 percent of GDP in 1992. The line shifted upwards only because of the sharp drop in oil prices in 1986, a bonus to a heavy importer of energy. Current account deficits year after year mean an ever-increasing foreign debt. Total external debt at the end of 1992 was 175 trillion lire, or 11.5 percent of GDP. It generated interest payments three times greater than net revenues from tourism. More than half the current account deficit was now due to interest payments. So the loss of competitiveness had started a vicious spiral.

Here lies the origin of the sharp devaluation of the lira in 1992, amplified by expectation-induced speculative capital movements. The lira lost more than 20 percent with respect to a basket of the major currencies. This had a strong beneficial effect on competitiveness since internal inflation was maintained on its declining course. The current account deficit turned into a net surplus in 1993, with an impressive improvement of over 3 percent of GDP in one year. A strong surplus in trade has emerged, providing the means to pay interest on the debt.

Now Italy's bond issues are highly attractive for world investors again and command a rapidly diminishing spread over issuing costs of the best debtors. When Moody's rating agency lowered the rating of Italy's debt in spring 1993, many indignant comments were expressed; in fact, Moody's pronouncement sounded like the recognition of an illness when recovery was well under way. The lira is now freely fluctuating as well as most other currencies. The whole EMS has been badly hit by the 1992 crisis and needs restructuring. Among the obstacles to reconstruction, though, no one can include Italy's external imbalance.

PUBLIC DEFICIT UNDER (SOME DEGREE OF) CONTROL

Increasing yearly deficits in the state's accounts characterized the 1970s for two reasons: rapidly growing expenses for social policies (such as the extension of social security benefits and health care to the whole population) and lagging (even though rising) revenues due to a structural inability of the tax administration to control evasion. In addition, a wide reorganization of the tax system—including the introduction of the value-added tax and the comprehensive personal income tax in 1973—brought a temporary but costly decrease in tax revenues. Revenues and expenditures have kept growing faster than GDP since, up to the present levels of 52 and 42 percent of GDP. The gap remained, fluctuating around 10 percent of GDP: over 150 trillion lire at 1993 values.

Efforts to reduce the deficit were made, particularly from 1976 onwards. Welfare benefits were reduced. For example, people had to pay part of the cost of medical services and drugs. Most of the adjustment was on the side of taxes and social security benefits. Yet all efforts were frustrated by the growth of interest payments on an endlessly increasing stock of debt. Primary (i.e., net of interest payments) deficits shrank, interest payments grew, and the overall deficit stuck at 10 percent of GDP. And the stock of public debt grew larger than the GDP itself. No benefit to the debtor could come from inflation in the 1980s since all public bonds were either very short term or carried indexed interest: nobody would have bought fixed-interest long-term bonds. How long such a trend could be sustained became a central question, stimulating for academic economists, frightening for everybody. Of course, sustainability depended on the volatility of financial markets.

At the annual meeting of the Bank of Italy in May 1992, Governor Ciampi suggested that an overall reduction of the deficit of 6 percent of GDP in eighteen months was necessary; that implied expenditure cuts and/or tax increases for about 100 trillion lire, much more than had ever been attempted.

Ciampi had underestimated the task. The "natural" trend of expenditures was stronger, a heavy recession hit tax revenues and inflated social payments, and the debacle of state-owned firms brought further burdens. The problem had been made intractable by a long neglect and by exceptionally high interest rates on the world's financial markets for over ten years. Now a twenty-year old problem had to be solved in twenty months, and at the worst possible time. Real incomes were declining and unemployment was soaring.

In July 1992 the Amato cabinet delivered the first package of measures, including new property taxes and a freeze on public sector wages. A new package came with the 1993 budget, and a third one was the responsibility of Mr. Ciampi himself, called to lead the next cabinet in May 1993.

The public sector deficit initially worsened due to soaring interest rates on short-term public debt during the crisis of September–December 1992. But the crunch was effective. Italy's public sector ran a primary surplus in 1993, and the overall public deficit declined to 9 percent of GDP.

Ciampi's hand has been lighter. The social costs of the recession advised against further action, and a rapid decrease in interest rates provided some help. The stabilization timetable has been diluted somewhat. According to government plans, the public debt, which now has reached 119 percent of GDP and is still growing, will stop just below 125 percent between 1995 and 1996. It is a high level since the Maastricht Treaty established that access to the future European Monetary Union will be barred to countries showing deficits larger than 3 percent of GDP and a debt-to-GDP ratio higher than 60 percent; but new terms will have to be negotiated anyway to meet the reality of other countries, including Germany. It will not be difficult to allow for a high debt once its growth has been stopped.

Other difficult years lie ahead, even if economic recovery will help. Demographic trends create a "hidden deficit" in the pension system since this year's pensions are paid with this year's charges, and the number of contributing workers is decreasing with respect to the number of retired people. Retirement age is gradually being postponed, although much too slowly for balancing social security budgets, but it is producing an undesired impact on unemployment.

The other great theme of the next years could be named fiscal federalism. The new drive toward local autonomy requires a transfer of taxing power—which is presently concentrated at the national level—to the regions, reversing the direction of the 1973 tax reform.

PRIVATIZATION BEGINS

In 1991 Italy had the largest public sector of any Western economy, and privatization was an exotic word. A powerful system of state enterprises included public utilities such as telephones, television, railways, air transport, and electricity; it dominated the banking sector and some manufacturing sectors such as oil and gas, steel and aluminum, and defense and telecommunications apparatuses; it had important interests in construction, food production, retail chains, insurance, and other businesses where a rationale for public ownership is quite hard to find.

Over the years, such unusual extension had originated from a few politically decided nationalizations, many rescue operations of ailing private firms (mostly in the 1930s and in the immediate postwar years), and from the ambitious growth plans of public managers. In some cases, public firms had succeeded in breaking private monopolies and speeding up industrial growth, particularly in the backward areas of the Mezzogiorno. State holdings IRI and ENI had commanded wide international respect as being well run.

In recent years, though, collusion in power between managers and politicians had increased and produced a host of insane industrial choices. The increasing opening of the economy to international exchanges introduced greater competition, reducing the need for public action. Public enterprises, rather than stimulating competition and efficiency, had come to operate largely in sheltered markets such as public procurement or regulated services and to demand continued protection.

A sudden change of official policy to wide privatization arrived with Amato, although some half-hearted initiatives had been taken by the last Andreotti cabinet in 1991–92. There was a powerful reason behind the change: most public enterprises were in urgent need of new capital, and some of them were in fact bankrupt. This was the result of three factors: in general, the deep recession; in some cases, such as steel, overambitious expansion plans; in others, such as the engineering-defense group EFIM and the construction sector of IRI, plain mismanagement.

During the 1980–83 recession the state had poured large subsidies into the system of public enterprises—in the manufacturing sector alone, more than 1 percent of GDP each year. Now another operation of the same amount was necessary just to keep the system afloat, and even more to provide fuel for matching the acquisitions and the research effort of international competitors. The state budget could not bear the burden. Moreover, there was an even more rigid obstacle: the European Commission had made it quite clear that it would consider each provision of new state capital to state-owned firms as a violation of competition rules if it was carried out under conditions that a private shareholder would not accept—and this was the case in most instances.

Italy was forced to privatize. Those who advocated privatization were now for the first time in a position to overcome the massive resistance of an ideological left, of (often redundant and well-paid) employees, and of a powerful body of managers who had been selected according to their allegiance to political parties.

Amato began with two sharp decisions. First, the bankrupt industrial holding EFIM was officially dissolved. An attempt to avoid extending a de facto state guarantee to all bank debts of the group started a rift with the foreign banks; it proved very costly in terms of financial standing for the whole public sector and ended with a belated pledge to full repayment. The EFIM firms were not closed: some have been sold; others merged into homogeneous (and better run) IRI concerns; others are still in the hands of a special commissioner in search of a solution. EFIM's annual report for 1991—its last one—showed a negative net worth of "only" 400 billion lire; Amato had to pledge 9 trillion to cover losses and debt; before the end of the liquidation procedure total costs will probably reach 15 trillion—almost 1 percent of GDP. The lesson is that a good share of the likely proceeds from privatization will be absorbed by the costs of making the state enterprises themselves ready for sale.

The second decision consisted in transforming all state bodies running or holding industrial and services production into private-law corporations and sacking most of the top administrators, leaving leaner boards and mostly new chief executives in charge. This was prepared in deep secret and decided overnight in order to prevent a response from the political-managerial complex. New men were then gradually brought in while most of the old guard was prosecuted for corruption or illegal financing of political parties. Thus soon after taking charge in May 1993, Ciampi had to find a new president for IRI and recalled Romano Prodi, a well-known economist who had already held the position in the 1980s.

Next, the Amato cabinet provided a comprehensive plan for privatizations, amid hesitation and internal conflicts. Only one year later, in the last months of 1993, had the first important sales been transacted. Part of IRI's food sector has been sold to Nestlé and part to a national private group. ENI's engineering unit, Nuovo Pignone, went to General Electric. Large banks such as Credito Italiano, IMI, and Banca Commerciale Italiana, are being offered to the public and to institutional investors in the hope of shaping new public companies.

The sale of such an important part of Italy's productive apparatus is going to change the property map and the power system of the country. A hot debate has thus begun around privatizations. Supporters of the public company model advocate wide share sales to the public, with limits to individual share ownership. In contrast, supporters of a French-style government activism advocate building a strong system of national business groups; existing large national private firms should then form the kernels of the command groups to which state enterprises should be sold. The debate produced an internal split in both the Amato and Ciampi cabinets and the resignations of two industry secretaries (both withdrawn after pressure from the prime minister). In any case, privatization is pragmatically going on. It may be faster or slower, but going back to a general and stable system of state holdings is now impossible. Economic necessity is pushing the process. The general philosophy of privatization is also now accepted by most of the left. The power apparatus that was identified with the political-managerial system has largely been dispersed.

Two issues remain unresolved. First, how much of Italy's production system will remain in Italian hands? Most Europeans still consider national control a relevant issue; Italians are probably less keen on nationalism than the average, yet not to the point of being completely indifferent. Second, the privatization of utilities creates an acute need for a good regulatory system. Regulation has been somewhat neglected since public enterprises were supposed to act in the public interest anyway. Price and tariff controls by government have been formally strict but supported by little analytical capability in the government offices assigned to the task. The new shareholders of utility companies will want to know more about tariff-setting procedures, quality requirements, and the extent of monopolistic concessions. The European Commission, on the other side, is pushing toward more competition in utilities, thus affecting the net worth of companies presently operating under monopolistic conditions.

"EXTRAORDINARY" POLICIES FOR THE SOUTH DISCONTINUED

The state apparatus for special interventions in the Mezzogiorno—a cabinet minister, a government department, and an autonomous state agency—have been suppressed: another result of the hectic legislation pushed by the Amato cabinet in the remarkable second semester of 1992. The agency Cassa per il Mezzogiorno had been set up in 1950; successive legislation had increased both money transfers and the size of the special administration. In forty years real per capita income in the South more than tripled, and so did national income, so the relative income gap shrank by a negligible amount. Things went better in the first thirty years. Although per capita income in the Mezzogiorno is higher than in Greece, Ireland,

and Portugal, there was some worsening in relative growth in the last decade, when unemployment soared.

The efficiency of public administrations declined in time. Besides useful public works and an effective use of industrial incentives, a series of wrong decisions was taken, the result of incompetence and sometimes corruption. Public works often proved to be just an employment-creating activity. Large industrial plants with little economic sense were dubbed "cathedrals in the desert"; they diverted employment from traditional activities, offering high wages in a business without a future. Responsibility by local administrators, entrepreneurs, workers, union leaders, and citizens at large was discouraged; the ancestral attitude of expecting everything—and particularly employment—from the national government was reinforced.

A partial change was effected by new legislation in 1986; Amato went further. The ministerial department, agency, and many public bodies with special tasks which had sprung around the agency were dissolved. Powers were given back to the sectoral ministries and the regions. Regional policies, now the responsibility of the ministry of the budget, are subject to a unique national discipline, and subsidies are graduated with respect to economic parameters such as per capita income and the unemployment rate, regardless of geography. This is what the European Commission requires, so even in this field decisive help in promoting change has come from Europe.

While traditional economic analysis on the backwardness of the South stressed the need for capital and recommended public works and incentives to investment by firms it has become rather common opinion in recent years that high priority in development policies should be given to reestablishing respect for the laws, maintaining public order, and providing basic public services with sufficient reliability. In a way, development is seen as depending less on specific economic policies than on general political and administrative reform.

FIVE ASPECTS OF A PERSISTING WEAKNESS

Italy needed a turnaround. Its economy, although growing as fast as the rest of Europe's, had been deteriorating in some important aspects. Action had to be taken to crush inflation, redress the external balance, slash the public deficit, privatize state enterprises (at least in manufacturing and banking), and destroy the waste-creating special administration for the Mezzogiorno. Action along such lines has been initiated and has progressed to a point of no return. This is good, but it cannot be the whole story. Other problems exist where the impact of change has not been felt so directly and effectively.

UNEMPLOYMENT

The most urgent among the open issues is unemployment. Italy has an unemployment rate of 10.5 percent (standard OECD measure)—very close to the average European level. Yet the labor market presents distinct national characteristics. Two-thirds of the unemployed have been out of work for over twelve months, while the proportion is lower than 50 percent in all other European countries—and lower than 20 percent in the United States and Japan. This means that there is little mobility in and out of work, and the social cost of unemployment is much more concentrated. The share of young people unemployed is higher than in other countries, and the unemployment rate in the South is three times higher than in the northern regions; the population of working age is growing in the South and diminishing in the North, so the imbalance is increasing. Some hope can be attached to a better recognition—by the unions first of all—of the need for wage moderation and for a greater flexibility in the labor market.

WEAK PRODUCTIVE AND FINANCIAL STRUCTURE

In a longer view, Italy's economic system is not well equipped for future growth and international competition. Industrial firms are too small and lack advanced technologies; banks are inefficient, and financial markets are still underdeveloped. The overall competitiveness, which is reflected in foreign trade figures, is partially due to a remaining degree of protection from imports in sectors such as cars and textiles and to the persistence of national markets for public procurement and most services. All legal and most de facto shelters are going to be dismantled with the enforcement of European and GATT agreements in the next years. Moreover, small firms although efficient, are disadvantaged in global markets and face the alternative of being either squeezed out or bought by bigger competitors.

On the other side, a number of active small firms and a high birthrate of new firms are the basis for an entrepreneurial selection process. The saving rate of Italian households is still among the world's highest, and recently produced legislation has opened the way for much needed pension funds and other institutional investors. So the growth of industrial firms should find a more favorable environment.

SLOPPY PUBLIC ADMINISTRATION

Even worse is the condition of the public administration, sometimes suggestive of the Third World. A rigid and centralized organization, designed in the nineteenth century on the French model and then maintained, has proved ill-suited to an individualistic and localistic culture. Some regional decentralization was tried in the 1970s, with disappointing results.

Although a minister "for bureaucratic reform" (then "for the public function") has existed for many years, the first real attempts at reform were by Amato and Ciampi. Amato set the legal foundations, obtaining a parliamentary mandate for far-reaching changes in labor relations within the public sector and in the reorganization of offices. Ciampi's Minister for the Public Function, Professor Sabino Cassese, is probably the most knowledgeable and experienced man in Italy on the topic. He has shown tremendous energy in revising and simplifying procedures. (In the Financial Act of 1994 he listed one hundred types of procedures and asked legal powers to streamline them.) He is now forcefully raising the issue before politicians and bureaucrats. He has published calculations showing that Italian firms waste 10 trillion lire (2 percent of total exports) due to the cumbersome procedures of the Ministry of Industry. He has ruled that firms are allowed to keep all documentation required by law on optical support, doing away with paper. He has played a major role in writing the state's 1994 budget by assisting the treasury minister in revising and cutting expenditures item by item, putting up strong resistance to the traditionally victorious requests of the various ministries, and making a first attempt to do away with incremental budgeting and build a zero-base budgetary process. The approach is pragmatic, but action is radical and merciless. If Mr.Cassese were allowed to work for a couple of years, Italy's public administration would undergo its first real modernization in half a century or more.

LARGE ILLEGAL SECTOR: BETTER STILL, THREE QUITE DIFFERENT ONES

Recent episodes have thrown new light on the extent of the illegal sector in the Italian economy. At least three quite different realities are commonly but mistakenly included under the term and should be looked at separately. First is the informal economy, consisting of a myriad of small family enterprises and individual workers, all operating with some degree of tax and social security evasion. It can be seen as characterizing an early stage in economic development and then gradually giving way to more formal units, usually behaving with a greater degree of legality. In general, tax obedience has certainly increased in most parts of Italy in recent years.

Second is corruption in business, often linked to political interference. This is now under the reflectors of the judiciary and the media. It appears to have constituted a pervasive machine, supported or at least tolerated by all political parties, which in fact are crumbling under the scrutiny and the general reaction. The economic impact of corruption will be better assessed in time: it is probably at the roots of the debacle of public enterprises and has something to do with the poor competitive performance of certain industries, such as those linked to public procurement.

Third is criminal business, run by the Mafia and similar organizations. This is a world in itself, mainly concerned with drug traffic, but also with local rackets. Organized crime is a powerful enemy of economic development in Sicily, Calabria, and other areas, making normal honest economic activity impossible and dominating all sorts of business for its own recycling purposes. It is tied to corruption in the economic activity of the public sector, to corruption in the whole of the political process and even in the judiciary and police. Much more than an economic problem, it is a threat to civil society and political life. The period under consideration has seen a historic turnaround in this area as well. All that can be said in an essay on economics is that the reestablishment of law and order looks more likely now than it looked two years ago, and this is a prerequisite for resuming normal economic activity and growth in the Mafia-affected areas, with fallout effects in the rest of the country.

CONCLUSION: IS THE ICEBERG MELTING?

Is the turnaround strong enough to overcome the inevitable resistance and rebounds? Is it general enough to set a new course for Italy's economy, not to mention politics? Let us leave something to the historian. The novelty and the extent of the change under way are nevertheless evident, and they support a cautiously optimistic view.

The strength of Italy's economy has sometimes been identified in its underground component, or *economia sommersa*. ("Underwater" is a less funereal image; it hints of the possibility of the ice melting away, with an ambivalent meaning: one can either imagine the criminal aspects fading and a sound economy and society emerging, or fear a dissolution of the largely informal but vital economic and social system itself.)

The well-known notion that weaker governments may produce more dynamic economies could perhaps be applied to Italy—up to a point. By the 1990s, Italy had reached the stage where weak governments do much more harm than good to the economy.

It seems close to a miracle that such sweeping changes in legislation and in the style of government have been produced by two emergency cabinets, who relied on very fragile parliamentary majorities and whose basic strengths lay in the weakness of their political supporters and controllers (in addition, of course, to the qualities of some of their components). The turnaround has been exquisitely political. If this is true, then the outlook for the economic future depends largely on the likelihood of a stable political equilibrium being reached. The work done in recent years, though, has greatly improved the starting conditions for any future government. Having overcome an emergency, Italy now has some time for working out the new equilibrium. Some time, but maybe not very long.

THE BURDEN OF TAX EVASION

Giulio Tremonti

THE CURRENT ITALIAN TAX SYSTEM

In the Italian tax system, formalism prevails over substance, the central over the peripheral, the state over the market. In short, the complex prevails over the simple. In a field like taxation, in which substance counts at least as much as form, this could not be worse. For this reason even simple tax reforms internally consistent with the existing Italian system—because they presuppose change in that system—are already out of the question. In fact, the system itself is capsizing.

The Italian tax system, apparently identical to a Western model, is in reality substantially based on an Eastern archetype. It is a Justinian system inspired by the authoritative formula "*Quod principi placuit.*" This implies a system that aims for enigmatic perfection, "modernly" developed following the formula for the perfect police state. In the perfect police state citizens police themselves. In the perfect tax state taxpayers should be their own assessors: declarants and auditors, owners and managers, certifiers and guarantors on their own behalf, as well as for their dependents, clients, and correspondents. It is a system in which the norms are measured in square meters (the square meter is asserting itself as the yardstick of entitlement in Italy), an order tempered only by the general nonobservance of the rules which constitute it.

If we stop at the superficial, this difference does not appear. However, if we delve deeper, it is precisely the Byzantine and Eastern matrix which emerges forcefully. The phenomenon below the epiphenomenon emerges. In the East, it is the sovereign who decides taxation, not taxation that decides the sovereign. The *potestas* is sufficient, and the *auctoritas* obsolete. Exactly like in Italy. The tax code descends from the state to the individual vertically and inflexibly (excluding amnesties, offered through the merciful grace of the sovereign).

The essence of tax collection is sacrifice, not benefit. The cause of taxation is axiomatic: taxes are paid by virtue of an abstract principle, almost an incumbent curse, an obligation of penitential expiation due to the simple fact of having something. This mysterious and religious background is always present, as much in primitive tax systems as in Italy's. One need only remember the tacit fervor of the "active repentance" formula, coined to denominate an ordinary pardon. Contributive capacity is not so much a guarantee, a legal limit of collection, or a criterion empirically derived from one's financial statement as it is a dogma descended from on high. Above all, in the ideological architecture of a tax system so constructed, the *agorà* remains above and the *mercatus* below. It is not taxation properly adapting to the economy, but the economy properly adapting to taxation.

It is in these terms that the difference between East and West emerges. The Eastern tax archetype is vertical and state-controlled, artificial and sacrificial, dogmatic and biblical. It is not written by chance (even if recounted here as a joke) that before confronting Goliath, David negotiates a tax exemption for himself and his sons with Saul, who graciously concedes it. David thus becomes the first independent contractor in history to request a tax amnesty.

The Western tax model is just the opposite. The *pactum unionis* is not here conceived and constructed as *pactum subectionis*. The tax burden is not conceived as an end but as a means. Agorà and mercatus combine in flexible forms. The tax code does not develop rigidly along a vertical line. Certainly it has a vertical flow, but then it also subdivides into diverse statutes, with aims differing from those of the state (local governments). The justifying grounds of tax collection are alternately constructed from sacrifice and benefit. Thus they are continually balanced by the citizen with his or her tax vote. The Western tax model is in particular and as much as possible pluralist and procedural, autonomist and consensual, flexible and transparent, empirical and contractual. The doctrine of benefit is pushed to the point that the Treasury is the "trustee" and the taxpayer is the "beneficiary," according to the doctrine of the trust. Tax power is not absolute, but subject to continual checks of the actual received benefit, to a diffuse possible electoral repeal. The empirical concept of consensus, in fact, prevails systematically over the dogma of *dominum*.

The Italian penchant for a tax system like the present one, a system more Eastern than Western, more deontic than economic, has been both cultural and instrumental. Cultural because in theory the Italian tax system coincides with the democratic model of popular despotism, exalting it perfectly. The fact is that in practice it has functioned to the contrary. It has penalized above all the largest and least affluent classes, which are forced to the highest possible degree of tax "equality" by automatic and mechanical taxes like payroll deductions and general market-based consumption taxes. This colossal fiscal injustice is still considered (and this is truly curious) a simple deplorable technical mishap. Instrumental because the Italian tax system is perfectly coherent with the political regime that generated and developed it. They coincide, forming a unified historic bloc, as much temporal profile (beginning in the mid-1970s) as ideal matrix (affirmation of a firm belief in a central state, of the solidarity of consociation).

In the last twenty years an extraordinary combination of politics and finance, of constitutional form and unconstitutional praxis, has developed into a complex and prodigious form. This was something not much different from a white coup. It became the "democracy of deficit," practiced and evolved in a progressive deficit of democracy. This is a political regime based on the model and expedient of debt, which is structurally removed from the constitutional vote *par excellence* from the tax vote. With the help of the illusion emitted from a collective and colossal Mephistophelian "IOU," this political regime believed, and made believe, the impossible possible, that financial wealth was not an alternative but could actually be the constitutive base of the social state.

In order to obtain this illusory effect, financial power was first manipulated (all financial power to the state; the state over the market), then reinforced by the power of debt (parliament, which historically sprang up to control the spending of sovereigns, itself became the sovereign of spending). Finally, it was used to create the illusion of a social state which was not only gratis, but actually profitable, as much in economic terms (the illusion of widespread wealth) as in political terms (the vote not only controlled by those who pay, but also—and above all—polluted by those who collect).

The tax system was a fundamental part of this regime for three reasons, relative to the concentration, postition, and application of financial and tax power. In particular:

a) Initially financial power was totally concentrated in the state through the extant financial autonomy of local agencies, which were transformed into mere centers of dispersement (something like 30,000 dispersement centers spread through the territory).

b) The financial power of the state was developed in the most radical manner possible. In fact, the "liberal" tax model was repudiated. This model is based on the reduction of tax on income that is saved and invested by individuals of their own free will and on the free market for socially worthy services: contingency funds, relief funds, etc. To the contrary, the most radically fiscal model was adopted, based on the taxation of all produced revenue (save for an immense exemption for evasion) and on its redistribution in the form of government spending. This evidently is the model of organization of government finances that ensures the state the possibility of exercising brokerage and arbitrage functions in the circulation and distribution of wealth. It is the state that collects and the state (not private citizens, not families, not the market) that decides what is socially worthy and produces it.

c) Tax power was legally modulated according to the model of exemption for evasion and of favor for debt. The exemption for evasion was guaranteed by tax legislation, based on accounting systems that grotesquely formed an impenetrable shield against the Treasury itself in favor of the tax-evader. Favor for debt, notable in general and particularly in the case of government debt, was then formalized, first by total tax exemption granted to government securities, and then by a purely symbolic direct taxation levied on the people—physical, anonymous bearers of these same securities. (Moreover, it checks a great many important residual forms of government securities' exemption through indirect taxation.)

On these bases two initial conclusions can be drawn:

a) This tax system is not perfectly coherent with the political regime begun in the mid-1970s; it is both the cause and the effect.

democracy of deficit would not have developed if there had not been a Treasury based on the model of evasion and debt: constituent evasion to the North, benefits raining down on the South, the country unified by government revenue. All of this is outside of the fundamental constitutional pact of "No taxation without representation." We have a political regime which, on the one hand, escaped the "tax vote," and on the other hand attracted the "electoral vote." This forms the essential base of the current political "cleptocracy."

b) The passage from Eastern to Western model, from the old deontic tax model to a new economic one, cannot be made with a tax reform internal to this tax system. And probably cannot be made by this political regime. As Sieyès, jurist of the French Revolution, noted, constituted or established power will never be constituent power.

For these reasons, the tax change, if it is to happen, can only be revolutionary (as the referendum movement, which primed a revolutionary political process, was revolutionary). The necessary revolutionary passage must be one toward a new tax constitution, which redefines the relationship between state and market and state and territory.

What *must* the state do, and what *can* the market do? What *must* the central government (the state) do, and what *must* the local governments (regional, provincial, municipal) do? Again, how many sacrifices are asked *of* the people, in terms of national solidarity, and how much instead can be asked *by* the people, in terms of particular benefits?

Caveat. Perhaps this picture is excessively pessimistic. Certainly at the base there was also a vast heterogeneity of ends. Many of the ideal and political forces that wanted the social state certainly did not want the involution of the democracy of deficit. They had high and noble ideals, and they simply thought that an efficient social state required a strong tax state. And they felt that the two states must be separated from each other (first the Treasury collects, then other agencies distribute), intermediated by a central national state, and finally superimposed on the market. In the long run, the model revealed itself as disastrous. The totally centralized tax state does not work. The same can be said of the social state.

Now the same objectives of solidarity can be reached with different political means, with a tax state more divided over the territory, a social state closer to the market. The national social state must guarantee social security and welfare services basic to the actually needy segments of the population—that is, to the minority of the population. The rest must be produced by the market and purchased on the market by families, which are sustained by the state with tax deductions. Requirements of financing this organization of social solidarity do not include a strong central rigidity in the application of tax regulations (which, among other things, no longer functions). This provides one more reason not to fear the tax revolution.

A TAX REVOLUTION: IT IS NOT NECESSARY TO DO IT, JUST WAIT FOR IT

It is, then, not necessary to carry out a tax revolution; it suffices to expect it. It is still difficult to say if the revolution will be carried out by a "big bang" or by a more incremental cascade of political and economic phenomena. But it is already intrinsic to the tax system. It has already begun. And as is always the case with revolutions, the fragmented revolutionary factors act on the old environment both internally and externally.

The internal factors—which will be more closely analyzed below—essentially act on three levels:

a) The Italian tax system is parasitic, progressively shifting wealth from production to debenture. It does so shifting assets equal to that of direct taxation (assets now equal to almost 200,000 billion). As is evident, this is the way the base case of tax policy is produced. The goal of a sole tax, in fact, becomes Verrian (Verrian in the sense of the rapacious proconsul Verre), aimed at the collection of revenue targeted to recompense debenture, with consequent and growing indifference to the necessities of equity, development, investment, or employment.

b) Next we move to a technique typical of tax cubism. Tax figures are divided and superimposed, from the center to the periphery, solely by multiplying the centers and collection points. The central state is strangling its collateral political structures: local agencies, social security agencies, etc. The mechanism is apparently virtuous. The state reduces the transfers to these structures, thus allowing the announcement of a spending cut. In conjunction, the state transfers to these same structures additional quotas of compensatory tax power in the form of healthcare taxes of the "poll tax" type, in the form of increases of employer contributions such as pension plan and insurance payments, additional or new local taxes, etc. Thus it can be announced that *state* taxes are not rising. The "state" mentality, in fact, deceives members of government that these are the *true* taxes, that the others are something else. It is a cubist device based on the decomposition and movement of figures, a mechanism that initially has a strong illusory content. The financial illusion mainfests itself most strongly when, with the announcement of a benefit, the state tax burden does not increase. A further spell is conjured: the local tax or parafiscal burden does increase. But then it has minimal possibilities of feasibility and political capacity. If government finance is in fact (perhaps) divisible (into state, parafiscal, regional, provincial, and municipal finance), the citizen is, instead, indivisible—like his or her wallet, which loses economic weight as it acquires political weight (thus developing the "wallet vote").

c) We pass finally from burden to oppression, assigning to citizens in general and to taxpayers in particular functions that should instead be carried out by public offices. This is especially evident in the transfer of growing accounting *corvées* to single taxpayers, to third parties (substitution duties), and among third parties (activation of conflicts of interest or of shrewd devices of "private police").

The external factors manifest themselves on four levels and depend on the pressure exerted by the immense stock of government debt, the growing erosion of the bases of the "modern" national state, the increasingly wide economic division of the country, and the change constituted by the diffusion of universal suffrage, as follows:

a) The crisis of the "modern" national state: The "modern" national state is too small with respect to the phenomena that are developing on a global scale and too large with respect to the needs of local government. In fact, the fundamental political chain—state-territory-wealth—is scorned.

b) The excess of government debt: The stock of government debt equals almost 2 million billion lire.

c) The division of the country: The country is, unfortunately, increasingly divided, horizontally and vertically. It is divided horizontally between reality and finances. Reality is made of people, houses, factories: super-taxed. Finances are essentially made of government revenue: super-recompensed—all the more so as government revenue is not fed only by social savings. The country is in fact characterized by a large propensity toward savings, including savings of taxes. Evaders collect three times in this way: they do not pay taxes, they have social services almost gratis, and they collect interest on money not given to the government. The progressive transfer of wealth from production to debenture has permitted the progressive descent of the country among developing nations.

The country is divided vertically between North and South, private industry to the North and employment to the South. It is clearly divided by different economies and ideologies, each one dominant in its own area of development: private industry in the North, government employment in the South. Sixty percent of private business owners and 75 percent of the partners in family businesses or partnerships are concentrated in the North. With the addition of the central area, these figures grow to 80 percent and 90 percent respectively. In contrast, in the South the dominant productive activity is constituted by government employment. It is precisely this economic differential that began to be transformed, in the first free elections after the fall of communism, into a political differential.

The population of private business owners and more generally of independents (in Italy there are more than 4 million "holders" of file numbers assigned by the government in order to collect or refund IVA [value-added] taxes—more than in France and Germany combined; counting relatives, it is almost a population) began to vote, not only with its head, but also with its wallet, as the rest of Europe has done for some time, and thus expressed a census vote. "Census vote" is not meant in the sense that only those who pay taxes vote or that one votes in order not to pay them—not even in the sense that only private businesses pay taxes, nor that all private businesses pay all taxes. Rather it is meant in the sense that with respect to government employees, private business owners have, and have begun to express, additional reasons to protest the mismanagement of government services.

Everyone is right to protest the inefficiency of essential government services: health, justice, education. However, the discomfort of private business owners goes beyond and even begins precisely where, with the frequently symbolic performance of a job, the discomfort of the mass of public employees ends. It is exactly in this sense that—right or wrong—the sensation of paying taxes twice spreads among private business owners—first as penalization of productive activity, then as outright taxes. From licenses to mail, from transport to union relations, from authorizations to embezzlement, from allocations to dispensations, the effect exerted on private business by the mismanagement of government services is more ballast than utility. Moreover, both government employees and private business owners pay taxes, but while the Treasury is avaricious toward the former, when it is not avaricious toward the latter it is nonetheless odious to them, for two reasons. The first reason (previously discussed) is that the state unloads its progressive inefficiency onto private industry, transferring to it a growing load of burdens destined to be substitutive in retaliation precisely for its inefficiency. Four accounts are needed to sell a kilo of bread; anyone who endorses a bank check is in principle presumed an evader or member of the Mafia, except when proven otherwise. For every real transaction a growing number of useless transactions are thus imposed—purely a "fiscal" ritual. The second reason is demagogy. Anti-evasion campaigns are proclaimed and publicized with the fastidious mind-set of a hunter, "black lists" and "red books," proof of receipt regulations imposed on children, etc. This is a political technique that causes everyone to lose: the state, which does not collect taxes; the evaders, who, however, sustain the cost of evasion (because evading also has a not insignificant price); and the parties that practice this technique and lose votes.

d) Universal suffrage: The absolute political novelty of the last years is the freedom of the vote, the effective diffusion of universal suffrage. Until now universal suffrage in Italy was more formal than substantive. Given with one hand, it was taken away with the other. The vote of the masses was polarized in the elementary and fundamental Pythagorean alternative between two opposing forces like night and day, good and evil: democracy and communism. These are forces that are perhaps ideological and therefore manipulated by the elite. It is true that at a certain point this ideology began to lose force. But to compensate the "democracy of deficit" is then begun—with analogous effects of manipulation of the political vote—which subverts the fundamental consitutional mechanism, "No taxation without representation." Half of the political vote was thus distorted because it was not "tax vote" but "electoral vote," from those who do not pay taxes but collect interest, unjust pensions, etc.

   It is no longer this way. The people no longer vote on the basis of an abstract and artificial opposition of ideological polarities, but on the basis of the quotidian needs of material life. They vote with their wallets. And they will do this forever more for two reasons. The first is that the "debt model," which complied with the old political system of persistence in spite of the progressive fall of ideologies, failed and ended. That which lost political vitality was compensated by social or financial profit. The second reason lies in the fact that the illusion thus created can no longer be maintained. In reality, this illusion is transforming into its opposite, in the electoral penalty for a political regime restricted as much by the enormous stock of self-generated government debt as by the crumbling of the financial illusion that through political retaliation fostered exactly the opposite of that which until now it actually did—increase the tax burden, reduce social "protection."

On its own account, the tie between the electoral system and the tax system is crucial and indeed should be the object of specific analysis. More particularly:

- Marginally, studying the meaning of the reserve of votes forecast to favor nonresidents (Italians abroad vote but do not pay; they actually vote in order to receive pensions);

- Principally, studying the new political "caucus" that progressively is taking shape within the new single-member constituencies, among other things under the heavy pressure of fiscal interests that will be represented by intermediary bodies like unions.

AGENDA FOR RECONSTRUCTION

"Oh, I want to become Swiss! Cursed sole tax that has reduced me to begging. But is it perhaps more just and honest to have three or four hundred taxes, the names of which are impossible to remember or pronounce?" Thus Voltaire ironically quipped in one of his famous tax stories. In reality, between one tax and hundreds of taxes, the *juste milieu* is found somewhere in the middle.

I suggest, in summary, that a tax revolution, coherent with the previously espoused principles, can be based on the following essential points:

a) There are five truly essential taxes: IRPEF, IRPEG, IVA, manufacturing and customs, and property. The others can calmly be eliminated, from the tax on inheritances and donations (which has a ridiculous yield—700 billion per year, meaning that in Italy one either does not die or dies extremely poor) to the tax on plastic bags, lighters, refrigerators, etc. The entire "bestiary" of Italian taxes is drastically thinned out.
b) Demolish progressiveness. No longer justified by ideology, overelevated rates do not produce but rather eliminate revenue. In conjunction, trifling controversies are eliminated. Minimum accounts (at least up to half a million) must be able to be defined by writ. In addition, the government must become stricter about all aspects of the system—particularly corruption, which is now not only exempt from regulation, but actually rewarded. The heavy taxpayer should interest the Treasury above all.
c) Extend the catalog of deductions, especially to favor families and their social security and welfare savings.
d) Eliminate the debt model, with the *par condicio* between loan capital and venture capital.

e) Restore power of taxation to local agencies, regions, and municipalities. Above all, local autonomy should not be considered as the power to impose new taxes, but as budgetary autonomy and responsibility, in which earnings and expenditures are voted on and balanced.

THE FOREIGN POLICY THAT WAS NOT THERE

Sergio Romano

The Italian "revolution" coincides with the sudden disappearance of the conditions on which Italian foreign policy was based. By a peculiar stroke of bad luck, the death of the Italian regime parallels its disappearance, after forty-five years, in the international arena. Italy functioned within a delicate mechanism whose pulleys and springs were European integration, the United States, NATO, and (on the other side of the wall) a strong friend-enemy, the Soviet Union. Now European unification is in jeopardy, the United States has not yet decided what its future global role should be, NATO is an empty house of unclear functions, and the Soviet Union is gone. As a result, the pulleys and springs have stopped functioning and the engine is broken. To have a foreign policy means having clear goals and the means to achieve them. The goals—real or fictitious, material or ideal—can be different: strategic collocation, construction of a vital space, regional hegemony, an empire, control of communications routes, freedom of trade, regional integration, or global security. The means too are various: economic power and the capability to use it, loans and credits, military force, an authoritative and reliable diplomacy, and a geopolitical position ready to be exploited. Right now, Italy does not know what it wishes its future to be, and in any case it does not have the means to achieve it. It lacks a foreign policy because it lacks both goals and means.

Let us start with European integration—the single most important goal for all Italian governments since World War II. Instead of considering "Europe" in abstract terms, let us look at what European unity has meant for Italy since the postwar period. The real Italian Europeanists—our "fathers of a united Europe"—can be counted on one hand: Luigi Einaudi, Altiero Spinelli, Carlo Sforza, and Alcide

De Gasperi. Einaudi and Spinelli became Europeanists after having realized that the nation-state born out of the Risorgimento had failed and that Italy needed to justify its existence with a new mission. In a speech in 1947 at the Università per Stranieri of Perugia, Sforza declared that European unification would mean for Italy what the legitimacy principle had meant for France after the Congress of Vienna. Like Talleyrand, Sforza wanted to transform the military defeat into a moral victory through an inspired political project which would erase the distinction between winners and losers.

Einaudi had come to similar conclusions since his exile in Switzerland before the end of the war. When the peace treaty reached the Senate, he voted to ratify it, motivated by the need to get rid of all nationalist nostalgia in order to move forward to a truly international policy. He certainly was not less "nationalist" than Benedetto Croce—who voted against the treaty—but instead of nursing a wounded pride full of potentially revanchist overtones, he elected to quickly turn the page on the entire war period. He had understood better than Croce that the lost war meant much more than just the end of fascism and that Italy's only chance of survival as a nation-state lay in forging an international agenda quite different from the one it had pursued between 1861 and 1943.

The integration of European people through the Marshall Plan and NATO also brought a pragmatic De Gasperi to share Sforza's political project. He used Europe as an argument to convince his fellow Christian Democrats to choose the West. He presented Europe as a promise of peace for all continental nations and used this vision to win acceptance for the military plans through which the United States aimed to counterbalance the expansionist ambitions of Soviet foreign policy. He did so with great conviction because to him a unified Europe looked like the modern version of the political system he had grown up with before World War I: a Christian Democratic Europe whose major leaders—Adenauer, Schuman, and himself—were all more or less fluent in the lingua franca of the Dual Monarchy, a Europe whose political shape in the postwar world would be as similar as possible to the Austro-Hungarian empire.

Spinelli, like De Gasperi, had never been a nationalist. Since becoming a Communist after the 1921 Congress of Livorno, he was a convinced internationalist. He discovered Europe once he understood that the Soviet Union was exploiting the "brother parties" to better accomplish its imperial ambitions, and he then devoted to the "European revolution" all of the energies he had previously invested on the ideals of the Communist revolution.

These four European forefathers came from completely different backgrounds. Einaudi and Sforza were products of national liberal democracy; De Gasperi and Spinelli belonged to the internationalist front, a dynastic one for the former, an ideological one for the latter. But they all shared the same lack of faith in the Italian state and its potential for surviving its defeat in World War II and the postwar world with all its original ideals intact. For all of them, Europe was thus a second love: for Sforza and Einaudi, it represented a new and broader nationalism which could replace the old and worn out nationalism of the Risorgimento; for De Gasperi, Europe represented an empire, a confederate yet Catholic democracy in which Italy, like a greater Trentino, would find a role for all its parts, from the Alps to Sicily; for Spinelli, it represented a new internationalism to which he could devote the passion and energy he had wasted on the deceitful Soviet internationalism. None of them, not even Einaudi, chose Europe for economic reasons. It was a political choice—especially for Einaudi and Sforza—based on the conviction that Italy had lost its reasons for existence.

The economy nevertheless played a major role. The battle for open borders and free trade was fought by Einaudi and Ugo La Malfa with the conviction that protectionism and liberalism were the political equivalent of nationalism and Europeanism respectively. But the European choice was politically motivated, especially for the two liberal democratic leaders, by the urgency to give a new moral constitution to the country. Sforza in particular recalled Mazzini and his young Europe to show that Italy had been the bearer since Risorgimento of a great European vision. This was his version of the "legitimacy principle," to be used to bring Italy proudly back among the family of nations. This was the bloodline to secure for the country and himself a leading role in the incoming Risorgimento.

The European vision thus became the ruling class's political investment for the salvation of the country. However, the people who succeeded these four forefathers were, with some notable exceptions (such as Gaetano Martino), skeptical, mediocre, and cynically opportunistic. From then on, Italy supported European integration more or less in the same way it had supported the Triple Alliance between

1882 and 1914: it made some coherent decisions but used much conformity, rhetoric, and cunning.

Italians believe in Europe in the same way they have believed in the many foreign powers taking control of their history. Europe is like the "Emperor" or the "Pope" or any other authority with a dominant role in the politics of the country. To the question "Are you in favor of Europe?," Italians will answer in the same positive way that the majority of people from Lombardy and Veneto would have in 1858 to the question "Are you for the Austrian emperor?"—an answer that only two years later would also have been given to the new question, "Are you for the King of Italy?" None of these positive answers would have changed Italian opinion that every system—national, imperial, or federal—must be endured and, if possible, flattered, circumvented, and deceived.

There are further considerations on the left. In the early stages, neither Communists nor socialists were "Europeanists,"convinced as they were—as Spinelli was until 1938—that the entire world would become socialist. From the internationalist perspective of the left, European unification was a bourgeois distraction, a final capitalist attempt to modernize and rationalize the citadel of bourgeois democracy. Later, when they found out—as Spinelli did—that internationalism was only the new disguise of Russian imperialism, the parties of the left became—with some ambiguities—"European." In particular for the Communist Party, support for European integration was the price it had to pay to find a pluralistic credibility. But European integration had to be coherent with the party's political agenda in order to recreate, on a European scale, a new internationalism. This led to two strategies: Eurocommunism and, when that failed, the formation of a progressive front with the left wing of the Labor Party and German Social Democrats. For the majority of the Italian left, Europe was essentially a certificate of goodwill, a safe-conduct to get out of the Leninist ghetto. However, once European unification was accepted, it ceased to be debated. With the Communists now solidly sharing a Europeanist policy, Italy became "European" in the same way it is Catholic: with rhetorical fervor, indifference, cunning, and many secret dealings. Europe is like a religious icon in front of which all politicians quickly cross themselves before moving onto other topics. European religion, as the first article of the Italian Statute declares, is a state religion.

The economy undoubtedly fortified this faith. It is sufficient to look at the statistics of Italian exports for the last forty years to understand the richness of the relationships among European countries. I do not claim that European integration caused the Italian economic miracle, but I have difficulty imagining Italy and its productive system without Europe. Business is quite aware of this. In 1947, when La Malfa started lowering border tariffs, and in 1957, when the government signed the Treaty of Rome, the business community resisted the change and looked at Europe with suspicion. Today it sees the Common Market as a necessity and would never survive without it.

These are the main components of Italian Europeanism. Lately they have been tarnished by a sentiment of "impotent Europeanism." In these years the number of people, especially of the ruling classes, who have invested Europe with the task of changing Italy has increased steadily. The more Italy sank into the shifting grounds of bad political habits, the more Europe—with its directives and agenda—grew to become the only Italian hope for redemption and reform. As a result, we witnessed a curious political schizophrenia. The same people who in Rome were deeply enmeshed in the wheeling and dealing of consociational politics were in Brussels calling for rigor, coherence, and orthodoxy. Sinners in Italy, they became saints in Europe. In almost every phenomenon of Italian political life in these recent years, we can see the conviction that Europe would eventually force us to clean house. This impotent Europeanism probably rendered Italian politicians even more nearsighted and carefree: it led them to hope that the emperor in Brussels would solve the problems of a province they only ruled by proxy.

History has pleased them well beyond any expectations. Italy has signed the Maastricht Treaty with the same irresponsible ambiguity and intellectual levity it used to join the European Monetary System in 1979 and to follow the obligations of a common market. Once again the government had trusted providence and left to Europe the task to reform Italy. But the Maastricht Treaty, unlike other communitarian tools, is like a railroad schedule: it sets up, with bureaucratic rigor, the times of the financial unification and prescribes the precise conditions of the financial health of all its members. Countries can become union members only if their inflation rate is within 1.5 percent of the average rate of the three states with the lowest inflation, if the national budget deficit is below 3 percent of GNP, and if the national debt does not exceed 60 percent of GNP. At the time of the Maastricht signing, Italy could not meet two of these three criteria: the deficit and national debt were 10 percent and 110 percent of GNP respectively. No decrees out of Brussels would alone have solved the situation of Italian finance. At that time Italy—or at least the most responsible sectors of the ruling classes—had to admit that the government had taken on an obligation it could not fulfill. Moreover, since deficit and public debt were only the fiscal expression of the decay of the Italian political system, many recognized that the regime was incompatible with Europe. The Maastricht Treaty, much more than the end of the cold war, was the single most important external factor in accelerating the Italian political crisis.

What happened was exactly what the Italian political class had waited and wished for: Italian renovation by European decree. However, the treaty pulled Italy in two completely opposite directions: it showed the necessity for a radical change of the political system, thus contributing to the regime's crisis; but by casting a shadow on the integration process, it also produced a crisis in the concept of the mission used by Italy to justify its existence since the end of the war. History will tell if the European turmoil following the Danish referendum in spring 1992 should be attributed to the foolish pride of technocratic enlightenment in Brussels or to a singular combination of historical events such as the high cost of German unification, American recession, unemployment, and the financial instability caused by antagonistic monetary policies (Bundesbank and Federal Reserve). I personally think that the treaty would not be in crisis if these historical circumstances had not shown up at the same time, causing instability in the free movement of capital. The crisis of the monetary system between the summers of 1992 and 1993, however, transformed the railroad itinerary agreed upon at Maastricht into an uncertain journey. At the same time, we must not forget that we will never have a strong common market if EC countries are not able to unify monetary, financial, and social policies. Sooner or later, Europe will start again from Maastricht.

The treaty crisis coincides with the Italian one, denying the country a European reference which has been, since CECA, the pivotal point of Italian international policy and national consciousness. If European integration becomes uncertain, Italy becomes uncertain.

With the crisis of the state and of national identity coinciding, the European crisis intensifies and deepens the Italian crisis.

When De Gasperi asked the Italian parliament to ratify NATO—as agreed upon by Sforza in Washington in 1949—he met with considerable opposition from important sectors of his own party. But he did not dare tell parliament that the major obstacle to Italian entry in the alliance had come precisely from the United States. The U.S. government was eager to save Italy from the Communists, as proved by the covert operations conducted by the CIA's Special Operations Group. But it was not ready to include Italy in NATO. At the State Department, many people wanted to avoid this for at least two reasons: they had little trust in Italian military capability, and they did not want to extend to the Mediterranean area the political and military protection spelled out in the treaty. However, the French had asked protection for Algeria and wanted to include among the signatories to the treaty another Mediterranean country. Truman conceded. He did not want Italy, but even less did he want a fight among Allies which could have benefited the Soviet Union. Thus, thanks to French diplomacy, Italy became the outpost of a geopolitical area which spread from the western Atlantic to the Adriatic and Sicilian seas (Greece and Turkey would join NATO later). This extension of territorial responsibilities transformed Italy into the southern border of the "Atlantic," assigning to its territory a strategic value.

We will never know how the United States would have tried to protect Italian territory from the Soviet threat if Italy had not been admitted into NATO. But we know that from the time that NATO was extended to the Mediterranean area, the United States did not hesitate to create the conditions for political and military control in case of need. It did so on three fronts: it set up military bases with full military autonomy, established a dominant relationship with the Italian intelligence community, and kept veto power over all major decisions of Italian politics. That did not mean daily interference with Italian governments, as the left naively claimed. The United States was too divided, "pluralistic," and quarrelsome to give precise instructions to a foreign government for its daily operations. But it ruthlessly intervened every time it felt the need to reaffirm the security and loyalty of the area. The socialist entry into government was possible only because at the end of 1963 the Kennedy administration approved the center-left; the Communist admittance became impossible when the Carter administration repeatedly opposed it in 1978 and 1979. At these times, the limits of Italian sovereignty became clear for everybody.

Other countries responded to American interference by refusing it, as did France and Spain, or by trying to transform it into a partnership, as did Great Britain and Germany. Italy chose a third way: giving to the United States what it wanted, provided it did not interfere too much with internal interests. It gave up intelligence autonomy but kept using it for internal power struggles and political favoritism. It gave up military autonomy but kept providing NATO with understaffed troops with only representative power. It accepted U.S. control over its political system, but kept the right to tangle with some of the United States's worst enemies: the Soviet Union, Arafat's PLO, Ghaddafi's Libya, Mengistu's Ethiopia. We can say that overall Italy—especially in these last thirty years—traded parts of its territory and political autonomy for the right to pursue a foreign policy that, though respectful of NATO, was dictated by internal power struggles. It was not a Gaullist policy because Italy did not care, as De Gaulle did, for independence and national pride, but a policy synthesizing all pacifist and Third World tendencies present among the political forces making up Italian consociational democracy. It was a faithful NATO member as long as a global war was not imminent and Italy could play the broker rôle between an Eastern and Western bloc that had no real intention of fighting each other. It favored mediations, reconcilements, dialogues, and ecumenical perspectives since this diplomacy pleased and suited the Catholic left, the socialists, the Communists, and the economic sectors eager to do business with Eastern Europe and the Arab world.

In all crucial moments, Italian governments always made orthodox decisions. In December 1979, for instance, Italy supported German Chancellor Schmidt's request for the deployment of American missiles as a political and military answer to the Soviet SS20 and accepted placement of the Cruise missiles in Comiso. But once again it traded national territory for the possibility of being unfaithful to the alliance. In the following months the government tried to lessen the orthodoxy with mediations and political winks meant for the progressive forces of Italian society. Andreotti, then foreign minister, winked to the Communists that he was against German unification; while Craxi, prime minister at the time, seemed to call into question, during a trip to Lisbon, the time schedule of missile deployments. At a time when German unification was unreal and the missile talks were firmly in U.S. hands, such declarations were purely formal. But they constituted signals to the Soviet Union and to progressive and populist sectors of Italian politics that although Italy was "Atlantic," it could, if need be and possible, act on its own.

This ambiguity entailed some risks. In October 1984, U.S. planes intercepted an Egyptair airplane and forced it to land in Sigonella, Sicily; Palestinian leader Mohammed Abu Abbas and four of his followers were on board. Several days earlier, this group had seized the Italian ship Achille Lauro in Alexandria, Egypt, and killed a retired U.S. citizen. The United States wanted these terrorists, but the Italian government refused to extradite them, preserving its Third World credibility with the Arab world and Italian left.

Apart from a few incidents, a wavering Italian foreign policy easily found its way through Atlantism and pacifism. The international conditions produced by the cold war were ideal for Italian diplomatic skills. The division of the world into two blocs kept it safe from a global war and kept a tight lid on regional conflicts. This "balance of terror" was in reality a long phase of stability and peace during which Italy assumed obligations no one would call upon and preached a peace no one would want violated.

With the fall of the Berlin Wall and the end of the cold war, these conditions no longer apply. The Gulf War, regional conflicts in the former Soviet Union, Yugoslav disintegregation, Somalia's collapse, and the confusion in Cambodia are proof that a world order able to prevent, settle, or limit international conflicts is over. The fall of an empire is an event that only fools and the idealistic carefree can welcome. Like a major earthquake, it sent waves of instability through the foundations of the international community, upsetting its balance. Those who hope for a drastic reduction in military budgets as a result of the end of the cold war should look at arms programs of countries such as Pakistan, India, China, Korea, or Japan, let alone other smaller Asian countries.

The end of the era of the impossible global war has crippled the diplomacy borne out of that unreal threat. The only countries with political programs are now those able to afford the tools to implement them: an army ready to fight, the financial means to assist newly formed states, a strong humanitarian organization able to aid civilians. There are three examples that show how inadequate Italy's means are: the Hexagonal, Yugoslavia, and Somalia.

The Hexagonal, also called the Central European Initiative, is a program initiated by Minister of Foreign Affairs Gianni De Michelis in 1989 to group some of the Central European and Balkan nations under Italian leadership. It was a good idea. On the economic level, it offered Yugoslavia, Hungary, Czechoslovakia, and Poland an opportunity to form an area of economic collaboration with Italy and Austria while waiting to become part of the EC. On the political level, it offered them the opportunity to escape German influence. The Hexagonal would have recreated a Mitteleuropa independent from Germany, opened possibilities for common work, and unbridled energies at a time when many countries were rejecting communism and attempting to reconstruct their economic and political systems. But it had costs, especially for shared infrastructures, that Italy could not afford. The comparison with Germany is telling. The FDR, in order to win Soviet approval, poured into its unification substantial funds, loans, and investments. Italy, on the other hand, offered its foreign minister's talkativeness, many meetings with ministers and bureaucrats, some conferences, but very limited regional opportunistic funds.

Following Yugoslavia's disintegration in 1991, Italy was excluded for historical and geographic reasons from contributing its forces to UN troops operating in the area. The presence of Italian troops in the same locations they had invaded only fifty years ago had been deemed inappropriate. But Italy could have helped the people, showing its solidarity and goodwill. However, it could not do so due to its lack of a strong relief organization. France has Médecins du Monde and Médecins sans Frontières; Great Britain has the Save the Children Fund and other relief organizations; Germany has an excellent Red Cross. Italy's Red Cross is unable to sustain a major relief operation, and the only other organization operating on its territory, the Caritas, is accountable only to the Vatican. This scarcity would have been a minor problem if the collapse of the world order had not provoked all around the world—from Bosnia to Somalia, from Kurdistan to Tajikistan—an array of regional conflicts in which the local population could play the role of victim, hostage, or torturer. In order to have a foreign policy under these circumstances, a government must project a caring, organized, and efficient image.

This is the best way to smooth the ground for future economic and political relations. To "show the flag" in a war scenario fought over men, women, and children, one has to deploy an army of doctors, nurses, drivers, social workers. Italy can sometimes use its troops as it did in Kurdistan or in Albania, but its lack of relief capability is hurting its ability to conduct effective diplomacy.

For the third example, let us briefly review the history of Italian participation in UN operations in Somalia. At the end of 1992, Somalia was one of the four or five countries around the world where civilians were dying from hunger and were continuously harassed by brutal warlords. Leaving Bosnia aside, the Liberian situation (where 250,000 people had died in four years of civil war) or the Sudanese one (where nobody knows how many southern Christians have been killed by Muslims) seemed more serious than Somalia. But everybody knew that aid relief in Somalia depended upon the whims of warlords and that flour was rotting in Mogadishu storehouses. UN Secretary General Boutros Boutros-Ghali wanted to do something but lacked the means. The United Nations is not yet able to mount and sustain a complex military operation on its own. It could patrol a border or monitor elections, as it did in Cambodia. But it lacks troops, special corps, intelligence, communications lines, and operative and logistic structures. Enter George Bush, who in December 1992—a month before Clinton's inauguration—decided to teach the president-elect a lesson on foreign policy by ordering the deployment of American troops in Mogadishu. They arrived amid a flurry of spotlights, flashes, and the noise of movie cameras. But the United States did not want to stay long, and after a few days announced the withdrawal of the majority of its contingent. In other words, the United States implicitly announced to the warlords that if they were patient, they could regain their territory. To deal with the U.S. withdrawal, the UN Security Council formed an international contingent to protect civilians and disarm the military factions.

The Italian government decided to participate in the operation by sending 2,500 soldiers. Italy wanted to make amends for having supported Siad Barre and for the suspicious dealings concerning its financial aid during the last years of Barre's regime. It also wanted to show its Third World sensitivity in this former colony. Once in place, the Italians found that they still had many personal contacts and used them to establish links with the warlords, especially with

General Mohammed Aidid. They operated as they did in Lebanon between 1982 and 1984, just as the Americans did in Mogadishu. This networking was interpreted by the United Nations and the United States as a sign of excessive boldness and autonomy.

The Italian relationship with the United States worsened after Aidid's attack against Pakistani troops and the U.S. response. The Italians thought they had a sort of tacit immunity, but they quickly realized otherwise once three of their soldiers were killed. Thus started a vicious circle of accusations and counteraccusations. The Americans and the UN command accused the Italian troops of lacking discipline and directness; the Italians replied by accusing the United States and United Nations of having transformed a humanitarian operation into a punitive expedition with civilians as primary targets.

The Somali imbroglio offers contradictory lessons and truths. In the first place, it shows that when the United Nations must make military decisions, it has to rely on the nation able to deliver ships, helicopters, airplanes, communications lines, strike capabilities, and, above all, political and military power. This nation has almost always been the United States. UN wars—from Korea to the Gulf War—have in reality been wars wanted by the United States and waged under the UN banner. In the second place, the Somali situation shows that the United States is too strong, independent, and proud to allow its troops to be under foreign command. It agrees to NATO unified command because American hegemony hides under the heading of unification, but it has always kept full control of times, means, and ways in any single operation.

Finally, Somalia teaches us that Italy does not want or cannot afford the risk of a military operation. The two major UN participants during the crisis—Americans and Italians—confronted each other from opposing and unsatisfactory positions. The former waged war without politics; the latter, politics without war. Both used the means with which they were more comfortable: Americans used their arms because they have them and because all through their history they have always looked for quick and decisive solutions. Italians used diplomacy because they have mediocre military power and public opinion will not accept loss of life. Both chose the most congenial strategy for their needs: Americans chose punitive expeditions because they allow fast incursions in and out of the political arena;

Italians chose diplomacy since it puts off the call for action. However, without weapons, money, and a strong relief organization, Italian foreign policy is only a rhetorical exercise.

Italy has lost the geopolitical capital it had during the cold war and currently lacks the means for the challenges and responsibilities of the present political situation. European integration will eventually absorb Italian diplomacy within a wider context, but the "promised land" of a common European foreign policy is not yet within sight. Before they can be heard on the international scene, Italian governments will have to work hard to provide the country with credible means of action. It is doubtful, however, whether they can effectively do so at a time when the Italian political agenda is so predominantly domestic. Eventually the new Italian foreign policy depends on the reconstruction of the Italian political system. In the meantime Italian foreign ministers and diplomats will have to talk softly and carry a very little stick.

REFERENCES

Are, Giuseppe. 1977. *L'Italia e i mutamenti internazionali 1971–1976: L'arretramento di un paese diviso in un mondo in trasformazione.* Florence: Vallecchi.

Cacace, Paolo. 1968. *Venti anni di politica estera italiana (1943–1963).* Rome: Bonacci.

Cesa, Maco. 1989. *Defining Security: The Case of Southern Europe and the Superpowers in the Mediterranean.* Pisa: Ets Editrice.

IAI (Istituto Affari Internazionali). *L'Italia nella politica internazionale,* a series of yearbooks. Rome.

Romano, Sergio. 1993. *Guida alla politica estera italiana dal crollo del fascismo al crollo del comunismo.* Milan: Rizzoli.

Santoro, Carlo M. 1991. *La politica estera di una media potenza: L'Italia dall'unità a oggi.* Bologna: Il Mulino.

Seton-Watson, Christopher. 1991. "La politica estera della Repubblica italiana." In R. J. B. Bosworth and S. Romano, *La politica estera italiana 1860–1985.* Bologna: Il Mulino.

Vigezzi, Brunello. 1991. *Politica estera e opinione pubblica in Italia dall'Unità ai nostri giorni.* Milan: Edizioni Universitarie Yaca Book.

THE MAFIA, COSA NOSTRA, AND ITALIAN INSTITUTIONS TODAY

Pino Arlacchi

CRIMINAL ACTIVITIES IN ITALY

Criminality in southern Italy and in Italy in general emerged in the 1980s as the major national problem and one of the most important factors setting Italy apart from the rest of Western Europe. The emergence of Italy's "criminal question" had been in the works for some time, but it has now imposingly assumed center stage. At the same time, law enforcement agencies have only recently come to recognize and evaluate its seriousness.

At first glance, Italian criminal activity can be broken down into four fundamental parts: the Mafia and organized crime, political and administrative corruption, financial criminality, and illegal lobbying. The Mafia and organized crime comprise a great number of family businesses (500 according to the Ministry of the Interior, with 15,000 members) which control most illegal economic activities on a national scale. These families also control a significant part of legal economic activity in wide areas of the South and in limited sectors in the North. Political and administrative corruption includes a range of illicit activities that are typical of wide sectors of Italian public administration. Hence the expressions *sistema delle tangenti* and *tangentopoli. Tangenti* are kickbacks. Financial criminality refers to group and market behavior which relies on and uses illegal methods in the management of legal businesses. Finally, illegal lobbying consists of pressure groups—which in Italy are prohibited by law—using a wide range of instruments to manipulate and intimidate officials and administrators. The Masonic Lodge P2 and similar associations are typical examples.

A number of closely related criminal activities specifically defies the Italian criminal question. In other European countries—in Switzerland and Germany, for example—illegal financial dealings are also widespread as a result of the size and international nature of the financial markets and in Switzerland through the secrecy laws protecting the banking system. But these countries do not have to deal with the armed power of the Mafia, which allows for the threatening and killing of competitors and adversaries (e.g., consider the Ambrosoli murder and the Ambrosiano affair). Even in the United States the Mafia is strong, but its effective influence on the high echelons of the federal government—through corruption, business relationships, and threats—is not comparable to that in Italy. In many Western countries, there are many examples of unethical or illegal management of certain affairs, some public, but nothing compares with what has happened in Sicily in recent years. There Mafia businesses, or businesses related to the Mafia, have been able to monopolize the majority of public funds coming their way, both national and international. Currently in Italy 2,600 public administrators are accused of corruption or other serious offenses, while 40 city councils have been dissolved because they were heavily infiltrated by organized crime.

The ability of Italian illegal elites to communicate with each other has made it possible for many Mafia families to interact easily with Milanese venture capital, P2 members, considerable sectors of the state bureaucracy (both in Rome and at the periphery), and local and national credit institutes. Each of these criminal sectors, at one point or another, has had contact with the others to operate various businesses which, without a common plan or goal nevertheless have had an overall destructive effect on society and the state. During the 1970s the different forms of organized crime became increasingly integrated, setting up an illegal national market in which multifarious goods and services are exchanged: arms, drugs, kickbacks, information, and specialized labor.

THE MAFIA AND COSA NOSTRA

The Mafia is the most powerful and dangerous component of Italian organized crime. This is due to its economic dimensions, the number of people affiliated with it, its ability to manipulate public institutions, and the complexity and sophistication of its organizational structure. Nobody else in the illegal market is simultaneously able to manage economic, military (its organized recourse to violence), and political resources as well as the Mafia. Corporate raiders and venture capital can control banks, businesses, and funds in significant ways, but they do not have hit men at their disposal. Illegal political lobbies can be extremely insidious and dangerous for political institutions, but they do not have large and autonomous financial resources, nor do they command military capability. The politicians involved in corruption schemes need partners able to guarantee their impunity, while always being under the threat of denunciation and public scandal. The current power of the Mafia consists in not being a single unique or simple entity, such as a political party, a pressure group, a business, or an army. Any analogy to these institutions, although seductive, is misleading. The Mafia's organization and behavior are polymorphic phenomena.

The Mafia's purpose is relatively single-minded and predictable: the acquisition and conservation of power and money are an easily detectable pattern that can be analyzed. But there are deeper and layered meanings underneath. In the last ten years, we have made great strides in understanding the composition, activities, and organizational structure of Mafia families. Since 1980 remarkable investigative progress has allowed us to focus on the Mafia structure more closely than ever before. This has not been without a price: many officials who "understood"—that is, discovered—the Mafia's hidden links and connections with Italian economy, society, and public institutions paid with their lives.

By virtue of this patrimony of knowledge, we can now be more assertive in the study of this phenomenon and in planning how to fight it. A point of significant analytic relevance is the distinction between the generic label Mafia and the criminal Sicilian cartel of Cosa Nostra (literally, Our Thing). This distinction emerged in the major investigative work done in Palermo between 1982 and 1991 by the Anti-Mafia Task Force led by Giovanni Falcone. This group uncovered the most intimate structural secrets of Cosa Nostra and also documented the scandalous relationship between Cosa Nostra and legal institutions.

Both the most important government witnesses of the Sicilian Mafia (Tommaso Buscetta, Salvatore Contorno, Antonino Calderone, and Marino Mannoia) and the investigators of the Anti-Mafia Task Force have consistently pointed to the existence of a formal and secret cartel of Sicilian criminal families. This criminal body is strictly governed by rules of conduct and has an executive board, organizational roles, and highly defined plans for action and recruitment procedures.[1]

The goals of Cosa Nostra are 1) the protection and advancement of its affiliates' interests—legal and especially illegal—in the economic, political, and social spheres, and 2) the regulation of internal conflicts among families. Cosa Nostra's distinctive feature is its tendency to challenge the Italian state with its representatives as an equal, as well as to infiltrate it through hidden relations with its representatives, bureaucrats, and officers, and even through the neutralization, by corruption and violence, of whoever opposes its plans. Cosa Nostra's brutality vis-à-vis the state results from the desire to safeguard its own economic interests and the interests of its associates. At the same time, it reveals a project for total domination which has been building for the last ten years with the rise to power of the Greco-Corleonesi family. Other large criminal constellations—the Neapolitan Camorra, the Calabrese 'ndrangheta, and other Sicilian criminal groups not belonging to Cosa Nostra—also confront, fight, and manipulate legal institutions, but only Cosa Nostra is able to do so systematically and with implacable efficiency, up to the point of using terrorist tactics.

In addition to their more developed use of political subversion and to their secret coordination, the families that make up Cosa Nostra can be distinguished from other groups generically labeled "Mafia" in two other ways: a) extremely selective criteria for the recruitment of new members, who for the most part must have Mafia background or be blood-related for several generations with a Mafia family, and b) a keen ability to regulate internal conflicts and monopolize violence to subject small criminal groups active in its territory. Cosa Nostra's strict recruitment procedures consist of a scrupulous review of a candidate's personal and family history to evaluate his criminal reliability. For instance, the candidate's father or close relatives should not work for the police or the judiciary; he must have been born in Sicily; he should not have leftist leanings or be otherwise affiliated with the left; he must have strong family values (no illegitimate offspring, no homosexual tendencies, no divorce, etc.); and he must not be a relative of Cosa Nostra's victims. Such admission criteria have recently become even stricter due to the judicial offensive of the 1980s and the increasing number of *pentiti* (literally, repenters, or turncoats). One of Cosa Nostra's responses to the wave of indictments and arrests has been an organizational restructuring that favors smaller and more cohesive families, with a greater differentiation of its personnel (the "men of honor") from people belonging to other groups of Sicilian crime.

The existence of formal bodies governing Cosa Nostra's affairs (such as the Provincial Commission of Palermo and the Regional Commission), as well as the discipline imposed by individual families on their own members, serves to limit violent internal conflict. In recent years, in fact, the number of homicides in areas controlled by Cosa Nostra has been slightly lower than in those under the control of other criminal groups. However, Cosa Nostra's better control of intra-family conflict should not be confused with the much exaggerated "ability to guarantee law and order" attributed to the Mafia. Today's Cosa Nostra shows no interest in repressing or containing the predatory activities of micro-criminality and common delinquency. Even though it retains capillary control of its territory and indisputable power with regard to petty criminal activity, Cosa Nostra tends to let a limited amount of illicit activity run unchecked. The provinces with the largest number of families belonging to Cosa Nostra report rates of common crime (including burglary, robbery, and extortion) that are among the highest in the nation. In 1990, 20 percent (13,623) of Italy's serious robberies were committed in the province of Palermo alone. The relative lack of interest among the bosses of Cosa Nostra in repressing petty crime can in part be explained by the need to keep the fullest reserve of possible criminal labor from which to select the best elements for its own ranks.

THE ORGANIZATIONAL STRUCTURE OF COSA NOSTRA

From the pentiti's statements and the results of numerous recent investigations, it is possible to compose a much more detailed picture of Cosa Nostra's inner workings. Even though it has a lot in common with secret societies known to historians and sociologists—e.g., rituals of initiation, selection mechanisms, management rules, and specialized roles—Cosa Nostra does not appear to be a rigid and unidimensional sect of conspirators.[2]

Cosa Nostra's internal life is regulated by two fundamental types of relationships: a) a "goal-oriented" relationship between individual and group dealing with the sphere of economic interest of the associate; it is marked by a high level of business freedom and personal autonomy for the individual with respect to the family to which he belongs; and b) a "status" relationship expressing an individual obligation of faith and absolute submission to the family and its representative organs. This may require that the man of honor put his own and other lives in danger for the execution of highly risky tasks (such as assassinations, homicides, punishments) having to do with the defense of Cosa Nostra's common interests. The status of "man of honor" is acquired through a contract for life, symbolically expressed through a blood oath. The distinction and hierarchy between the two relationships are crucial. They allow the group to realize a balance between the restrictive dimensions of the normative apparatus (the "militancy" in Cosa Nostra) and the economically pragmatic aspects of daily life. Without such a double dimension of belonging, Cosa Nostra would not have its tremendous elasticity and economic power.

Business relations among members of a Cosa Nostra family require rigorous respect for private property and allow freedom of venture for each individual. Every man of honor manages his own quota of legal and illegal activities (bars, restaurants, usury, gambling, construction, swindling scams, robberies, etc.) in full autonomy. Partnership with other family members is frequent but in no way mandatory. The family can regulate, tax, and in certain extreme cases prohibit certain criminal activities (for example, kidnapping in Sicily) in the name of general interest or territorial principles, but the concept of economic freedom for each man of honor and for each family with respect to the others is never questioned.

Mafia families are ventures, and the members are vested entrepreneurs. But the essence of Mafia families and the meaning of being a Mafioso, a man of honor, cannot be understood by simply looking at the market with its accumulation of wealth and power. Cosa Nostra's families are not mere capital ventures, and Cosa Nostra's commission is not a simple cartel for legal or illegal activities. The Provincial Commission of Palermo and Cosa Nostra's Regional Commission are essentially political organisms. They constitute a kind of Mafia government, a rough attempt to introduce coordination among entities which were traditionally sovereign and independent. Cosa Nostra's commission is not the administrative council of a large criminal venture, and as such the Mafia is not a "multinational of organized crime." The expenses for the management of coordinated activities are minimal since many of the crucial services are provided by the individual families. Legal help, for instance, which represents one of the highest costs for the American Mafia families, has not been a problem for the Italians given the large number of lawyers who in recent years have become men of honor.

Multinational expansion in illegal trade is the product of investment decisions undertaken by individuals and families who from time to time and from deal to deal decide to form ad hoc ventures. Common, for example, is the constitution of joint ventures, or investor pools, among families in the field of international narcotics. Also common is the constitution of true and proper oligopolistic cartels in the appropriation of public funds. The commission in this case can function as a regulatory organ and can arbitrate disputes. But such functions are not necessarily performed by the commission.

All this does not prevent important Mafia profits from being invested in a seemingly coordinated and concentrated way through banks and financial institutions in certain parts of Italy and Europe, which might lead one to suspect a common plan or strategy. When one goes deeper into how a decision was made, one often discovers that people in constant interaction have come to react individually but in convergence to new factors. Such was the case after the implementation in 1982 of the Rognoni-La Torre law, which called for the seizure of bank accounts set up with funds coming from illegal activities. The response within Cosa Nostra was to redirect its investments to Germany.

COSA NOSTRA AND INSTITUTIONS

Current newspapers are full of more or less sensational "revelations" about the relationship between Cosa Nostra and politics, Cosa Nostra and the judiciary, Cosa Nostra and the intelligence service, Cosa Nostra and the Masons. Many of these revelations come from the pentiti and need to be thoroughly studied and verified. There is relatively little new, but what there is is serious and meaningful. A picture is emerging about a network of historic relationships among organized crime, politicians, and state officials that is much more solid than was heretofore imagined or suspected.

My impression is that regarding relationships between Mafia and politics, in Sicily there has been a fundamental continuity which is now being questioned for the first time. I think we must accept the distinct possibility that relationships between Sicilian politicians and Cosa Nostra—in the form of formal affiliations, oaths, and consequent obligations of obedience—have been more frequent than we thought. This holds true for the relationship between Cosa Nostra and professionals (mainly lawyers, but also doctors and others), not to mention employees and functionaries of the state. In other words, the number of men of honor unknown as such but occupying powerful positions in public institutions and in the professions has been, and perhaps still is, much larger than we imagined. I have come to this conclusion on the basis of a logical deduction, based on both my interviews with Antonino Calderone during recent hearings before the Anti-Mafia Commission and the news appearing in recent months in the press. Calderone told me of four members of the House that he knew as men of honor, formally affiliated with Cosa Nostra, and of an unspecified but large number of Cosa Nostra regional representatives in the 1970s. Other pentiti under questioning have recently involved other politicians, and about forty Sicilian politicians are currently accused of Mafia association and other crimes. Among them there are a former minister and six members of the national parliament. There is no reason to doubt that direct participation in the Mafia, in terms of formal affiliation and submission to the norms and obligations that derive from it, has been a common practice among Sicilian politicians since World War II.

As far as the politicians of past legislations are concerned—from the period immediately after World War II to the beginning of the 1970s—it is necessary to acknowledge their double loyalty to the Mafia and to democratic institutions. We need more articulate explanations than the simple invocation of split personalities—although there have been such cases lately. An explanation of this phenomenon can be traced to two factors: a) the sharing by traditional Mafiosi and "associate" politicians of an identical ideology and subculture based on friendship and the code of honor; and b) the absence in the past of a direct confrontation between Cosa Nostra and the state. Moreover, the relations between Mafia and politics in the not too distant past were sustained by the role assigned to the Mafia as safeguard of the existing sociopolitical order. Historically many Mafia bosses exercised their power with the conviction that they were acting in the name of legality: as mayors of numerous Sicilian towns during the Allied occupation, as auxiliary police in the repression of banditry and farmer revolt after World War II, and as judges in civil and penal matters. These roles were recognized and publicly praised by state representatives.

In 1955 the complementarity of traditional Mafia authority and state authority was actually theorized by one of the highest ranked Italian judges. On the occasion of the death of Calogero Vizzini, a well-known family head, Giuseppe Guido Lo Schiavo, public prosecutor general for the Supreme Court, wrote:

> It is said that the Mafia despises the police and the magistracy. This is inexact. The Mafia has always respected the judiciary and its judges, and it has bowed to their decisions; it has not gotten in their way. In the prosecution of bandits and outlaws it has stood side by side with the forces of order. Today we heard a new name as successor to Don Calogero Vizzini as head of that occult group. May his work respect the laws of the State and serve the betterment of the common good (*Rivista Processi*, no. 5 [January 1955]).

If this is the view of one of Italy's most powerful judges, one can only guess at the attitude of local administrators vis-à-vis the Mafia—and how minimal their discomfort must have been to serve Cosa Nostra and the state at the same time!

In more recent times, the relationship between Mafia and politics has been altered by the withdrawal of the mandate to the Mafia to mediate and repress social and political conflicts. After the institution of the first Anti-Mafia Commission, and above all after General Della Chiesa's murder in 1982, the legitimization of Mafia power came to an end. Relationships with Mafia bosses were no longer shown off but hidden and covered by a thousand cautions; in some recent cases, such relationships had begun to be causes for unpopularity and damaged reputations and careers. Moreover, the expansion in the 1970s of Cosa Nostra's economic power can be traced to growing political autonomy, which eventually turns into distinct conflict. The string of assassinations of high-level officials that began in 1979 and culminated in the massacres of 1992 expresses the emergence of Cosa Nostra's "subversive face." This tougher attitude is accompanied by an increase in the rigor and secrecy of the recruitment of political figures. Cosa Nostra continues to accept ruthless politicians, but the cartel is aware of a growing lack of trust and quality in the available pool. All this has probably helped reduce the number of politicians looking up to the Mafia. But this reduction is amply balanced by the decision of many men of honor to directly enter politics, especially in local administrations. Nor should we forget the greater involvement of politicians in financial partnerships with the Mafia or in the networks of clandestine organizations outside of Cosa Nostra such as secret Masonic lodges and special interest groups.

LAW-ENFORCEMENT STRATEGIES

The outline of a fighting strategy for the next years emerges from what has been discussed so far. The difference between Mafia and Cosa Nostra is not in their diverse economic and social structures or in their different cultural meaning. The Mafia remains the great socioeconomic and political problem of Italy and hence a possible future problem for a unified Europe. Cosa Nostra is an integral part of the Mafia; it is the organized quintessence of Mafia power. Our first goal must be the attack of the secret society as such: the bosses must be arrested, the leadership disassembled, the funds of its affiliates seized, and its protectors in the political arena, public affairs, and the professional world identified and nailed. At least five years of judicial offensive are necessary to dissolve Cosa Nostra, to subject it economically, politically, and militarily to the state and civil society. This is Italy's task, the job of its government both present and future.

At the same time, Cosa Nostra as a secret society is but one aspect, however important, of the Mafia problem and of crime in its larger dimensions. Even with Cosa Nostra destroyed, the Mafia remains an integral element of society and culture for a large part of southern Italy, one that cannot be easily fought or eliminated by arrests and convictions. The Mafia remains a compound phenomenon linking together criminal family business, financial ventures, networks for power, corruption, and "clean" investments. As such it spreads all over Western Europe. Neither five years nor Italy's dwindling resources are sufficient to face the complexity of this phenomenon.

NOTES

1. According to Calderone, "It is better to understand from the very beginning that the Mafia as a word does not exist, at least for us. The Mafia is really called 'Cosa Nostra.' In fact, we never say the word 'Mafia.' Cosa Nostra is secret; it is the criminal élite" (Arlacchi 1992: 3–4). See also the opening statement of the Tribunal of Palermo in the case against Abbate Giovanni and 706 others (that is, the preliminary document for the "maxi-trial" against Cosa Nostra): "This is an indictment against the Mafia's organization called 'Cosa Nostra.' A very dangerous criminal organization which, through violence and intimidation, spread and is still spreading death and terror."

2. In Calderone's words, "Cosa Nostra's cleverness consisted in being an association of 'men of honor,' a secret thing for the very few, but at the same time being connected with everyday activities. It is well spread among professionals and tradespeople. Everybody can be found within the Mafia; apart from judges and policemen, there are all kinds of people. The Mafia has infiltrated every nook of society" (Arlacchi 1992: 27).

REFERENCES

Arlacchi, Pino. 1986. *Ordinanza di rinvio a giudizio contro Abbate Giovanni + 706.* Palermo: Procura della Repubblica.

———. 1992. *Gli uomini del disonore.* Milan: Mondadori. Tribunale di Palermo.

THE DISCOURSE ON MIGRATION: RACISM IN CONTEMPORARY ITALY

Marco Jacquemet

Italy has become the promised land for many disenfranchised migrants looking for prosperity and a sustainable way of living. Starting in the second half of the 1980s, people from north and west Africa and Eastern Europe increasingly crossed the borders into Italy and established a stronghold within this society intentionally constructed as monocultural. Social responses to this phenomenon did not take long to surface as explicit intolerance of migrants, producing a situation of racial animosity that will be one of the permanent features of the Italian sociopolitical landscape for years to come. This contribution will document the nature, scope, and features of this migration; analyze Italian responses through everyday interactions and accounts; and address some of the intercultural conditions stemming from the new political framework of the Second Republic.

A NEW AMERICA

In the Loreto subway station in Milan, it is easy to discern the new multicultural Italy. Every noon Senegalese migrants gather at a cafe there to exchange letters from home and information about jobs and housing. In one corner, an Italian-speaking migrant helps a newcomer fill out a form for a merchant's license. In another, two men with braided hair and African robes discuss going to Belgium, where pay is said to be high. "A lot of people in Senegal have never heard of Rome, but everybody knows Loreto," says Youssoupha Kalla, a street merchant in Italy for two years. "I am just doing what Italians did in America 100 years ago. This is the place you come to get rich" (*Wall Street Journal,* 14 August 1990).

The heavy migration from Africa, the Far East, and Eastern Europe marks the final act of Italian integration with the rich and industrialized North. Italy's migratory "pull" factors derive from both its inclusion in the rich North and some features intrinsic to its sociopolitical landscape:

1) Italy's high standard of living, at par with other industrialized nations, has been achieved through an unregulated but prosperous economy. The trend toward a service-based economy has increased the number of temporary, low-paid, and unreported jobs. The porous state of many undocumented or underreported businesses makes it easier to absorb migrants willing to work as a shadow labor force, forfeiting social benefits, control over work conditions, and unionization. Even Italian unions have acknowledged the shadowy nature of migrant labor by signing in Turin a contract with Fiat for Saturday and Sunday jobs open to migrants. The agreement met with few objections, with the notable exception of Democrazia Proletaria, a small left-wing organization that objected to the clear pattern of exploitation and treatment of migrants as "second-class citizens." Migrants' associations lauded this opportunity to work (Cocchi, ed. 1990).

2) A weak and chaotic Italian public administration has produced a mass of conflicting regulations, with the result that Italy still does not have a clear policy concerning migration. Exploiting the arbitrariness of the system, migrants can enter Italy and even in some cases acquire a work permit. Competing policies abound. The various regulatory programs of 1987–88, the "amnesty" included in the 1990 Legge Martelli—through which 200,000 migrants obtained residence and work permits—and talk of a new amnesty in 1993 must be weighed against the many administrative decisions (such as the *circolari amministrative*) which gave such great discretionary power to the local governments and/or police to deny permits, resulting in many cases in a reversal of the Legge Martelli.

3) Italy's geopolitical position as the southern border of the EC has meant easy access for many migrants, especially from Africa, willing to illegally cross the Mediterranean Sea. In many cases, southern Italian organized crime has provided routes and means to migrants in exchange for money and/or the willingness to be exploited as cheap labor once in Italy.

4) Northern Italy has the world's lowest fertility rate (1.26 percent in 1992; in comparison, the minimum rate for sustaining a long-term stable population is 2.1 percent; Rampini 1994). This has produced the perception of a future need for migrant labor. Since the northern Italian economy is near full employment, new jobs in industry and services will be occupied by migrants. Incidentally, by importing migrant laborers, northern Italian capital can avoid exporting its factories to southern Italy, thus bypassing the 2 million unemployed southerners (Bolaffi 1993).

The pull factors must be counterbalanced with the "push" factors of the home countries, such as the following:

1) The deepening global crisis of developing nations, especially in north Africa, where the economic crisis is combined with a sociopolitical one. This means that migration from these areas is no longer just an economic phenomenon but is the permanent displacement from the area of entire strata of the population.

2) The demographic explosion witnessed almost all over the Third World, again especially in north Africa. The population of the five African countries on the Mediterranean shores, after having doubled in the first half of the century (from 22 to 45 million in 1950), increased to 90 million in 1980, will pass 140 million by the end of the century, and is projected to be 200 million by 2025 (Trifa 1989; Iaquinta 1990). These trends in population growth, coupled with internal problems in the distribution of resources and the siphoning of national wealth into the First World, will have a major influence on migration patterns.

If in the 1960s and 1970s the pull factors were the predominant reason to migrate, in the 1980s and 1990s the push factors have had the upper hand, creating a situation much more difficult to regulate from the European side. According to the last available figures provided by the Ministry of Interior, in 1992 there were 925,000 legal aliens in Italy, 770,000 of them from non-EC countries; 264,000 had work permits while 150,000 were unemployed and 150,000 were family members. Among the countries better represented are Morocco (93,000), the United States (80,000), Tunisia (49,000), the Philippines (42,000), the former Yugoslavia (38,000), Senegal (27,000), and Albania (27,000). In comparison with other European countries, these numbers are not very impressive. The percentage of migrants in the Italian population is one of the lowest in Europe. The last available statistics, from 1990, show that migrants were 1.4 percent of the population, compared with 6.4 percent in France, 8.2 percent in Germany, 9.1 percent in Belgium, and 16.3 in Switzerland (Rampini 1994).

These official statistics, however, are unable to clearly trace migratory patterns. Statistical studies on migration, as almost all studies on the subject, tend to apply synchronic models to documented entry in a country, never really addressing the temporal length of stay, the possibility of repeated comings and goings, and internal mobility once a migrant is in the country. Migratory movements, like all nomadism, are de-territorial and de-temporal: land ceases to be occupied space and instead becomes simple support for movement; time ceases to be segmented intervals for work and leisure and instead becomes duration between arrivals and departures.

It is thus imperative to look at migration from a qualitative perspective, to be less interested in hard figures and try to elucidate the social phenomena underlying the movement of people. If we adopt such a qualitative lens and look at macro patterns, we shall see that one of the clearest consequences of migration in Italy is a deepening of Italy's own "southern question." Migration has aggravated the gap between North and South, both economically and socially.

Until recently, the migratory phenomenon in Italy had very peculiar characteristics compared with other industrialized countries. While the migrant labor force in countries such as Germany, the United States, and France was concentrated (due to state intervention) in the most heavily industrialized areas of the country, in Italy it was the reverse: a large number of migrants found their first job, usually part-time or underground, in the less industrialized and more unemployed area of the country (Bolaffi 1993). The South, with the already chaotic management of public policies made worse by local inefficiency, was a mixed blessing for migrants: on one hand, it was easy to get in and stay unchecked; on the other, with very little demand for labor, the only work to be found was seasonal farm labor, construction, or through the black market. Moreover, in a context where migrants' willingness to be exploited found no laws granting them legal work but no actual enforcement of restrictive measures, another consequence was that many business activities in order to exploit migrants' needs for a job, any kind of job, de facto went underground. Thus while the industrialized North has lately started taking measures to accommodate the migrant labor force through unemployment offices and unionized training courses, the South keeps swallowing an increasing number of clandestine workers into its unregulated economy, becoming a transit area, a zone for reconstituting the social group through chain migration thanks to a less controlled territory.

Socially these different economic patterns have produced responses to migrants which once again show the historical division in the social consciousness of the country between North and South. The historical tradition of internal (South to North) migration in the 1950s and 1960s and the response to it from northern Italians provide the context for articulating the division between North and South in dealing with foreign migrants. In order to account for reactions to migrants, we must look at the double-step nature of social identity in a country already folded in two having now to confront the "south" of the world. As a result, we are confronted with two different phenomena: a) northern Italians view all migrants as "them," an undistinguished group (though social differences among the northern hosts affect perceptions of migrants); and b) southern Italians perceive differences between migrants in terms of whether "they" are "more like us" or "more like them." The next two sections will explore this dichotomy.

POSSIBLE RACISMS IN NORTHERN ITALY

Foreign migration has rekindled northern Italian racial animosity toward southerners. Though historical intolerance for internal migrants had been dying out, a new and more antagonistic form has lately surfaced in dealings with foreign migrants, especially now that ethnic signs have made it quite simple to immediately identify foreign migrants as "others." In this region with the lowest birthrate in the world, we found reactions to migrants split among social classes. Recent studies using survey techniques have uncovered a multifaceted approach to migrants depending on social factors pertaining to the polled Italians (Balbo and Manconi 1992). It has been found that being middle aged, male, lower middle class, or having received an education before 1968 (when schools and universities became the center of a new consciousness in relating to the social world) influences one against migrants. On the other hand, we find a decidedly more friendly approach to migrants among young people, mostly female, and among people who received their education after 1968. Both the upper and working classes, with a more liberal and/or progressive frame, are generally found on the migrants' side. Nevertheless, the dominant representation of migration seems to be firmly in the hands of the antagonistic camp. In a poll taken in 1993, the majority of Italians (64 percent) thought there were too many migrants living in Italy. This survey showed Italians as the most intolerant among Europeans (*Eurobarometer;* cited in Rampini 1994). According to Manconi (1989), this is the result of three forms of intolerance:

1) A *compounded* racism, where offensive and/or discriminatory behavior is the result of awareness of ethnic differences combined with a perception of crisis and emergency. This form of racism a) stresses the criminal side of migrants' activities (for instance, in 1990 Bologna witnessed a neighborhood candle march against migrant prostitutes, despite Bologna's long-standing tradition in tolerance of sexual trades); b) represents migrants as marginal subjects unable to properly function in Italian society; they are depicted as ignorant of modern practices, deprived of language skills, and living a shadowy life; and c) denies migrants' everyday life, their "human side," in order to view them as threatening episodes of unregulated social disorder.

2) A *rivaling* racism, derived from a perception of the need to compete for limited resources; this racism breeds over the defense of a symbolic and material control of the territory and the competition for (among many components) a) housing; in the north there has been much uproar against migrant settlements, such as the 1990 firebombs against a migrant camp and near riots in Milan and the 1993 summer nights of violence in Genoa's older district; b) services (schools, hospitals, transportation); and c) employment (for instance, the 1990 Florence chase by local shopkeepers of street vendors from the Maghreb or Senegal). A symptom of the symbolic nature of this defense was clearly displayed in a questionnaire taken

among Milan high school students: 14.5 percent of them were afraid of migrant competition over jobs (Balbo and Manconi 1992).

3) An *ethnocentric* racism, resulting from cultural stereotypes called upon to defend Italian culture and lifestyle against outside influences deemed "backward." This racism wants Italy to be a monocultural society with strong rules of proper behavior and an even stronger ideology of hospitality, which dictates that guests must conform to local customs (the well-known "In Rome do like the Romans"). A questionnaire in Milan asked, "In Milan would you consider the foreigners to be citizens like everybody else?" Forty-four percent answered, "Yes, if they conform to the rules of our society" (Balbo and Manconi 1992). This third form of racism will be the greatest challenge for Italian society since it is at the cultural level that a balance between integration and a right to differences must be found. Various social sectors are already experiencing some of the more controversial issues. For instance, the Ministry of the Interior is confronted with the issue of legal bigamy in the case of multiple wives asking for residence permits to join their husband. Labor relations are also confronting multicultural issues, such as Muslim workers' demands for work holidays to respect Ramadan.

To these three forms Melandri (1990) added a fourth—namely, *exploitative* racism, which seizes upon the migrants' willingness to be exploited and provides them with unhealthy and dangerous jobs, without paying any attention to their need for social benefits or good working and living conditions. Two health surveys conducted by NAGA in Milan and Caritas in Rome have found that the most common diseases of migrants are not those stereotypically associated with them (such as tropical or sexually trasmitted diseases or AIDS), but rather are the consequences of poor living conditions, such as colds, muscular tears, gastrointestinal disorders, and depression.

PECULIARITIES OF THE SOUTH

Of the four forms of racism discussed above, only the last one can be clearly identified in southern Italy. As we have seen, the South is increasingly accepting large numbers of clandestine workers into its unregulated economy. However, outside of being exploitive of the labor force, the South offers fewer opportunities in a traditionally illegal and underground economy.

Preliminary research in southern Italy has found two major players in the management of migrant labor:

1) *Organized crime,* which controls north and west Africans' access into Italy in exchange for work in the fields and/or the sale of counterfeit and stolen goods door-to-door and in the streets. Most migrants controlled by organized crime are males, usually with a non-Christian religious background.

2) The *church* (through its organizations Azione Cattolica and Caritas), which provides housekeepers (from the Philippines, Cape Verde, and Somalia), mostly females and Christians. Thanks to the church's humanitarian efforts, many middle-class families can again afford a full-time maid (as in the first half of the twentieth century, when peasants from the impoverished countryside came to urban areas).

Surveys in Naples by Caritas have found that southerners' perceptions of migrants, instead of being differentiated according to the social status of the interviewees, depend largely on the ethnic background of the migrants. Thus Asians are better perceived, being viewed as "clean and good workers," while Africans in general are viewed as being "just like us," a populace which brings diseases and is a dirty, noisy, violent, and sexually threatening wild bunch.

COMMUNICATIVE INTOLERANCE

The multiethnic fabric of contemporary Italy, combined with the emergence of an aggressive ideology of intolerance, has created a crisis of exclusion for the newly arrived social groups. Italy is now permeated with a discourse through which latent or tacit forces of exclusion are at work in a manner which is all the more pernicious as it is invisible to its dominant practitioners. This discourse—articulated in the media, the arts, and everyday communication—constitutes the basis from which denigrating policies are routinely implemented and forms the basis upon which racist politics can be expressed and enacted. More or less implicit biases, stereotypes, and derogatory metaphors form a polymorphic discourse strategy of exclusion and ultimately provide a pseudo-legitimation for racist, xeno phobic, and intolerant social and political behavior. This racial intolerance is thus found in an array of linguistic practices available to Italian speakers. Two of them are particularly telling of the process: *labeling* and *forms of address*.

LABELING

Since the capacity of discourse to denote and represent the social world is fundamentally implicated in relations of domination, control of the representations of reality constitutes a tool in the hands of the dominant groups for carrying out their hegemonic agenda (see Voloshinov 1973[1929]; Bourdieu 1977). Among such discourse practices, labeling constitutes one of the more efficient instruments for the construction of dominant representations of the social order. It should thus not come as a surprise that the labeling of migrants has constituted one of the fields for the definition of minority status.

One of the first words used to label migrants was produced by public discourse in the mid-1980s and is still going strong. The success of *vù cumprà* (a stigmatic expression from the Calabrese dialect, loosely translatable as "D'you wanna buy it?") is clearly identifiable in the dual movement which wants the stigmatization of migrants to come on top of southern Italians' stereotyping. At the same time, the expression's focus on the most identifiable of migrant work activities displays an inability to see migrants as anything else but marginal subjects. The reality, though, is that only 15 percent of migrants are actually street vendors.

Another popular word used to label migrants is *lavoratore straniero* (literally, foreign worker). It is descriptive, neutral, less emotionally charged, and defines identities based solely on work, thus again reducing migrants' existence to their single most visible activity while denying them the status of whole human beings. *Straniero* (foreigner) is apparently neutral, but it discriminates between Italians and others on a potentially menacing us/them dichotomy. (All Italian schoolchildren are still familiar with a World War I song whose refrain is "Non passa lo straniero" [The stranger will not get by here], implying that Italian territory must be protected from these threatening foreigners).

From bureaucratic lingo comes *extra-comunitario* (non–EC member), which has spread to many communications forums, from the media to political debates. As a term specifically used to define migrants, it is found only in Italy and is unknown in the rest of the EC. Here again we find no reference to the home country, the migrant being defined only in reference to locals, in this case the Europeans (the notion of a Fortress Europe clearly marks the boundary between ins and outs). Finally, there are labels which take the home country into account. Here, however, a "bundle mechanism" is used to group various ethnic groups into single ensembles. Thus *marocchini* (Moroccans) becomes the stereotype for people from the Maghreb; *neri/negri/negrambi* (all variations of Negro) bundle together all West, East, and Central Africans; and *albanesi* (Albanians)—or less frequently *polacchi* (Polish)—is used indiscriminately for all East Europeans.

FORMS OF ADDRESS

In Italy the concept of respect constitutes one of the most salient cultural values in social interaction in public. Thus Italians devote keen attention to the etiquette attached to this notion. The etiquette is evident in various forms of discourse, but it is especially focused on forms of address. These carry great weight in social exchanges and are read as indicators of an individual's social standing and position within a community. In north and central Italy, the address system is based on two forms: *tu*, the second person singular, used as the familiar form, and *lei*, the neuter form of the third person singular. In the South the formal lei is often combined with *voi*, the second person plural. The last two express respect. It is not always easy to determine why people use one of the three forms; the choice depends on social, cultural, historical, and class factors. Broadly speaking, however, we can say that for most people tu is used either among friends and in the family or with people perceived to be of an inferior status. Lei is reserved as a respect form in institutional or formal settings for unfamiliar superiors and/or distant acquaintances.

Personal observation and recent studies point out that most of the interactions concerning migrants, especially Africans, are conducted in the tu form. This form can in fact be used as an asymmetric marker of social standing, making it possible to create a superior/inferior interaction, with the superior party using tu and receiving lei or voi. Domestic relationships between masters and servants were traditionally managed in this way, and still today it is not uncommon to address waiters in the tu form and expect a lei form in return. Migrants are easily made to fit into this asymmetrical relationship by the nature of interactions in public places—i.e., according to the conventions of respect, local people should control the first move, so migrants are usually addressed with tu. However, the migrants' relative unfamiliarity with Italian makes it difficult for them to understand the asymmetrical distinction of tu/lei, with the result that most of the times they elect to reciprocate with the tu form. By using the tu form, migrants violate expectations of the frame of address, which can trigger racial animosity against them, people who "clearly could not stay in their place."

RACIAL INTOLERANCE

Linguistic denigration, stereotyping, and racial animosity are the foundations from which many racist events are bred, eventually leading to a full-scale racist situation. According to Balbo and Manconi (1992), we are moving from the scattered manifestation of racist events to a serious racist situation, especially in the less tolerant cities of the North (Milan, Florence, or Genoa).

Contrary to the French or German situation, there is not yet a party whose political agenda is centered around the issue of intolerance to migrants. What we have is an undefined archipelago of organizations exploiting this intolerance. Two political organizations are notable in this respect: the Lega Nord (see Diamanti 1993; Mannheimer in this volume) and the right-wing Alleanza Nazionale (AN), formerly Movimento Sociale Italiano (MSI). These two parties are polarizing the geopolitical landscape, producing a clear break between North and South as the result of their racist positions.

The Lega Nord, an umbrella organization covering six regional leagues, has grown dramatically in the period 1990–94. It has ostensibly campaigned on a vague platform of federalism, but in reality, it aims to appeal to the northern dislike of anything and anyone from further south, including the government in Rome. Thus the Lega Nord has become the reference point for all policies of northern intransigence against the South. To be sure, the Lega has an anti-immigrant agenda, but this is not yet its defining core; this organization's central ideology is above all anti-centralism and anti-parties (that is, anti-Rome). However, its championing of strong local communities could turn into intolerance against nonlocal forces, the migrants again becoming the main target.

In the case of the AN-MSI, a strong nationalism tinted with xenophobic components made it emerge as an effective force from the South to counter the Lega's separatist claims. The strong neofascist vote in the 1993 local elections and the 1994 general elections clearly shows the lack of historical consciousness among many of the less-educated voters. This is especially serious among young people, who have never had a chance to understand fascism because the history they typically learn at school ends before World War II. The AN's growing presence in many areas of the South, where it has adopted the posture of protector of local benefits received from Rome, makes it likely that it will adopt a negative position vis-à-vis foreign migrants in the name of national interests.

As Balbo and Manconi (1992) have pointed out, however, we do not need a racist party to have racist practices. Three forms of racist practices have been identified so far:

1) Militant racism based on aggression and violence. This is a very territorial and violent form, usually found among skinhead-type groups (see Berardi 1993).

2) Opportunistic racism. Associated with institutions, it surfaces during specific crises (such as the Milan riots for migrant housing or the Albanian boat people crisis in summer 1990) when the government or governmental agencies decide to intervene in the name of a "national" emergency to get rid of the disturbing foreign element.

3) Monothematic racism. These are practices sought by social groups to target single sore points in interactions with migrants, such as the competition over work opportunities or sexual competition. It has been found that the latter, especially in regard to West or Central African males, is an important factor in male peer group

animosity against migrants perceived to be competitors for women. The myth of African sexual potency, combined with a different code of what constitutes beauty, makes many migrants into threatening rivals to be contained and coraled. This creates resentment and violent responses.

CONCLUSIONS

In the 1980s Italy witnessed the emergence of a *lumpenbourgeoisie* which profited from the economic transition from an organic industrial system to a polymorphous information system. In this transitional period from industrialism to "immaterial" capitalism, wealth was found in mass media and advertising, speculative financing, covert bribery, and the cycle of drug and weapons sales. As a result, we witnessed the development of an economic system no longer based on productive capacity and competition but one which has at its core Mafia-like strategies based on raw force and a sentiment of belonging, making the system profitable only for people with the right connections and the proper attitude. This situation, emblematically represented by the corruption scandals of 1993, has produced a public discourse in which people are designing a new national consciousness based on a cycle of depression-panic-anxiety pivoting around the issue of what constitutes a national identity.

Belonging and identity constitute the two poles of interethnic tension. They are intrinsically connected through their communicative nature: individual positions (i.e., identities) are provided with meaning by a social group which has as its only requirement an individual's membership in it. Social identity is accepted, understood, and shared only from within an environment providing the tools to account for this belonging. However, identity and belonging within a social group are never perceived as constructed, as the product of an ongoing negotiation among various social actors and forces. They are viewed as natural, as tied to an origin, a territory, a clan. Identity discourse looks for roots and sets up boundaries.

This practice of looking for roots and setting up boundaries is at the core of identity discourse. In Italy, this discourse has been brewed primarily in the media, and particularly in the private national networks of Italy's new prime minister, Silvio Berlusconi. Berlusconi, the owner of the three private national networks, many print media, and holder of 80 percent of the nation's advertising business, began to transform the social imagery of Italian viewers in the 1980s, during the years of C-A-F (Craxi-Andreotti-Forlani). Now his power in shaping Italian politics promises to reign unbound, with serious consequences for any social groups that do not conform to the sociopolitical context of the Second Republic. More intolerance to "deviant" behavior is to be expected.

With Berlusconi's rightist government this intolerance is compounded by an explicit unwillingness to help migrants. The hardliners seem to have taken the upper hand: they want to put a stop to work and stay permits, to implement forced repatriation, to tolerate only underground activities—since the reality of low-paid, unreported labor is still necessary (and profitable). Berlusconi—and whoever else is behind his electoral program—stated that Italy must have all the migrants it can decently afford, based on the needs of the free market. In fact this is another way of saying that Italy already has all the migrants it can handle.

Given the state of the Italian economy and since the strongest animosity to ethnic differences comes from a situation of limited resources, the outlook for migrants in Italy is not reassuring. The future of the many documented and undocumented migrants will be very difficult. At the same time, their presence constitutes a great challenge for Italian society: it calls for a common project of negotiating equal access for different identities within a truly intercultural society. Only then will Italy finally find its place in the European landscape.

REFERENCES

Balbo, L., and Manconi, L. 1992. *I razzismi reali.* Milan: Feltrinelli.

Berardi, F. 1993. *Come si cura il nazi.* Rome: Castelvecchi.

Bolaffi, G. 1993. *Immigrazione fuori dall'emergenza.* Rassegna di Sociologia, Il Mulino.

Bourdieu, P. 1977. *Outline of a Theory of Practice.* Cambridge: Cambridge University Press.

Cocchi, G., ed. 1990. *Stranieri in Italia.* Bologna: Istituto Cattaneo.

Diamanti, I. 1993. *La Lega: Geografia, storia e sociologia di un nuovo soggetto politico.* Rome: Donzelli.

Ferrarotti, F. 1988. *Oltre il razzismo.* Rome: Armando.

Iaquinta, P. 1990. "Sviluppo demografico differenziale nell'area del bacino mediterraneo." In Cocchi, ed.

Manconi, L. 1989. "Molti razzismi." *Democrazia e diritto* 24, 6.

Rampini, F. 1994. "Paura dei 'barbari' e difficoltà ad essere Italiani." *LIMES* 1, 1: 191–98.

Melandri, A. 1990. *Razzismo come, dove, perchè.* Rome: CIES.

Trifa, C. 1989. "La transizione demografica nel mondo arabo." In *Abitare il pianeta: Futuro demografico, migrazioni e tensioni etniche,* vol. 1. Turin: Ed. della Fondazione Einaudi.

Voloshinov, V. 1973 [1929]. *Marxism and the Philosophy of Language.* Cambridge: Harvard University Press.

UNION EXPERIENCE AND INDUSTRIAL RELATIONS

Guido Baglioni

A MOVEMENT NOT IN DECLINE

In this brief contribution I propose to furnish the readers of other countries (and those unfamiliar with the topic) with information on and assessments of the essential characteristics of the union experience in Italy and its important contribution to the configuration of Italian industrial relations. After an introduction on the current situation, I shall develop the discussion along the following three lines: a comparison with the experiences of the United States and other European countries, the post-World War II genesis and successive evolution of union activity, and the current problems that unions must face.

In the beginning of the 1980s, particularly due to the recessive processes of capitalist economies, many observers believed that an inexorable decline of union activity had begun. In fact, economic, political, and social factors (such as reductions in the numbers of workers) determined a notable, comprehensive "withdrawal" of such activity as compared to preceding decades, but, at least in Europe, it cannot be called a decline.

The loss of bargaining power, political clout, and representativeness was more evident in the first part of the 1980s than subsequently; in addition, it hit countries with already weak unions (France and Spain) more strongly than countries with strong unions (Germany and Sweden). Italy is considered among the countries with strong unions. Its current situation does not support the "decline hypothesis." However, this does not mean that one can ignore the changes and difficulties which currently concern organized labor in our country.

ITALY, THE UNITED STATES, AND EUROPE

A notable difference exists in the United States, where union activity from the end of the 1970s saw a period of gradual (probably not definitive) decline. But the differences between Italy and the United States are not limited to this period. They involve their constitutive characteristics, principally the following:

In Italy the level of recognition of the union on the part of the political, entrepreneurial, and cultural-informational world is decidedly higher than in the United States;

In Italy the union is not only an agent of contracts or demands, but has also always demonstrated a political propensity and a strong presence outside of the workplace;

In Italy the unions developed a generalized protection of the workforce in all sectors (the opposite of the American tradition of "fragmented" union action);

In Italy three trade union confederations exist, and (in comparison to the United States) the autonomy of union action is less at the business level than at higher ones (territorial and national).

The differences just listed are also noticeable when we compare the United States and other European countries. Other, more specific convergences between these countries and Italy can be added. Italy approaches other countries of Central Northern Europe (particularly Germany and Sweden) for the high recognition obtained by union players, their bargaining power, and active presence in businesses working toward the effective regulation of employment criteria. On the other hand, Italy's union experiences are similar to those of the Mediterranean region in two aspects—namely, the marked division of the three trade union confederations (more in the past than in recent years) and the influence that political events assume within these confederations and in their outside associations.

Even given these similarities, the Italian situation, like every other, demonstrates its own peculiarities. We shall underline two of them relative to the order of industrial relations. The first has to do with the fact that this order is normally expressed on two levels of negotiation—the national level (general or occupational) and the company level. In Italy we have had phases of major centralization and phases of major decentralization, but never exclusively one or the other. The second is recognizable in the low level of legislative or contractual formalization of bargaining processes, a characteristic which has been corrected in recent years by agreements between social partners and the government.

THE POST-WORLD WAR II PERIOD: GENESIS AND EVOLUTION

The Italian union experience was fraught with severe difficulties until the 1920s. During the twenty years of the fascist regime, its tortuous course was abruptly interrupted and a sole union established. This was a government institution, controlled by the state, which allowed neither freedom of association nor the right to strike. In the immediate postwar period, a union situation emerged which was destined to be of major import in the following decades. In spite of vast recent changes, its repercussions are still felt today.

For a brief period beginning in 1945 there was a large unitary confederation of all workers, who were responding to the climate of the struggle with fascism and the German occupation and to the pressing need for the material and moral reconstruction of the country. However, only three years later, in 1948, the components of this confederation broke into factions. The most important one, tied to the Communist and Socialist Parties, remains the CGIL. Another faction, made up of managers, Catholic activists, and lay reformists, promotes the CISL, which officially began in 1950. At the same time, the UIL was born, a small organization sustained by lay, non-Communist unionists.

The fundamental reasons for the breakup were primarily political—directly so as the split was seen as a way to remove the union experience from Communist objectives and concepts. (In fact it was called the union "transmission belt" of the party.) Indirectly it was caused by the repercussions of the cold war and the fact that the Communist and Socialist Parties were driven out of the government (1947). However, there are additional reasons for the division. The constitution of the CISL heralded a change from the Italian politico-union tradition. In its place the "hallmark" of North American unions was initially recalled. This differs intrinsically from the former tradition in the following salient ways:

Autonomy of the unions from political parties (for the CISL this means autonomy from the Christian Democrats, among whom are many of its managers and members);

Primacy of collective bargaining with respect to the legislative regulation of employee-employer relationships and denial of juridical recognition of the unions (provided for by the constitution);

Union as "ensemble" with members and occupational structures, opposed to the union as political bargaining movement of the working class.

In the 1950s and also thereafter, Italian union life was dominated by the disputes and confrontations of the CISL and CGIL. The CGIL remained the strongest trade union confederation, but with a low aptitude for foreseeing necessary strategic changes and with a mix of approval and opposition regarding the evolution of industrial relations. The CISL gradually increased its organizational foundation and demonstrated a major strategic insight via important shifts, from the promotion of integrative collective bargaining at the company level (1950s) to the acceptance and promotion of collective agreements (1980s).

In the 1950s, the dispute between the CGIL and CISL was sharp, the contractual power of unions modest, and negotiation normally stopped at the thresholds of companies. In the 1970s, in concomitance with a development called the "economic miracle," the CGIL and CISL found growing forms of competitive coexistence. The unions gradually augmented their bargaining power, and the diffusion of collective bargaining at the company level began.

The greatest change in the Italian union movement occurred with the "cycle of struggles" (1968–73), the manifestations of which appeared larger and more profound in our country than in other European countries. The following were the principal manifestations:

The explosion of a generalized mobilization of workers and of labor unrest, an event that brought out a deep-rooted propensity for labor unrest in the Italian unions;

The growth of unionization until more than 50 percent of the population was active (a high proportion if we take into consideration the Italian productive structure, in which small businesses are prevalent);

Collective bargaining shifted to the level of companies, with the role of manager of stipulated agreements in big businesses, and with new contents, like the egalitarian wage policy (equal wage increases for different types of workers);

Full recognition from employers and the political system of union players and representatives (particularly through the Workers' Statute Law of 1970);

The assumption of a direct political role by the unions (direct in the sense that it no longer passes principally through the mediation of political parties); unions became interlocutors of the government and were quite important, especially in the development of welfare.

At the end of the 1970s, a long phase began in which the Italian union movement substantially maintained the recognition and power it had gained but increasingly had to face economic realities, industrial restructurings, and soaring inflation (certainly contributed to by the contractual mechanism of wage indexation). In this phase the disputes of the CGIL and CISL reemerged periodically: the former was more given to the defense of gains obtained between 1968 and 1975, and the latter more disposed to revising bargaining strategies in the light of new economic situations and the attendant requirements of competitiveness.

Also during this phase, the assessments of observers of the Italian union experience differed notably. For some, after the years of the cycle of struggles, tendencies and events began that brought its progressive weakening and frequently the sacrifice of the interests and rights of the workers. For others, myself included, these years represent an exceptional moment, after which, for objective reasons, union action reentered a "situation of normalcy," with problems analogous to those of union movements in other countries of advanced capitalism.

The major reason for disputes among the various union components and for the differences in the assessments concerns collective actions. These were agreements among the government, unions, and entrepreneurial organizations to construct social and wage policies which would allow for the reduction of inflation and stop the heavy public debt, principally through income policy. These agreements were stipulated in 1983 and 1984. Afterwards, negotiations between the government and social partners continued, always with the aim of collective agreement. However, given the disputes or suspicion that they provoked, these negotiations were less emphasized.

On the other hand, the same collective bargaining produced negotiations concerning claims which were much more heedful of economic restraints than those of the past. This process of adaptation came about with the limits imposed by the income policy on national occupational bargaining and, in a decentralized and spontaneous fashion, with the integrative agreements at the company level.

The collective agreements and adaptive bargaining concerned workers of the production sectors exposed to international competition. Two other large groups of workers remained relatively at the margins of one or the other choice (for almost all of the 1980s): government employees and pensioners. The former especially, in addition to having full job security, succeeded in obtaining consistent wage increases which created intense and insidious labor unrest and conflicts (notably in decline in industrial sectors) due to the initiatives of a plurality of unions that represent specific groups of workers (for example, railway engineers and pilots) outside and often opposed to the most controlling lines of the trade union confederations (CGIL-CISL-UIL). For pensioners it meant that at the rate of the aging of the Italian population, they became a consistent part of these trade union confederations (almost half of the CGIL members), altering their traditional organizational makeup and creating serious problems for the social security supply and system (which has a higher distribution rate than that of many other European countries) from which they benefit.

CURRENT PROBLEMS

Italy, as noted, entered the 1990s with serious problems—old problems that have become more acute, as well as new and explosive problems. The most important of these problems were the profound political crisis (which assailed the balances of power of recent decades), the undeniable necessity to reduce the public debt and zero out the current deficit, the loss of competitiveness and the structural weaknesses of the industrial apparatus, and a high unemployment rate. The first three problems, particularly the first, concern our country much more markedly than other European countries; moreover, we also face them because Italy has full "citizenship" in the processes of European integration. The fourth problem is not more dramatic than in other European countries, but it cannot be tackled with historical solutions (the enormous emigration of the Italian workforce). The union movement and industrial relations are obviously involved in such problems, with a special position in relation to the first one. The Italian unions, despite ties to cultural and political circles, have not been substantially touched by the political crisis and its consequences.

The political crisis has its most evident (but not only) manifestation in the "sins" of party leaders, particularly those of the majority. These sins (personal interests, illicit financing of the party, abuses of power, and administrative improprieties) so far have not plagued the vast majority of union management at all levels. There are many explanations for this. This management does not have a managing role in politico-institutional processes. Union organizations (unlike parties) have a regular cash flow of membership dues. They are not normally employees of services with economic substance (banks, building cooperatives, real estate). In the union sphere a simple lifestyle dominates, and there is a rather high level of social control of this characteristic. The most ambitious managers (at times also the most capable) do not spend their entire life in the union and are able to transfer into the political arena with relative ease (prevalently as members of parliament). The most convincing proof that the political crisis did not involve union players is evident in their rather important role in the operation and adaptation of industrial relations vis-à-vis the economic and financial problems of the country. In fact, while the political scene was dominated by the destruction of the old balances, in industrial relations there was a distinctly constructive and innovative period (1992 and 1993) with the resolute aid of the Amato and Ciampi governments (decidedly more autonomous from the parties than preceding governments). During this period, unions, employers, and the government garnered positive results in the areas of public budget problems and the competitiveness of productive apparatus. This especially came about through an evident revival of collective negotiations.

After preliminary agreements, beginning in December 1991, a binding agreement was reached in July 1993. With it came a renewal of the income policy, the negotiation structure was set in order (distinguishing the functions of the different contractual levels), margins of flexibility in the labor market were introduced, and the connection between decentralized retributive increases and productivity or profitability of business was confirmed. The discipline of labor cost dynamics favored (together with the devaluation of the lira) the revival of Italian exportation and—a no less important fact—allowed the nominal and real wages of government employees to be held under control. During the same period, a significant reform began for these employees that aims for privatization of their employee-employer relations to reduce excessive advocacies of civil liberties, to introduce flexibility and mobility, and to reach connections between career and other duties. This is a wonderful reform in theory, but in probability it will take a long time to effectively implement, given the longstanding habit of many government employees of working too little and with too few service controls.

Along with the collective agreements, another dimension directly concerning industrial relations appears equally positive. The climate within businesses has become more collaborative, and those involved have begun to speak seriously of common interests between employers and unions and those they represent. The adaptive connotations of business negotiations have in fact become more marked (introducing major flexibility in the employment of labor). In addition, particularly in mid-to-large-sized businesses, agreements in which workers share in the results have multiplied (gain-sharing and profit-sharing), and programs of "total quality" have been realized, with the good will of the unions and with congruous contractual mediations.

This process of participation, with negligible precedents in Italy's tradition, has brought the system of industrial relations nearer to those of the countries of Central Northern Europe and demonstrated that productive and organizational innovation of businesses (with respect to market demands) can be achieved without deregulation and with the cooperation of workers' representatives.

It is very difficult to discuss positive results regarding the unemployment problem. Government and social partners have experimented with partial solutions, like job training contracts (not necessarily permanent hirings for workers under thirty) and solidarity contracts (the division of jobs arranged among employees in a company). In Italy the Workers' Insurance Fund (Cassa Integrazione Guadagni) also exists and guarantees a high wage share favorable to company workers in situations of economic crisis or structural difficulties, even for long periods. The government in office is preparing a series of interventions to support employment, along the lines indicated in the aforementioned agreement of July 1993. On the whole, these are nondecisive, costly measures which are not capable of cracking the hard nut of unemployment, which will remain conspicuous even with an economic recovery.

Unemployment constitutes a thorn in the side of union organizations. It creates strong social tensions and introduces a weighty dualism (employed and unemployed) in the labor market. It is at the center of the burning political debate in progress, but no one is in a position to propose and sustain wide-ranging socioeconomic policies (of a Keynesian nature). This situation poses a serious dilemma for unionists. On one hand, it is their duty to protect the workers; on the other, they cannot *not* involve themselves heavily in helping those without jobs. On one hand, they want to defend the wage levels and many guarantees of the former, and this implies higher labor costs and mechanisms of labor market inelasticity; on the other, they know that the employment rate can improve if the cost of labor becomes more flexible and if further aspects of flexibility are introduced.

With respect to this situation, some place their hopes in the will and ability of the government majority which will come out in the elections of spring 1994. Others think of the generalized application of the Volkswagen formula (at least at the European level): strong reductions in working hours, with accompanying wage reduction). Still others maintain that de facto we will coexist with a consistent unemployment rate, reduced in tandem with the economic recovery, with the mitigation of its harshest effects through a growing gamut of social shock absorbers and specific measures, rendered bearable by the level of wealth produced on the whole and by distributive processes.

MYTH AND REALITY ABOUT THE ITALIAN FAMILY

Chiara Saraceno

A SILENT REVOLUTION

Both in Italy and abroad there is a widespread notion that the Italian family is not just holding on but has remained essentially unchanged for at least the last fifty years in terms of the values and the relationships that hold it together. Barbagli (1990) notes this in his research on matrimonial instability. The thesis of persistent familism is also sustained by Paul Ginsborg (1989) to explain the specificity of the Italian political case. The fall in the birthrate might induce pessimistic reflections on intergenerational solidarity (see Donati 1991, Sgritta 1991), but the extended stay of children at home well after they become adults (granted its meaning is ambivalent) is taken as indicative of the traditional bonds of family solidarity and dependence. (Scabini, ed. 1988; Cavalli 1993). The unemployment rate of married women with children is no longer (or at least not always) considered an indicator of the disintegration of the family (as it was by Ardigò and Donati 1976), although the rate is considered by many scholars and opinion-makers to be indicative of the potential risk (or dysfunctionality) at which a family finds itself. This rate, however, is not seen as a potential element in the redefinition or reorganization of the family.

Social policy in Italy continues to refer to a model of the family which takes for granted the gender division of labor and the economic and caring solidarity through the generations. As recent provisions of health reform confirm, family makeup and family income—not individual rights and needs—are among the prevalent criteria used by legislators to distribute and ration services and benefits. This makes Italy a variant of a type of welfare regime that Esping Anderson (1990) has defined as corporate-conservative. While social policy that supports the family exists in other countries in this category (Germany, Belgium, France, and Holland), in Italy such policy is almost totally absent. Rather, the family and its organization along precise lines of responsibility, both generational and gender-specific, are taken for granted (Saraceno 1990, 1992).

Taking the family for granted has made things more difficult not just for individuals (women in particular, as well as children, who only with difficulty have the economic resources for autonomy, and the dependent elderly whose well-being depends on family solidarity), but also for the family itself, concretely existing families themselves, which in the last thirty years have been changing the behaviors and priorities that have typified the so-called "Italian family." From the mid-1960s family relationships and behavior have in fact seen a constant and visible transformation of their principal dimensions: marriage and procreation. This process is tied to phenomena less immediately visible and documentable in statistical terms, but nonetheless significant: the redefinition and renegotiation of the relationship between men and women.

Since the baby boom of the early 1960s—more a result of the size of the cohort of marriage age than of a reversal of the sixty-year-old trend of decline in fertility—the number of children per couple has begun to decline, settling at about two, then dipping below this figure. In the 1980s and 1990s, not only third children, but also second children have been rarer in the central and northern regions. In the large cities of the South as well, they have come to constitute an exception. The phenomenon of a fast and significant decline in births is even more interesting if one considers that in Italy disseminating information on contraceptive methods, the sale of contraceptives, and abortion were illegal until 1975 and continue to be condemned by the Catholic Church (except for periodic abstinence or the rhythm method). This disconnection between behavior and normative models signals not only a secularization of sexual and procreative behavior—from which the judgment of the state and the Church is removed and which is seen to be a dimension of personal liberty—but also a change in the idea of family and couple, which are ever less defined on the basis of their reproductive responsibilities. Today Italy has the lowest birthrate in the Western world, with 1.3 children per woman.

These changes have brought a redefinition of the role of procreation in the lives of adults, particularly women, and the place of children in the family. The latter are seen to be the result of choice rather than of chance or destiny. For this reason, along with a systematic reliance on contraception (even by the most traditional means) to control the number of children and to decide when to have them, there is also an increasing use of artificial reproduction to produce the desired child or children. Recent research has shown that the majority of couples desires at least one child and that the importance attributed to children increases when one already has one (Palomba 1991). Therefore procreation remains of great importance for Italian men and women. For the most part this is procreation within marriage, given that the number of children born out of wedlock in Italy is statistically negligible among Western countries and substantially stable. But one child, and at the maximum two, is sufficient to give weight to this importance.

Even before 1970, when the law that allowed divorce was introduced, the number of separations had begun to rise noticeably, quadrupling in a span of twenty years. In 1990 the number of separations (44,018) equaled about 14 percent of the marriages that were celebrated in that year. In 1988 there were 37,224 separations, equal to about 12 percent of the marriages. (In 1971, when legal separation became a required step for those who wished to dissolve their marriages, there were 11,796 separations.) The number of divorces, stabilized in the second half of the 1970s, began to rise, doubling in four years (15,065 in 1984, 30,876 in 1988, and 27,682 in 1990). Such a phenomenon affected all regions, although conjugal instability remains notably lower in the South than in the central and northern regions. (Some of the latter rates—in Emilia Romagna, Piedmont, and Lombardy—approach the German and the English.) Owing to these regional differences, which in large part correspond to diverse economic, cultural, and family traditions, as well as to different employment rates for women, matrimonial instability in Italy is notably lower than the European and Western averages in general—either a fifteenth or a ninth lower, depending on whether one considers divorces or separations. In contrast to other countries, Italian matrimonial instability is more prevalent among the middle and upper classes and among the more highly educated, probably due not only to the bureaucracy involved in the procedures which require resources and ability, but also to the relative newness of the phenomenon.

The rise in matrimonial instability accompanies two other phenomena which are even more noticeable in other Western countries: a reduction in the propensity to marry and an increase in unwed couples living together. The first phenomenon essentially has to do with first marriages and the younger cohorts. It is the youngest who are reluctant to marry or at least desire to delay matrimony. Note that the age at marriage in Italy has remained stable and higher than in other industrialized countries for almost the entire past century: twenty-three years for women and twenty-seven years for men.

The second phenomenon concerns people of differing ages, with perhaps a prevalence in the middle years. In other countries (except Sweden, where living together has become a type of family as widespread and legitimate as matrimony) it is primarily the young who live together without or before marrying. In Italy one often finds middle-aged adults and elderly living together, although in any case this is apparently a very limited phenomenon: only 1.8 percent of all couples were not married in 1983. This Italian particularity is due in part to culture and religion, which often consider cohabitation without marriage reproachable, especially for young women, and in part to legislation. While young people living together do not have the understanding or support of their families and do not have access to forms of social support such as rent control or low cost housing, many adults who want to live together find incentives not to marry. On one hand, the long period required by law to divorce restricts those who want to build a new life and live together; one must first legally separate; then one must wait a minimum time before asking for a divorce. Until the divorce reform of 1987, which reduced the waiting period to three years, it was necessary to wait five years. On the other hand, the rules for allowances to a divorced person, the transferability of pensions, and inheritance make it such that many divorced women (as well as widows) choose to live with their new partners out of wedlock in order not to lose their allowances or pensions and not to complicate inheritances to their children.

Many observers believe that the cultural restrictions indicated above cause the underestimation of cohabitation in Italy. Research on university students who study in a city away from their own and where they keep their official residence and on adults who live alone would seem to suggest that unwed cohabitation is more widespread than appears in official data, even if differing by geographic regions and social classes.

Living alone as a life choice or as a phase before matrimony or cohabitation seems to be a more prevalent phenomenon abroad than in Italy. So-called one-person families are on the rise. But this is due to an aging population and a greater number of widowed elderly, and only marginally to the phenomenon of young adults who leave home to live on their own (Menniti, ed. 1991). Moreover, the Italian university is neither conceived nor organized to encourage living independently of the family; many students who study away from home do not find housing support, services, or part-time work which would allow them clear autonomy from their families. The phenomenon of living alone, perhaps in part underestimated, is more present in the urban areas of the central and northern regions, which are not only magnets of immigration for both work and study, but also offer greater possibilities for work and therefore economic autonomy, as well as protection from restrictive social controls.

The infrequent incidence of either young people living together or young adults living alone outlines a family that has few children, who live at home for a long time with more or less total economic dependence, given the difficulty that young people face as they seek to enter the labor market. At both the cultural and legal levels, young people have acquired greater rights in terms of behavioral and consumer choices, so in the life cycle of the Italian family there is now a relatively long phase in which two generations of adults live together and negotiate responsibilities and rights, expectations of reciprocity, and needs for autonomy. The results of this long cohabitation of generations—which is certainly not new behavior in Italy but which persists even with changed expectations in the relationship between the generations—are for the most part interpreted in terms of prolonged dependence and difficult emancipation "for lack of conflict." Recent data from the third Study of the Condition of Youth in Italy (Cavalli 1993) interpret long cohabitation in this way as well. However, I believe that this is only a partial reading, if for no other reason than that it presupposes an earlier period in which children left home in greater numbers on the threshold of adulthood, which is not the case.

Negotiations and continual redefinitions of reciprocal expectations and responsibilities outlast the period of cohabitation, inasmuch as a greater lifespan extends the kin network for three generations—children, parents, and grandparents. Recent research has shown the importance of the flow of help and the exchange of resources in the kin network (especially between generations), both in affective terms and in terms of the quality of life (Sgritta 1986; Barbagli 1991; La Mendola 1991; Oppo 1991). To be able to count on the support of the family is an important resource in Italy, perhaps more than elsewhere, and above all for the young and the elderly. For a young person faced with difficulty and the long waiting period prior to entering the labor market, the possibility of being at least partially supported by parents for a more or less prolonged period constitutes a crucial element in the strategy of integration and exploration of chances. For the elderly, in the absence of an adequate system of social services and in light of the large number of elderly who receive only a small pension, the capacity of the family to provide economic support can make a crucial difference.

The phenomena described above indicate how crucial a resource the family continues to be in Italy, in terms of both affective and material support. However, this family in certain ways seems to maintain a clear continuity with tradition in name only. It is precisely because behaviors of women and in the intergenerational relationships—which in the past sustained the functioning of the traditional family—today seem radically changed that expectations inherent in much social policy as well as in common sense that the family continues to function in traditional terms seem to be resting on a rather shaky foundation. There are ever fewer daughters to take care of the invalid elderly, not only because they are more involved in work outside the house, but also because fewer of them have been born. Intergenerational solidarity will experience interruptions and redefinitions as conjugal instability renders the bonds between grandparents and grandchildren less obviously certain. At the same time, the obligation to support one's children longer because of widespread unemployment among youth and the wait children face before entering the work force imposes new tensions on family relationships within those social strata—for example, industrial workers and artisans—in which there is a tradition of early economic autonomy among children, who were traditionally asked to contribute to the family budget rather than to depend on it for a long time.

In any case it is certain that if for none other than demographic reasons, the extended family network, with grandparents, children, sons and daughters in-law, and grandchildren seated at the same table for the major family holidays—which plays a part in Italian mythology, as well as in the present generation of fifty-year-olds—will not easily play a part in the experience of the younger generations.

AT THE CENTER OF CHANGE: WOMEN'S TRANSFORMATIONS

Among the changes that ought to be underlined are the relationship between the genders and, above all, the behavior of women both within and outside the family. The drop in the birthrate is not only the cause of the radical change in the lifecycle of women, whose procreative and child-rearing years are much reduced. It is also a result of a different attitude among women toward motherhood as the principal and fulfilling expression of adult feminine identity, paid work, economic independence from their husbands, and the personal costs of the gender division of labor both inside and outside the family. The increase in conjugal instability too in Italy is related to the increased employment rate among women. As in other countries, it is the women rather than the men who initiate separation (Barbagli 1990; Francescato 1992).

In the last twenty years the number of women in the paid work force has increased (although it remains at levels lower than those of northern Europe), and it involves mothers with small children (Abburrá 1989; Carmignani and Pruna 1991). In particular the decade from 1978 to 1988 shows a strong increase in the participation of women in the paid work force in the 25–50 age group and includes women of all educational levels. The rate of employment reaches 77 percent for women with either a diploma or university degree (for those with only the minimum education, the so-called *licenza media*, the rate of employment is 46.4 percent). This increase is all the more remarkable if one observes that even though 43 percent of the work has been transformed, at least in the short term, into prolonged unemployment, this phenomenon has not had the "traditional" discouraging effect—not even in the South.

Official employment among women, as well as part of unofficial ("black") employment, is mostly full-time. (Tables 1–3 provide some comparisons of female employment in Italy and in other developed countries.) It ought to be underlined that the relatively small wage difference between men and women in Italy is due not so much to the strength of the feminist movement or to specific positive action measures, which are still relatively recent and of doubtful effect, but rather to the efficacity of trade unions, especially in the 1970s, in defending low-income workers. Women are in fact disproportionately represented in this group. A second factor is the high number of women working in public administration and social services, where wage discrimination is less pronounced than in the private sector, at least at the lower and middle levels (Bettio 1988; Nassisi 1990; Pristinger 1992).

With a time lapse of about ten years, there was also an increase in the level of education of women, although in Italy, in contrast to the central and northern countries of Europe and the United States, the difference in level of instruction between the sexes remained constant until the mid-1970s. After 1975 the difference rapidly diminished, and in recent years some scholars have noted that women are overtaking men (Dei 1987; Schizzerotto 1988; Campani 1992). For this reason, it is among the youngest that men and women are closest to each other in level of instruction, and to a lesser extent in the type of instruction and in expectations with regard to the labor market. Much recent research indicates in fact that among younger women, only a minority renounces work in favor of family responsibilities; the figure reaches only 20 percent in southern regions for women with little education and where the unemployment rate is high even for men (IARD 1991; Saraceno 1993).

De Sandre (1991) provides an interesting and probing analysis of the interworking of the lower birthrate, the increase in education, and employment among the various cohorts of women who have reached adulthood in the period since World War II. In particular, he observes that the fall in the birthrate for the third child, then the second, begins with the cohort of women born between 1939 and 1948—that is, with the cohorts that began to appear in greater numbers in the labor market. De Sandre provides an explanation for this triangular connection:

Table 1

Selected Labor Force Statistics for Eighteen OECD Countries, Ranked by Female Share of Labor Force, 1960 and 1990

(Percent)

Country	Labor Force Participation 1960 Male	Labor Force Participation 1960 Female	Labor Force Participation 1990 Male	Labor Force Participation 1990 Female	Female Share of Labor Force 1960	Female Share of Labor Force 1990	1990 Labor Force in Services	1990 Labor Force in Government
Sweden	98.5%	50.1%	85.3%	81.1%	33.6%	48.0%	67.5%	31.7%[a]
Finland	91.4	65.6	80.6	72.9	43.7	47.1	60.6	22.4
Denmark	99.5	43.5	89.6	78.4	30.9	46.1	66.9	30.5
Norway	92.2	36.3	84.5	71.2	28.2	44.9	68.8	27.7
United States	90.5	42.6	85.2	68.1	32.5	44.9	70.9	14.4[a]
Canada	91.1	33.7	84.9	68.2	26.6	44.5	71.2	19.7
New Zealand	93.8	31.3	80.8	62.1	24.5	43.3	64.8	18.1[b]
France	94.6	46.6	75.2	56.6	33.3	42.9	64.0	22.6
United Kingdom	99.1	46.1	86.4	65.1	32.7	42.8	68.9	19.2
Belgium	85.5	36.4	72.7	52.4	30.2	41.6	69.0	19.5
Australia	97.2	34.1	86.1	62.3	25.1	41.3	69.0	22.8
Austria	92.0	52.1	80.1	55.4	39.4	41.0	55.3	20.6
Germany	94.4	49.2	80.7	56.6	37.3	40.7	56.8	15.1
Japan	92.2	60.1	87.8	60.4	40.7	40.6	58.7	6.0
Netherlands	97.8	26.2	79.6	53.0	21.5	39.2	69.1	- -
Switzerland	100	51.0	93.6	59.3	34.1	38.1	59.5	14.7
Italy	95.3	39.6	78.1	44.5	30.7	36.8	58.6	15.5
Ireland	99.0	34.8	82.2	38.9	25.6	31.6	56.2	13.7

Correlates of female share of labor force 1990:
Labor force in services (percent): 0.549 ($P < .05$)
Labor force in government (percent): 0.642 ($P < .01$)

Sources: OECD, *Economic Outlook,* 1992, Historical Statistics; O'Connor (1992).

[a] 1989.

[b] 1985

Table 2

PART-TIME EMPLOYMENT IN EIGHTEEN OECD COUNTRIES, RANKED BY FEMALE SHARE OF LABOR FORCE, 1979 AND 1990

(Percent)

	Part-Time Employment as a Proportion of Male Employment		Part-Time Employment as a Proportion of Female Employment		Women's Share in Part-Time Employment	
Country	1979	1990	1979	1990	1979	1990
Sweden	5.4%	7.3%	46.0%	40.5%	87.5%	83.7%
Finland	3.2	4.4	10.6	10.2	74.7	67.8
Denmark	5.2	9.0	46.3	41.5	86.9	79.4
Norway	7.3	8.8	50.9	48.2	83.0	81.8
United States	9.0	10.0	26.7	25.2	68.0	67.6
Canada	5.7	8.1	23.3	24.4	72.1	71.0
New Zealand	4.9	8.5	29.1	35.2	77.7	76.1
France	2.4	3.5	16.9	23.8	82.2	83.1
United Kingdom	1.9	5.0	39.0	43.8	92.8	87.0
Belgium	1.0	1.7	16.5	25.0	88.9	89.6
Australia	5.2	8.0	35.2	40.1	78.7	78.1
Austria	1.5	1.6	18.0	20.0	87.8	88.8
Germany	1.5	2.1	27.6	30.6	91.6	90.5
Japan	7.5	8.0	27.8	31.9	70.1	73.0
Netherlands	5.5	15.8	44.0	61.7	76.4	70.4
Italy	3.0	3.1	10.6	10.9	61.4	64.7
Ireland	2.1	3.8	13.1	17.1	71.2	68.2

Sources:

Table 3

Ratios of Female to Male Hourly Earnings for Manual Workers in Manufacturing in 1988 and Dissimilarity Indices for 1970 and 1986 for Eighteen OECD Countries, Ranked by Female Share of Labor Force in 1990

Country	Female to Male Earnings Ratio	Dissimilarity Indices 1970	Dissimilarity Indices 1986
Sweden	90.0	44.3	37.9
Finland	77.2	38.7	43.0
Denmark	84.4	45.4	40.5[a]
Norway	84.3	47.7	46.6
United States	65.0	44.0	37.4
Canada	65.0	48.7	40.2
New Zealand	74.6	42.8	- -
France	- -	38.9	- -
United Kingdom	68.0	42.4	- -
Belgium	74.5	39.8	- -
Australia	79.6	47.2	47.8[a]
Austria	- -	35.9	44.4
Germany	73.0	35.1	37.8[b]
Japan	48.9	25.3	23.1
Netherlands	78.0	45.1	40.0
Italy	74.3	23.4	- -
Ireland	68.9	46.0	42.9

Correlates of female/male hourly earnings in manufacturing:
Labor force in government (percent): 0.858 ($P < .01$)
Union density: 0.591 ($P < .05$)
Correlates of percentage labor force in government:
Union density: 0.645 ($P < .01$)

Sources: OECD—*Employment Outlook,* 1991, table 2.16 for ratios of female to male earnings; *Employment Outlook,* 1988, for dissimilarity indices; O'Connor (1992).

[a] 1985.

[b] 1984.

The combination of two tendencies (education and employment), both growing, certainly affects the so-called "opportunity cost" of children by discouraging fertility. Since it is the woman's time that is mostly at stake in reproduction and in raising children, the opportunity cost is at least equal to the lost salary while the woman dedicates to her child that time in which she cannot work for pay. Better professional opportunities for the woman tend to increase the opportunity cost of children.

In effect, the mass entry of women into higher education outlines new paths of entry into adult life for women, and for this reason new patterns of being a woman. Recent research indicates that the level of education is a crucial variable not only in the timing and manner of entry into the labor market for young women, but also in their life plans as a whole. For example, a study by IARD (1991) shows that the prospect of becoming a housewife and dedicating oneself entirely to the family as soon as one reaches adulthood—considered by only a minority at all social, educational, and geographic levels—is more significant among women with only the minimum education. This phenomenon signals not only new forms of inequality among women, but also the continued persistence of gender differences. A male with little education does not have the (certainly doubtful) choice of resolving his difficulties in the labor market by leaving it or by rejecting work as an indispensable part of his individual and social identity.

With the rise in education, the spheres and models of participation for women in the labor market have changed. There is ever less factory work and ever more clerical work; fewer women work at a very young age and then abandon it to raise a family (to then turn to unofficial work in the case of need); there is ever more full-time work and lifelong commitment to work. Young women today are entering the labor market later than their mothers due to the double effect of a higher level of education and a longer wait (Gesano 1990), but once they find a job they tend not to abandon it. They are supported in this regard by some of the most liberal legislation favoring working mothers in the West, although the laws are applied differently in the public and private sectors.

The phenomenon of increased employment among women cannot be attributed solely to emancipation and feminist movements, which in the 1970s and early 1980s were highly visible. Much married female employment is a result of family need: a two-income family can respond better to its needs, to economic crisis, and to unforseen events.

The greater female employment rate brings about renegotiations within married couples regarding the organization of daily life and the distribution of power and responsibility, which are seen as important as procreation and its timing. On this last issue, it is worth noting that in Italy, that which is for the most part implicit in the model of procreation as choice was made explicit with the law on abortion, approved on a wave of the feminist movement and confirmed (though narrowly) in the following referendum: if it is true that one is often dealing with a couple's decision, it is also true that the desire and choice of the father must in every case be subordinated to that of the mother. We are here in the presence of a discontinuity which is not merely symbolic, noteworthy in a culture in many ways steeped in patriarchal models which until the beginning of the century held the juridical sway of marital authorization, to which every choice of a woman on almost every issue was to be subordinated, and which until 1975 had a family law that was among the most hierarchical in the Western world.

It is only in the sphere of procreation that the woman's will is given precedence in conjugal negotiations. In other spheres, not priority, but simply parity seems to continue to be problematic, in practice if not in law. According to much research, women still take on the majority of domestic work and care, whether they have a paying job or not, and it is they who most often must give up a career or promotions (if not simply the job) in order to take on family responsibilities; research suggests that it has been easier for women to enter the work force than it has been to get men to take on family responsibilities (Saraceno, ed. 1980; Balbo et al. 1987; Roveri 1990; Palomba and Sabbadini 1992). On the other hand, access to paid work allows for "exit" for those who do not succeed in finding satisfaction via "voice." Part of conjugal instability, like hesitation in getting married, is due to the unwillingness of women to remain in relationships that lack reciprocity and are strongly assymetric (Barbagli 1990; Francescato 1992). This does not prevent women from running a greater risk of economic impoverishment because of matrimonial instability, precisely because of the division of work and responsibilities between the genders in marriage. The risk is particularly great when there are young children, who are most often entrusted to the mother in the case of separation. Child support, while highly variable, is generally low. Only a minority of women (10 percent, and as many as 20 percent in the South) receive any support for themselves upon separation, and even fewer do so upon divorce (Barbagli 1990). In other words, Italian men, as soon as they are freed from the bonds of matrimony, seem to feel even less than their European counterparts the need to continue in their traditional role of breadwinner for either their children or their ex-wives. In this, they are supported by judicial practice.

LEGISLATIVE CHANGE: SHADOW AND LIGHT

Changes in behavior and in the ways families are organized have seen only partial recognition in legislation and social policy. In effect—above all in the 1970s because of the strong women's movement, whose claims were heard in part by the lay parties and the left—laws relating to the family have changed profoundly, and questions of gender have become part of public discourse. Between 1970, the year that divorce legislation was introduced, and 1978, the year in which abortion was legalized, a series of laws that regulated family relationships and the rights of women was changed radically. In addition to laws that directly regulate the institution of family and procreation, others should be noted—for example, a law in favor of working mothers was broadened to include all categories of female workers and rendered better in terms of guaranteeing income and length of leave, and the so-called law of equality in 1977 confirmed equality between men and women at work and also introduced paternity leave in specific circumstances. In those same years the basis for a local system of family support services was established: nursery schools for children under the age of three of working mothers, widely available kindergarten for children between the ages of three and five, elementary school with a longer schedule than the traditional half day, at home services for the elderly, etc. In reality, in the decades following, this system of services has seen unbalanced development (e.g., kindergarten has developed more than nursery school and more than services for the elderly), creating different models of social citizenship. Today, even in the regions in which these services are more developed, they risk being reduced for budgetary reasons. However, especially where these services have created concrete expectations, they have radically changed the needs and the rights of both the family and its individual members. For example, in Emilia Romagna, where nursery schools cover 30 percent of the age group, even housewife mothers seek to enroll their children because they consider nursery school an invaluable educational experience, whereas in other times or in other regions to send a child to nursery school signified either a minor sin or maternal inadequacy and in any event was perceived as risky in that it signified lack of affection.

The legislation on the family that resulted from the reform in 1975 reaffirms conjugal equality, already present in the republican constitution, and at the same time erases the ambiguity of the constitution, where it states that in matrimony "Husband and wife are equal, granted that the family unity is preserved." The notion of a family head and his right to determine the residence of all family members, particularly that of the wife, on the basis of convenience is in fact eliminated. The traditional patrimonial system of matrimony is defined as a system of communal wealth, whereas before upon separation, a greater advantage was given to men. The communal concept is explicitly formulated to recognize the contribution each person makes for the common good and therefore recognizes the household work performed by women. Barbagli (1993) indicates that cultural transformations have surpassed the notion of community in marriage which seemed so innovative and responsive to the need for greater equality between spouses. The younger generations in growing measure have opted for a regime of separation, notwithstanding the greater risk of women, who earn less than men and do more domestic work for free. Maybe this means that equality based on marriage as a community is giving way to a notion of equality based on marriage as an association of individuals who do not so much want to mingle their economic resources as they want to share expenses.

A large portion of legislation regarding work (schedules, minimum age of entry, retirement age, etc.) continues to favor a male worker model with no responsibilities for the family, while women workers continue to be considered the titleholders of these responsibilities, in the name of which they receive some special facilitations; however, they encounter difficulties in getting their abilities and rights as workers recognized. On the one hand, social policy and services consider working mothers to be the bearers of particular demands (above all for the care of the youngest) whose satisfaction represents a social cost. On the other hand, policies and services refer to a model of family organization and relationships in which women are always available to care for those who are not totally independent (infants, dependent elderly, the sick, and the handicapped). Services for infants cover only a small number of children, even though there is great variation from area to area; schools operate half-time and provide no cafeteria service; dependent elderly receive help only if they are poor and lack a daughter or daughter-in-law to look after them; the hours of social services do not always correspond to the schedules of those who need them.

Social and work policy seems also to take for granted a specific model of intergenerational family solidarity; such a model can be very restricting. Social and health policy refers to family rather than individual income, and in some cases (services to invalid elderly) even to that of noncohabiting relatives. The young are considered children for an extended period under labor policy, so that entry level salaries and contracts are proposed until the ages 28–30. And so on.

Social policy and services have undoubtedly contributed to the redefinition of resources and the quality of family life, albeit unequally from region to region. However, in the fragmented and partial social state in Italy, families, and in particular women in families, are considered crucial partners, of whom one expects not only intelligence in utilizing the resources, but also flexibility, adaptability, and an ability to fill in the gaps of the social policy itself.

Legislation, moreover, seems to totally ignore the emergence of new family forms and the obligations and expectations that these engender. Particular problems can emerge in a one-parent (usually mother) family, on an economic as well as organizational level. Such problems find only partial recognition in services for young infants and in the way the entitlement to the family allowance is calculated. Above all, there is absolutely no legal recognition of relationships that emerge in reconstituted families—among children of different parents, between these children and the spouse of their natural parent, etc. A new husband has no responsibility for the children of the latter, even if he in fact contributes to their support. The very labels to describe these types of relationships are lacking. Moreover, the obligations and expectations in common-law households are hardly recognized: if one of the partners dies, the other cannot inherit, take over the lease on the home or apartment, and so on. In case of separation, the partner who subordinated her job to family responsibilities or worked in the firm of her partner does not have the recourse of having the economic value of her choices and services acknowledged. Certainly to legislate in such cases is no easy task, in that it risks creating bonds of marriage that are not accepted by those involved. However, the hesitation of Italian legislators, unlike their European colleagues, seems to stem from a difficulty in recognizing the legitimacy of these ways of having a family—that is, to move from the singular "family" to the plural "families."

REFERENCES

Abburrá, F. 1989. *L'occupazione femminile dal declino alla crescita.* Turin: Rosenberg and Sellier.

Ardigo, A., and Donati, P. P. 1976. *Famiglia e industrializzazione.* Milan: F. Angeli.

Balbo, L.; May, P.; and Micheli, G. 1987. *Vincoli e strategie nella vita quotidiana.* Milan: F. Angeli.

Barbagli, M. 1990. *Provando e riprovando: Matrimonio, famiglia e divorzio in Italia e in altri paesi occidentali.* Bologna: Il Mulino.

———. 1991. "I genitori di lei e quelli di lui: Un'indagine in Emilia-Romagna." *Polis* 5, 1: 71–86.

———. 1993. "Comunione o separazione dei beni? I rapporti patrimoniali tra i coniugi in Italia: 1975–1991." *Polis* 1: 143–62.

Bettio, F. 1988. *The Sexual Division of Labour: The Italian Case.* Oxford: Clarendon Press.

Campani, G. 1992. "Donne a scuola in Europa." In *Educazione e ruolo femminile,* ed. S. Ulivieri, pp. 245–82. Florence: La Nuova Italia.

Carmignani, F., and Pruna, M. L. 1991. "Le donne nel mercato del lavoro: Vecchi problemi e nuove opportunità." *Sociologia del lavoro* 43: 137–48.

Cavalli, A. 1993. "Senza nessuna fretta di crescere." *Il Mulino* 42, 345: 35–42.

De Sandre, P. 1991. "Contributo delle generazioni ai cambiamenti recenti nei comportamenti e nelle forme familiari." In *Secondo rapporto sulla famiglia in Italia,* ed. P. Donati, pp. 109–55. Milan: Paoline.

Dei, M. 1987. "Lo sviluppo della scolarità femminile in Italia." *Polis* 1: 143–58.

Donati, P. P. 1991. "Equità generazionale: Un nuovo confronto sulla qualità familiare." In *Secondo rapporto sulla famiglia in Italia,* ed. P. Donati, pp. 31-108. Milan: Paoline.

Esping Andersen, G. 1990. *The Three Worlds of Welfare Capitalism.* Oxford: Polity Press.

Francescato, D. 1992. *Quando l'amore finisce.* Bologna: Il Mulino.

Gesano G. 1990. *Dieci anni di evoluzione del mercato del lavoro italiano: 1978–1987, Un'analisi per generazioni del Nord-Centro del Mezzogiorno.* Rome: IRP/CNR. Working Paper No. 1.

Ginsborg, P. 1989. *Storia dell'Italia dal dopoguerra ad oggi.* Turin: Einaudi.

IARD. 1991. "I percorsi femminili di transizione dalla scuola al lavoro." Report by M. Palumbo and F. Sartori. Milan. Mimeo.

La Mendola, S. 1991. "I rapporti di parentela in Veneto." *Polis* 5, 1: 49–70.

Menniti, A., ed. 1991. *Le famiglie italiane degli anni '80.* Rome: IRP/CNR.

Nassisi, A. M. 1990. "Primo rapporto: Il lavoro femminile in Italia tra produzione e riproduzione," pp. 101–52. Rome: Fondazione Istituto Gramsci.

O'Connor, J. S. 1992. "Citizenship, Class, Gender and the Labour Market: Issues of Decommodification and Personal Autonomy." Paper presented at the conference on Comparative Studies of Welfare State Development: Quantitative and Qualitative Dimensions, Bremen, 3–6 September.

Oppo, A. 1991. "Madri, figlie e sorelle: Solidarietà parentali in Sardegna." *Polis* 5, 1: 21–48.

Palomba, R. 1991. "Gli italiani e le opinioni sulla natalità e le politiche demografiche." In *Famiglia, figli e società in Europa,* ed. A. Golini et al., pp. 301–32. Turin: Edizioni della Fondazione Giovanni Agnelli.

Palomba, R., and Sabbadini, L. L. 1992. "Fertility, Family Structure and Time Use in Italy." Paper presented at the IUSSP seminar on Gender and Family Change in Industrialized Countries, Rome, 26–30 January.

Pristinger, F. 1992. "Il lavoro delle donne: Passato e presente." In *Educazione e ruolo femminile,* ed. S. Ulivieri, pp. 143–76. Florence: La Nuova Italia.

Roveri L. 1990. "Indagine multiscopo sulle famiglie e l'uso del tempo in Italia." *ISTAT notiziario,* Series 4, Folio 41, 11, 10 (December).

Saraceno, C. 1990. "Statuto di genere e cittadinanza nelle società di welfare." *Problemi del socialismo* 5 (May–August): 137–56.

————. 1991. "Changes in Life-Course Patterns and Behavior of Three Cohorts of Italian Women." *Signs* 16 (Spring): 502–21.

———. 1992. "Continuities and Changes in the Gender Structure of the Welfare State: The Italian Case." Paper presented at the conference on Comparative Studies of Welfare State Development: Quantitative and Qualitative Dimensions, Bremen, 3–6 September.

———. 1993. "Elementi per una analisi delle trasformazioni di genere nella società contemporanea e delle loro trasformazioni sociali." *Rassegna italiana di sociologia* 24, 1.

Saraceno, C., ed. 1980. *Il lavoro maldiviso*. Bari: De Donato.

Scabini, E., ed. 1988. *La famiglia lunga del giovane adulto*. Milan: Vita e Pensiero.

Schizzerotto A. 1988. "Il ruolo dell'istruzione nei processi di mobilità sociale." *Polis* 2, 1: 83–124.

Sgritta, G. B. 1986. "La struttura delle relazioni interfamiliari." In ISTAT, *Atti del convegno "La famiglia in Italia." Annali di statistica,* Series 9, vol. 6.

———. 1991. "La condizione dell'infanzia." In *Secondo rapporto sulla famiglia in Italia,* ed. P. Donati, pp. 207–80. Milan: Paoline.

IS ITALY STILL A NATION?

Gian Enrico Rusconi

A nation can cease to exist. A nation is not in fact a fixed and indestructible political structure. Nor is it a pure ethnic phenomenon, disembodied from political forms. A nation is a delicate and complicated social construction composed of common culture and history, of manifest and shared consensus, and therefore of reciprocity among citizens. A democratic nation in particular is a bond of citizenship motivated by loyalty and common memories. Only through this interlacing of motivations and ties are the political relationships established that can claim to be democratic. Only in this way can the institutional framework of a "nation of citizens" be created.

When politics produces inefficiency and corruption, however, the bonds that hold a nation together are damaged. At that point, a shared sense of historical belonging is no longer considered a value. National identity no longer sustains political life, nor does it replace it. At this point, a nation ceases to exist. This can happen in many ways—not necessarily in the sensational secession of some of its parts. It is enough simply that the reasons for staying together be lost.

A democratic nation is made of both good political reasons for coexistence and ethnocultural roots. But these roots can become dry or torn and the reasons can be lost or falsified, even more so in a country like Italy, where democracy matured as laboriously as did Italy itself into nationhood.

When the institutional fabric of a nation constructed in this manner frays, as is happening before our eyes in Italy today, it is not strange that the desire should emerge to search for—or to invent—roots that are "more ethnic original" than the historic nation. Upon these roots a "custom-tailored" democracy is then anchored, cut along territorial borders and according to opportunistic and discriminatory sociocultural criteria—according to the motto: "Democracy, yes, but in my house, and with whom I choose." In this way, a democratic nation meets its end and regional ethnodemocracies emerge, perhaps behind a façade of formal unity. Is this the future of Italy?

To ask this question is in itself a symptom of uncertainty. In Italy for some time now, hypotheses of more or less radical regional autonomy with very confusing practical consequences have been superimposed upon the inertia of the sense of national belonging. The most striking product of this climate is the proposals made by the leagues to disarticulate the nation into macroregions—proposals that were first announced and then either withdrawn or suspended. These proposals have always remained operatively vague but, precisely for this reason, effective as a threat: they represent a playable card in political negotiations among parties.

It is time to get past alarm or complaint about this situation. It is necessary to begin thinking again about whether and how we are to remain a nation, whether and how we must become a "nation of citizens" in the strongest sense of the term.

Above all, the complaint about a lack of any sense of national identity in Italy conceals a misunderstanding—shared even by the best-intentioned scholars and historians. On the one hand, they insist on showing how difficult it was to build the Italian nation. On the other hand, they hardly provide Italian citizens with convincing arguments for considering themselves a nation in a meaningful way today. There is a lack of arguments that go beyond the traditional ones that have been revealed to be weak and biased by obsolete experiences. In my view, there has been a change in focus in the historiographic controversy on whether the nation in Italy has ever effectively played a role of collective identification, and therefore whether the nation has performed its function of civic, even more than political, integration, without which a democracy is not vital. Many historians deny that it has. Above all, they assert that the nation has not performed such a function since World War II. I will attempt to demonstrate that things are not exactly so.

To start with, let us note that all too often historians and observers in general have looked at the persistence of forms of a popular "national" (sub)culture with an attitude of intellectual superiority and have therefore totally devalued them. The inventiveness of Italian artists, writers, and intellectuals—for which they are praised abroad—does not hold true for their own history and culture. Here, there is no symbolic creativity. Why so-called "high" culture in Italy should have abandoned the national theme decades ago by giving it only hasty, summary criticism does not find an easy answer: it was incapacity truly to separate nationalism from a sense of national identity; it was impatience toward a certain residual, traditional, historiographic rhetoric; it was the absorbing centrality of other ideological paradigms; it was the "provincial complex" felt in the face of great European cultures (which are themselves unequivocally marked by national characteristics).

On the other hand, the same intellectuals have never taken regional identities seriously. The "small homelands" (*piccole patrie*) were merely biographical and literary pretexts, not a source of civic feeling as an alternative to the detested centralism of the nation-state. Regionalism in Italy has produced literature, folklore, and recrimination (side by side, it is understood, with both good and bad administrations). Notwithstanding its abundant sentimentality, it has never represented an authentic alternative to the nation.

In the 1980s the national question came to the fore again in all European countries, which of course have a different tradition from ours. Not only regionalist movements contributed to this reawakened national question, but also phenomena of a much different nature that should not be ignored. In France the problems of immigration were politically exploited by Le Pen's movement, whose slogan stressed the priority of the "national choice." In Germany it was a combination of the question of immigration and the persistent one of "German identity" which reawakened nationalistic attitudes in a xenophobic setting even before the violence of the Nazi skinhead groups. But more generally, unexpected questions about the role of nations and about national identities in Europe are born of the difficulty of the construction of political Europe.

In Italy in the 1980s there seemed to be a renewal of interest in the national theme with the publication of several books dedicated to the question of "Italianness" (*italianità*). It appears to me that a positive discourse has not emerged from these books; what has emerged is a confirmation of the insurmountable difficulties surrounding these problems. To make up for it, the first socialist-led government seemed to coincide with a brief political-cultural trend promoting a sort of renewal in national pride that was linked with several socioeconomic programs—a "made-in-Italy" nationalism. Everything ended with a rapid deterioration in the climate at the end of the 1980s and the beginning of the 1990s, years of economic recession and above all of paralysis in the political party system. So the leagues began to expand.

Having outlined these premises, I do not intend at all to ignore the most serious reason that is put forth to justify the abandonment of the national theme: the belief that an advanced democratic society can get along without a national reference. A discussion of this thesis ought to accompany that of the challenge by the leagues—that is, demonstrating, if only in an instrumental way, how precarious the link is between solid democracy and national integration. My considerations do not aim at digging up the nation itself, but at reconsidering it in the light of the rights of mature citizenship. My considerations are an invitation to rediscover, in the historical roots of national belonging—a belonging that ignores neither regional articulations nor supranational identifications—the reasons for resuscitating a gasping democracy.

I shall not analyze the leagues politically here; analyses run the risk of being flattered by the tumultuous chronicle of short-lived words and maneuvers. In this case the growth of the leagues, or "leaguism" (*leghismo*), is simply a symptom to be taken seriously, a symptom that the inertial sense of Italian national belonging does not have solid defenses against local involutions that put into play (as we shall see) not only abstract national integrity, but also the concrete values of democratic citizenship. It is possible that the leagues, by becoming politically national, will lose their most coarse characteristics in the face of coherent regional-based projects and practices. But processes of an ethnodemocratic type may infiltrate surreptitiously into these practices. All the better if none of this materialized, but this simple possibility is reason enough to reopen the discourse on the nation or (better still) on its link with an adult democracy.

Leaguism today is culturally weak and uncertain about the feasibility of its projects of regional autonomy and federalism—in short, uncertain about the national question. Under the pressure of local and national political necessities, its plans, with their indefinite outline approximating secession, have changed into simple threats. But these plans continue to be an integral part of the original motivations of the movement.

Leaguism has two underlying and equally indispensable causes. The first is an intransigent, ever-present, and noisy protest against what does not work in this wretched country, filling the news reports and editorials of our newspapers. When everyone is criticizing everything, the voters of the leagues need not listen every day to the exponents of their movement to find confirmation of their own behavior. Above all, after the electoral success of the leagues in April 1992, and thanks to able political direction, the attitude of the mass media changed considerably. The media moved from sarcasm to attention. Leaguism realistically presents itself as a candidate to replace the political class.

This replacement is forced not by an ideological and political revolution, but by very concrete and electorally effective slogans and formulae. One of these formulae is "If Rome has failed, let us do it alone, with our people." This is another cause of leaguism: the pride and credit of political endowment in regional belonging as such, if not in true and proper "ethnic identity." The rediscovered interest among people to exercise their own political citizenship in a local, regional, or ethnic setting shows leaguism to be our homespun and original variation of a phenomenon present in varying forms in other parts of the world. It is ethnodemocracy: democratic practice exercised within borders that are self-defined, capable of self-definition, and therefore controllable. One is truly a citizen only in a territory declared one's "own," even if the cost is discrimination against those who are not welcome. It is not necessary that such ethnodemocracy assume institutionally explicit forms. One need only consider the unpleasant sensation of feeling like an unwelcome guest, as Italian citizens sometimes feel in certain parts of the South Tyrol/Alto Adige area, a region which, given certain understandable historic motives, is virtually at a stage nearing secession from the Italian state.

With the spreading of terms that conjugate in many variations "ethnicity" and "nation," some true and proper polemical identifying constructions have become available in political communication. The improbability, the historical inconsistency, or the simple opportunism of an imaginary "nation" or "ethnicity" (Lombard or Venetian or Piedmontese) does not eliminate the fact that they perform identifying functions that motivate action among people disgusted by traditional politics. Technically these are mythopoetic operations in the same sense that the operations that forged the historic nations were mythopoetic. I do not believe that leaguism can renounce these operations entirely, even if it uses them only instrumentally. Whoever studies the ethnic or national revival that has been under way for years in all the world (well before the fateful year 1989) is struck as much by the degree of inventive selection by the emerging ethnic identities as by the symbolic charge they succeed in unleashing, rekindling ancient memories, however weak. In the cultural muddle of the proponents of the leagues there are elements of this type, even if their principal characteristic is polemic, emphasizing the reasons for differentiation, juxtaposition, and antagonism. These elements become a strategic resource in an effort to obtain something for the proponents and to deny others.

That this attitude could lead to a profound change in the Italian national identity as it was historically constituted, with heavy costs for the value of citizenship in general; that ethnodemocratic variations should be established de facto by means of regionalisms obsessed with their authority—these are questions that league proponents confront lightly, something that responsible citizens cannot afford to do.

It is obvious that the danger of the nation's disintegration or the emptying of its civic contents does not depend on the hypothesis of regional federalism as such, but rather upon the combination of federalism and ethnicity in the first league proposals. Once this combination is rejected, the debate on the regional redrawing of the Italian state opens up, with all the difficulties typical of every project of regionalization: optimal geographic dimensions; economic and fiscal autonomy; new political, administrative, and fiscal authority, without forgetting the space to be reserved for local cultural and linguistic expressions, and so on.

My reasoning begins with the assumption that a democracy needs civic loyalty and solidarity to function; these civic virtues, in the hearts and minds of the people, do not simply derive from the universal principle of citizenship, but they demand identification with some concrete community where a person belongs. Traditionally this cultural and political community is called a nation. What happens when this reference no longer functions? When the term "nation" itself is pronounced with embarrassment and with a thousand precautions? When it rings obsolete and pathetic?

In Italy the theme of the nation has never been freed conceptually and emotionally from the treatment it suffered at the hands of historic nationalism—above all at the hands of fascism. This fact, nonetheless, risks becoming an alibi. It is a commonplace that by using and abusing the national sentiment of the Italians and by leading them to the disaster of World War II, historical fascism profoundly damaged the idea itself of nation and homeland. As a result, after nationalistic and fascist degeneration, patriotism and a national sense of belonging would no longer be a civic and political resource employable in a democracy.

I do not believe that things are so. Or at least they should not be so, if we are to understand the nation as a form of democratic and civic integration, finally freed from the conceptual horizons fixed by historic nationalism. The idea of the nation therefore can be removed from its historic subordination and instrumentalization by the state. It can be linked with the universe of values of civil society and therefore with the logic of democratic citizenship, already projected into a European perspective. It is well to remember, however, that this nation of citizens is not a spontaneous fact, but the result of a cultural and conceptual effort that recovers its own roots and historic memories in a most reflexive and critical way.

History and common memory are an integral part of the self-recognition of a nation. In contemporary Italian culture, the most serious lacuna is the incapacity to recount the nation's history in a convincing way—in such a way, that is, as to create identification, notwithstanding and even through its immense contradictions. Common history has not become an irreplaceable moment of democratic "public discourse." To find the correct historical depth at which to hold a sensible discussion and to achieve the informative quality needed in a society dominated by mass media requires a great effort.

I am not sure whether someone somewhere can recount this history and avoid neonationalist rhetoric or class counterhistories. I am not sure whether it should be the historian or the writer who recounts a history of community composed not only of literature, arms, and blood, but also of shared work and effort, internal migration, and mixing that have established ties that cannot be broken without wounding the historic identity of all Italians, from both the North and the South. It is with this operation that the chatterings of certain league exponents ought to be challenged. Without the critical and solid reconstruction of a common memory, no civic sense of belonging will be created in Italy.

How far back must one delve into national history for this operation? To the Risorgimento? To the end of World War I? To the Resistance and the birth of the republic? To the years of postwar reconstruction and rapid modernization that are studied exclusively in socioeconomic terms or for the debate among political parties? National identification begins to lose strength only after the first years of the republic. It is undeniable, in fact, that the Resistance was guided by patriotic and national vindication and at the same time, at least in some of its representatives, envisaged perspectives of European federalism and regional autonomy.

Between 1943 and 1945 two ideas of homeland and nation clashed in Italy: the national fascist idea, which had no other motivation than a fideistic call to honor in spite of the catastrophe it provoked; and the idea of a new nation oriented toward a democratic and European civic sense, to be built anew, even if it might be linked to an old sentiment. Hence the character of civil war which the struggle for national liberation inevitably took on, because it redefines the criteria of a new national and political identity with arms and blood. Today we are able to measure in all their breadth the motivational complexities of the protagonists of yesterday, complexities that are transmitted problematically to the nascent democracy.

If Italian democracy meets its first challenge by avoiding a potential civil war of a type different from the one just ended (no longer fascists/antifascists, but Communists/anti-Communists), this is due to the loyalty of men in the Resistance who, despite having different passions and different conceptions of democracy, acknowledged their common membership in a community of history and destiny. They identified themselves in a nation capable of moderating the tensions of the parts in the very moment when new political rules were being redesigned. In other words, the founders of the republic were guided by an authentic constitutional patriotism, a concept that ought to be understood in the integrative sense, not in the surrogate or antagonistic sense with respect to the traditional feeling of belonging to a historical nation.

A brief excursion into the variants of Italian patriotism is appropriate at this point.

The subjective identification between nation and constitution (constitutional patriotism) is possible in Italy in the period surrounding the war of liberation because the sentiment of those involved in the Resistance found resonance in what I would call the "expiative" patriotism of a part of the Italian population. By "expiative," I mean the sentiment that was diffused amid the people with the disastrous course of the war, following above all the tragic withdrawal from Russia in the winter of 1942–43, an event that enters deeply into the Italian collective memory as few others do. Around that episode a spontaneous feeling of national solidarity develops through a common suffering perceived as not wholly undeserved. Only a few, however, have the courage (above all after 8 September 1943) to formulate a comprehensive ethical and political judgment that leads from dissent against the fascist regime to the choice of the Resistance. The majority of the population feels obscurely like a punished nation, resigned to expiate by means of a war fought on its own territory and in the form of a civil war. All of this does not falsify but rather confirms—if only in a passive way—the community of national destiny.

This complex of sentiments fades and changes after the institution of democracy, with the operation of the "republic of parties" and its new tensions. The new, bitter social and ideological struggle—especially in the frontal clash between communism and anticommunism—gradually obscures the ethical and political relevance of constitutional patriotism and the traditional national feeling that had been salvaged and kept in such patriotism. The substantial loss of sovereignty with regard to the outside in a world solidly closed in the ideological and military bipolarity of the two superpowers leads the majority of Italians to make the "national interest" coincide with Atlantic and then European integration. The governing political class, as soon as this choice is made, renounces any autonomy of action.

The loss of external sovereignty corresponds to the weakening of internal sovereignty, understood as the predominance of the common interest over the parts. Political parties conduct their confrontations and encounters using only rhetorically the reference to a common national belonging that is considered both obvious and electorally expendable. Political contenders reproach each other for selling the national interest to foreigners (to America, Moscow, or Belgrade). But these are ever more ideological and instrumental affirmations. For the culture of the left (not necessarily the most unwary) the idea of the nation gradually becomes a "rightist" idea. For Catholic culture, and therefore for the Christian Democrats, the idea is cumbersome.

Even official ritual is uncertain and divided among 25 April (in honor of the Resistance), 2 June (the establishment of the republic), and 4 November (in memory of the "victory" of 1918). Therefore the result of the "republic of parties" is not (as one might expect) a sort of extraparty safeguard of the idea and the value of the nation. On the contrary, one of the most negative long-term effects of the deep conflicts in the first years of Italian democracy is that of having created, at the level of popular culture, a strong sense of "separate belongings," excluding the sentiment of common citizenship.

Further analysis should be devoted to the 1960s and 1970s in order to emphasize the link between wild social and cultural modernization, the new model of social integration on the basis of consumerism, and the definitive expulsion of the nation from the horizon of Italian civic values. The nation slides into popular subcultural forms or into literary memoirs. The collective concentration on standards of well-being attainable either individually or by means of sectoral mobilization, and the parallel growing faith in the compensatory mechanisms of the social state, make an appeal to a higher "national solidarity" a slightly pathetic polemic motif rather than a realistic political project.

Meanwhile, since the beginning of the 1950s Italian culture has been exposed without any filters to the most massive invasion of European and American authors and works in its history. The comprehensible and justified desire to catch up is quickly transformed into a dependence on foreign cultures and into a sense of inferiority from which Italian culture would never free itself. All that is Italian is obscurely felt to be "provincial." The affirmative reference to the nation is left to the subcultures and as such is snubbed by the intellectuals that count. When sociologists and political experts apply themselves to the analysis of the mechanisms of the cultural and political workings and failings of the Italian state, they take it for granted that the nation for the Italians is a historical residue, deprived of relevance and incapable of identification. But the same social scientists and political experts, far from making a drama of it, consider the weak sense of national belonging to be a peculiarity, and not a negative one, of the Italian social structure, otherwise rich with friendly human qualities. On the other hand, to compensate, essayists and literary figures successfully cultivate the literary genre of "the original characteristics" of the Italians, often with great acumen, always with self-irony, sometimes with self-deprecation.

But the crucial point of our argument lies not in discovering nor in describing indicators and characteristic or cultural traits of Italianness (which foreigners attribute to Italians in massive and homogeneous doses more than the Italians themselves are inclined to admit). What counts is the contribution that these ethnocultural characteristics make (or can possibly make) to the smooth functioning of political and civil society, to its livability. Recently, taking into account a thesis diffused in the scientific community, Alain Touraine repeated that "in Italy, the consciousness of Italianness is much stronger than the idea of a nation state." But the French sociologist does not ask himself if and how this presumed "consciousness of Italianness" might replace the civic virtues and spirit of citizenship that the historic nation-state as such has not been able to create.

The lack of reflection and public culture in Italy on the relation between democracy and nation used to be concealed contentedly behind the announcement of the end of nation-states and the birth of a supranational and regional Europe. It was a rash announcement. Reality is being revealed as something else. The countries of the European Community are certainly proceeding toward political unity, but with extreme circumspection. Only reluctantly are they willing to reduce their traditional prerogatives. When arms or currency are at issue (the establishment of one bank and a single European currency, the creation of a common army, judicial cooperation), one goes to the heart of the sovereignty of the nation-states. And this sovereignty, however much it is redrawn, is still a resource that the European governments do not intend to deny themselves. This was seen during the confused and emotional debate on the Maastricht Treaty and in the reservations formulated from time to time by the various national governments.

Naturally in the end the same governments try and find meaningful agreements. But the understanding between nation-states is one thing; ceding their prerogatives to a supranational authority is another. Who knows how much longer political Europe will live upon the balance of the (however redrawn) sovereignties of existing nations, in an equilibrium of strength where some states obviously count more than others? Only European rhetoric prevents judging the full significance of the dualism present in the construction of the Community between Brussels and Strasbourg, a dualism that the project of the Union does not seem to be able to overcome with clarity. I mean the dualism between, on the one hand, a European Commission that communicates directly with the national governments and with state agencies, and, on the other hand, a supranational European Parliament limited in its authority, even if legitimized by direct elections (held, one notes, with heterogeneous electoral systems).

While political Europe, caught between vague federalist aspirations and powerful nationalist defenses, struggles to give itself precise political and legal form, other phenomena embarrass its presumptively homogeneous culture. Consistent layers of the populations of the most politically solid countries (France, Germany, and Great Britain) have become sensitive to the question of their own "national identity" in the European context. The issue is not simply compensation for the reduction in their legal sovereignty.

More subtle processes are involved here, touching upon the memories of nations separated in the past and far from spontaneously producing feelings of a common belonging. Behind the emphasis on a common European civilization there remains the worried and irreconcilable memory of the laceration of Europe which not incorrectly is called the European civil war. It is a laceration that, begun in the distant year 1914, has continued in varying forms, through civil as well as international wars, wars between nation-states and ideological states, settling into a long cold war, at the end of which there was the unexpected return of the ethnic wars and ancient conflicts in the Balkan area and elsewhere. The consequence of this process is the paradox of a Europe full of good proposals but with memories unified by the reciprocity of the wounds. One might be surprised that these affirmations are made after two or three generations, but the new generations have been shielded from those historical memories. They are generations without historic memory, or, in the best of cases, self-taught.

From this point of view, the construction of Europe, as it is occurring, does not perform any integrative role. Nor can it do so automatically according to the model that has worked historically for the single European nation-states. Given the foreseeable persistence of traditional national cultures, in the long term one might hypothesize a European federal state with a very peculiar identity. In the short to mid-term a more realistic forecast is an organism of the confederation type (however labeled) in which the historic nations will continue to play an important role. Against this background it is pure demagogy to emphasize a hypothetical "Europe of regions" that might risk turning into regions without Europe. When a solid national culture is lacking, so also is a serious vision of European regionalism.

Against this background, it is urgent that Italy rediscover itself as a nation again in the full civic sense described above—that it not cease to be a nation. What is at stake is the capacity to agree and to deal with the most solid European partners upon the whole of the legitimate interests of a historical community that has everything to lose by its disintegration. What is at stake is the relevance of Italy's cultural identity, otherwise abandoned to the chance that some eminent Italian intellectual will gain access to the European salons.

A somewhat different version of this article was published in *Archives européens de sociologie* 34 (1993): 309–21. For a more systematic development of these arguments, see my book, *Se cessiamo di essere una nazione* (Bologna: Il Mulino, 1993). For Italian sociological publications on the leagues, mention should be made of R. Mannheimer, ed., *La Lega Lombarda* (Milan: Feltrinelli, 1991), and I. Diamanti, *La Lega: Geografia, storia e sociologia di un nuovo soggetto politico* (Rome: Donzelli, 1993). On the national question in Italy, see G. Spadolini, ed., *Nazione e nazionalità in Italia* (Bari: Laterza, 1994).

The Political Actors

THE CHURCH AND POLITICS IN ITALY

Giacomo Sani

When I began working on this paper, I was not too happy with the working title, "Persistence and Ambivalence of Religiosity." In retrospect, I must give credit to those who devised it: the subject is indeed full of complexities, paradoxes, ambiguities, and nuances. There are no straightforward answers to many of the questions that one may legitimately raise about religion and the role of the Catholic Church in Italy. To be sure, a few things are clear. In the early 1990s, Catholicism in Italy is not what it was half a century ago. In the peninsula, as in other places, the process of secularization has left its mark in many ways, as I will attempt to show below. At the same time, evidence as to the decline of Catholicism during the last decades is not clear-cut. For example, while only one adult Italian out of three goes to church on Sundays, a large majority of parents still want their children to receive Catholic education in public schools. There are some partial explanations for the discrepancy. Yet the very fact that different indicators support a number of alternative interpretations is in itself telling.

The agenda of this contribution is as follows. I shall start with a brief description of the organizational strength of the Catholic Church and the changes that have occurred in recent decades at this level. I shall then turn to the evidence pertaining to the crisis of secularization and to the linkage between organized religion and politics. In the concluding section I shall raise some questions about the possible role of Catholicism in the present phase of deconstruction and in the eventual restructuring of the Italian polity.

ORGANIZATIONAL STRENGTHS (AND WEAKNESSES)

A management consultant hired to study the Italian Catholic Church would be impressed, at least at first sight, by the strength of the institution and its pervasive penetration of Italian society. At the end of the last decade, religious personnel, including priests assigned to parishes and members of the various orders operating in other capacities, amounted to about 200,000. This means that there was one member of the Catholic institution for every 300 inhabitants. The figure compares favorably, or even more than favorably, with the strength of the Italian military or with the number of people employed by the largest industrial firms. With 224 dioceses, 100,000 churches, 26,000 parishes, almost 300 seminaries, 135 weekly publications circulating at the provincial level, a national daily (*Avvenire*), and a weekly newsmagazine with the second highest circulation, the Church can count on what our hypothetical consultant may call a highly ramified "distribution network" comprising a number of "local outlets" scattered throughout the peninsula, on par with the number of post offices and police stations. To this one must add the presence of Catholic personnel in nurseries, schools, hospitals and various social service centers catering to the elderly, the handicapped, the homeless, orphans, drug addicts, immigrants, and the like.

But this is not all. The inventory of Catholic assets should necessarily also include the vast number of Catholic voluntary associations, ranging from the largest of them (Azione Cattolica—some 600,000 members) to a myriad of smaller groups operating in various walks of life from sports to social welfare and from health to political action, or the many specialized organizations bringing together Catholics with common interests, goals, or backgrounds (university students, graduates of Catholic schools, elementary school teachers, businessmen, workers, artisans, etc.). It has been estimated that membership in the various Catholic associations—what is called *volontariato cattolico* (Catholic volunteer work)—may involve as many as 4 million Italians, or approximately 10 percent of the adult population of the country. Since there is probably some overlap among the various organizations, a more realistic estimate must be scaled down somewhat. Even so, the adjusted figure is still impressive, and it confirms that the Church remains an important part of Italian reality.

However, even a cursory glance at the trends of the last decades produces a different and much less optimistic picture. Over time comparisons of various statistics show that the organizational strength of Catholicism has been declining. Just about every indicator points downward. There has been a decline in priests working in parishes, ordained members of various orders, nuns, newly ordained clergymen, and young people attending seminaries. The two indicators pointing upward confirm the existence of a problem. First, there has been an increase in the number of deacons (nonordained members of the clergy), but this was a measure meant largely to compensate for the reduction of ordained personnel. Second, the mean age of priests has gone up, a sure sign that turnover is eroding the demographic base of the lower clergy. Between 1970 and 1986, approximately 7,500 new priests were ordained, but they could not entirely replace the 11,500 people lost through demographic attrition. It should be noted that these various trends have been quite gradual. As far as one can tell, there have been no sudden collapses followed by surges in the figures. From year to year, changes in the statistics have been rather modest; their cumulative impact over the long haul has been pronounced, however.

THE IMPACT OF SECULARIZATION AT THE MASS LEVEL

Most observers of Italian affairs would agree with the proposition that over the last half century the country has gone through a process of "secularization." To be sure, there is no consensus on either the definition of the term or the most appropriate indicators to "measure" it. While some Catholic scholars tend to deemphasize somewhat the degree to which secularization has permeated Italian society, lay (or anticlerical) observers take it for granted that contemporary Italy is by and large a secularized society.

There is quite a bit of evidence backing the secularization hypothesis. To begin with, there has been a steady decline in the rates of church attendance from the mid-1950s to the mid-1980s. In the early part of the postwar period, seven out of ten adults could be classified as regularly practicing Catholics. The figure dipped to about 50 percent in the late 1960s, and by the late 1970s and early

1980s it had further declined to a new low ranging from 31 to 36 percent. By the middle of the 1980s, the percent of individuals going to church on a regular basis appeared to have stabilized around the 30 percent mark. Since then, not much change appears to have taken place. In this respect, there is a remarkable convergence in the findings of various studies even though based on different methodologies.

Second, there has been an increase in the number of marriages celebrated by civil authorities and without the traditional Catholic rituals. In the 1981–91 period, city hall weddings increased from 11 to 17 percent of all marriages. Considering that according to Church doctrine matrimony is a sacrament, the fact is not without significance. A parallel development is the increase in the number of legal separations and divorces. From 1986 to 1990, for example, the rate of divorces per 100,000 inhabitants almost doubled (from 29 to 48), and the figure for legal separations—normally a preliminary step on the way to a divorce—jumped from 62 to 76 per 100,000.

Third, there has been a sharp decline in birthrates. In 1976 there were fourteen live births per thousand inhabitants; in 1990 the figure dropped to nine per thousand. Between the population censuses of 1981 and 1991, there was practically no growth. Indeed in the last few years several regions—generally those more developed from an economic point of view—have been posting a negative demographic balance. Whatever the reasons that lead couples to have fewer children, one could plausibly interpret the sharp decline of birthrates in the country as evidence that a large proportion of Italian couples do not heed the doctrine of the Church in the matter of contraceptives.

The same argument could be made, and with greater force, in the case of abortion. The number of procedures for the interruption of pregnancy performed in public clinics has actually declined somewhat in recent years. However, the rate of abortions per thousand live births is still relatively high (287 in 1990, down from 355 in 1986). Moreover, recent surveys show a widespread acceptance of current laws on divorce and abortion. In fact, rejection of practices condemned by the Church is not total even among practicing Catholics. Young Catholics, for example, display surprisingly liberal attitudes toward forms of behavior not approved by the Church, such as living together without being married, premarital sex, and even homosexuality.

Some scholars, mostly within the Catholic tradition, while not denying the existence of these trends, find some silver linings in the clouds. They note, in the first place, that when asked, only a tiny minority of Italians define themselves as non-Catholic. Moreover, some studies show that the belief in God is generally shared by a huge proportion of adult Italians and that most of these also believe in the Catholic Church. It is also remarked that the rates of church attendance are no longer declining and seem to have leveled off, and some observers feel that there may very well be a reversal of the trend. Additionally, one could point to the fact that an overwhelming number of parents still want their newborn children to be baptized. In 1988, for example, the number of baptisms (530,000) was only slightly lower than the number of newborn babies (578,000). Although there are no statistics on funerals, it seems likely that the rate of religious ceremonies may be even higher than that of baptisms. As to the increase in the number of civil marriages, one could argue that with eight out of ten couples still preferring to get married in a church, the goblet is considerably more than half full.

Two additional and significant points could be made to cast doubts on the secularization hypothesis. First, Italian law now allows taxpayers to donate a small portion of their taxes (0.008) to religious and civil institutions of their choice. It turns out that three out of four taxpayers who take advantage of this option choose the Catholic Church as their beneficiary. Second, instruction in the Catholic faith is provided in public schools to all children unless their parents request otherwise. While there are no precise figures on this, the impression is that only a very modest proportion of parents goes through the procedure needed to get their children excused from attending religious instruction. The reasons behind this are not entirely clear, but the result is that a very large percentage of Italian youngsters are still exposed to the tenets of Catholic doctrine in the public education system. This is not exactly what one would expect in a fully secularized society.

As one can see, the picture is rather contradictory. The advance of secularization has not been uniform; the impact is more evident in some dimensions than in others. Moreover, even within the same dimension change has been a matter of degree. Analyses of the social and territorial patterns show that secular ideas and behavior are more pronounced in urban than in rural contexts and among the younger generations. While some observers feel that ritualism and conformism account for much of the survival of religious patterns, others believe that traditional indicators may not adequately tap the different and newer forms of religiosity which have been developing in recent times. In this controversy over the interpretation of different indicators, the points of view of the analyst are more important than the actual evidence.

INSTITUTIONALIZED RELIGION AND POLITICAL LIFE

The role of the Catholic Church in Italian politics in the last century and a half has been the object of a large number of scholarly analyses by both historians and social scientists. Within the space of a few paragraphs it would be impossible to give a succinct summary of the facts and interpretations which have been proposed over time. However, in this massive body of evidence there are a few key propositions that can be listed in capsule form as follows.

(a) The temporal power of the Church in the middle of the peninsula constituted an obstacle to the achievement of national unity.
(b) The breach between Church and state, formalized in the Encyclical Letter "Non Expedit" of 1874, placed the Catholics at the sidelines of the political arena for decades.
(c) The political system that emerged from Risorgimento was thus deprived of the benefits that would have come from an early integration of the Catholics into political life.
(d) The reconciliation between Church and state took place during the fascist regime, with advantages for both parties: the regime obtained a greater degree of legitimacy, and the Church recovered some of the privileges it had had earlier.
(e) Catholic support of the fascist regime was neither particularly intense nor equally and fully shared by all segments of the clergy and laymen; indeed from the early 1940s on there were significant contributions to the Resistance movement by Catholics at both the mass and elite levels.

(f) At the end of World War II, the "Catholic world," as Italians call it, reemerged as strong as ever and was well positioned to play a key role in the new democratic regime.
(g) Catholic personnel became the backbone of the leadership of the reconstructed Christian Democratic Party (DC), while the clergy and a variety of organizations closely aligned to the Church acted as agencies for securing mass support for the party.
(h) In the early postwar years, the DC, with the strong backing of the Church, became the major component of the anti-Communist bloc, and in the polarized climate generated by the cold war, it received massive endorsement at the polls in 1948, not only from practicing Catholics, but also from other segments of society terrified at the prospect of a Communist takeover.
(i) By the end of the 1940s, the position of the Church in Italian society could be considered quite satisfactory. The Concordat of 1929 had become part and parcel of the new democratic constitution, the DC had a majority of the seats in parliament, and a pious DC leader was at the helm of the government.
(j) In the following two decades, in spite of the gradual decline of the share of the vote for the DC and the partial transformation of its social base, the position of the Church as an institution remained largely unchanged. To be sure, the personality and philosophy of the various Church leaders made some difference. Under John XXIII, the directives of the Church and its relations with the DC were certainly different from what they had been under Pius XII. But in terms of Church-state relations the overall picture changed only very little.
(k) With the passing of time, however, it became apparent that modernization was taking its toll. The Catholic movement was defeated in the "divorce battle" of the early 1970s and on the more critical issue of abortion some ten years later. The results of these two referenda indicated that even on questions central to religious doctrine the Catholic world could no longer muster the votes necessary to support its positions.

Throughout the postwar period, the key has been a call for the "unity of Catholics," issued by the Italian Episcopal Conference (CEI), time and time again on the eve of each election, from the contest of 1946 all the way down to the election of April 1992.

Though the DC was rarely mentioned explicitly, the message, amplified and diffused by the lower clergy and by Catholic organizations, was clearly understood. At the elite level, the call for unity discouraged any attempt by Catholic politicians and intellectuals to bolt the DC and form a new group, even though they may have been unhappy with the policies and governing style of the party. There could be no bright future for a second Catholic party as long as the Church endorsed the DC. At the mass level, the appeals by the Catholic Church could work as long as two conditions obtained: the existence of a large pool of practicing Catholics exposed to the message coming from the Church, and the willingness of the flock to comply with it. Both conditions have changed over time. As we have seen, the pool of practicing Catholics has been gradually shrinking, thus eroding the reservoir of potential votes for the DC. Perhaps more important is the fact that the second condition no longer fully obtains. Though the evidence is scanty, it appears that the linkage between religiosity and voting behavior is not what it used to be. In earlier decades, it was assumed—on the basis of good evidence—that the appeals of the Catholic hierarchy would fall on fertile ground. With the passing of time, this could no longer be taken for granted. To be sure, the DC never had a complete monopoly of Catholic electors. Within the Catholic world there have always been some voters deviating from the predominant pattern. Some of them supported moderate political groups of the center and center-right; others voted for leftist parties. The novelty is in the fact that while in earlier times the proportion of these "deviants" was quite modest, it appears to have increased considerably in the last decade. At the end of the 1980s, it was estimated that a substantial proportion of the Catholic vote (approximately 40 percent), went to parties other than the DC.

The events of the last few years have eroded the linkage between institutionalized religion and politics even further. With the disappearance of the threat of international communism and the metamorphosis of the Italian Communist Party, the cogency of the appeal for unity has lost some of its strength. Anticommunism no longer wins elections; voters focus on other issues and pay more attention to appeals from other quarters. The "unity of Catholics" call was issued again in the course of the 1992 campaign, but it did not help to prevent massive losses by the DC. The fact that these occurred in the "white provinces" of the North, once a Catholic stronghold, is a good indication of the degree to which the linkage between religion and politics has been eroded. Eroded but not yet severed, however. In the early 1990s, militant Catholic movements such as Comunione e Liberazione could still deliver an impressive number of votes and assure the election of selected candidates.

CRISIS, DECONSTRUCTION, RECONSTRUCTION: WHAT NEXT?

Politics in Italy has always been characterized by a great deal of surface turbulence: endemic cabinet instability, piling of new problems on top of old issues, rumors of crises, occasional scandals, bitter polemics, debates over coalition formulas, and the like. Most observers, immersed in the climate of the story unfolding before their eyes, have generally tended to overemphasize the lasting significance of issues of the day. The First Republic has been pronounced dead, prematurely, at least a dozen times in the past.

Things may be different this time around. Turmoil has increased since April 1992. The country has been swept by an unprecedented wave of scandals involving high-ranking members of the political elite, public administrators at both the local and national levels, and business managers of the largest public and private corporations. Cabinet members and mayors have resigned in record number, and quite a few members of parliament are under investigation. Needless to say, the legitimacy level of political personnel has reached rock bottom.

The DC has been at the center of this storm. Though most DC leaders have escaped—as of this writing—the fate suffered by the socialists, there is no doubt that the party is in trouble. There are several components of this sad state of affairs. To begin with, the disclosures of heavy involvement in various episodes of corruption have seriously tarnished the image of the party. House-cleaning efforts designed to revitalize the organization and rebuild it from scratch have met (thus far) with a fair amount of skepticism. Images are hard to rebuild once they have deteriorated.

Not unexpectedly, polls indicate a further slide in the level of popular support for the DC. It seems likely that given a chance, more former DC voters will migrate to one or another of the groups, such as Lega Nord or La Rete, which have sprung up in recent times. While the Lega may appear to be an attractive alternative to moderates and lukewarm Catholics fed up with "Roman parties," La Rete may become a pole of attraction for militant Catholics interested in a regeneration of politics.

An additional and rather serious complication comes from the appearance on the scene of the Popolari per la Riforma, led by Mario Segni. A self-avowed Catholic elected as a DC in Sardinia, Segni has been an outspoken critic of the party and a leading proponent of change. So far, he has chosen to keep his troops within the DC, but under certain conditions he may be tempted, or forced, to lead some sort of a Catholic diaspora away from the DC. How many will follow him remains a question.

How about the Church? During the turmoil of the last year or two, it has maintained a rather cautious stance. To be sure, the hierarchy has repeatedly condemmned corruption. In fact, some Catholic critics have managed to turn the issue to their advantage by blaming the degeneration of politics revealed by the scandals on the materialistic and hedonistic attitudes nurtured by secularization. It was only natural that with communism out of the picture Catholicism would focus most on its other traditional antagonist. Equally predictable was the issue of a call for a regeneration of politics. But the Church has stopped short of either reendorsing the DC or encouraging Catholics to find a new home (or more than one) elsewhere.

For all Italian political actors, the Catholic Church included, the definition of new strategies designed to cope with the situation of the 1990s is made more difficult by the uncertainty surrounding the rules of the game. While it appears likely that they will be changed, it is very difficult to predict what will come out of the reform process which has been going on for some time. Though little progress has been made to date, the time seems ripe for decisions as pressures from different quarters have been mounting. However, given the variety of positions taken and the interests at stake, it is difficult to predict what kind of compromise will eventually be reached.

Some clues are offered by the new legislation on elections for local government bodies (mayors, municipal and provincial councils). The decision to let voters choose their mayors directly is certainly a departure from the past. Additional clues are likely to come from the results of a referendum involving the electoral law for the Senate which is scheduled for mid-April 1994. If the proposition passes, Italy will move away from the strict proportional representation system used in the past. The adoption of a predominantly majoritarian rule will likely have a number of conquences: (a) a weakening of the traditional party structures; (b) a greater emphasis on candidates and their ability to win in single-member districts; (c) restructuring of the party system resulting from the disappearance of some of the small groups, mergers, or the emergence of new political groups.

REFERENCES

Barnes, Samuel H. 1974. "Italy: Religion and Class in Electoral Behavior." In *Electoral Behavior: A Comparative Handbook,* ed. Richard Rose. New York: Free Press, 1974.

Brunetta, G., and Longo, L., eds. 1992. *Italia cattolica.* Florence: Vallecchi, 1992.

Cartocci, Roberto. 1990. *Elettori in Italia.* Bologna: Il Mulino.

————. 1993. "Misurare la secolarizzazione." *Rivista italiana di scienza politica* 1.

Cavalli, Alessandro, and De Lillo, Antonio. 1988. *Giovani anni 80.* Bologna: Il Mulino.

Cipolla, C., and Martelli, S., eds. *Immagini della religiosità in Italia.* Milan: Angeli.

Garelli, Franco. 1991. *Religione e chiesa in Italia.* Bologna: Il Mulino.

Gubert, R. 1992. *Persistenze e mutamenti dei valori degli italiani nel contesto europeo.* Trento: Reverdito.

Guidorossi, Giovanna. 1984. *Gli italiani e la politica.* Milan: Angeli.

Leonardi, Robert, and Wertman, Douglas. 1989. *Italian Christian Democracy: The Politics of Dominance.* London: Macmillan.

Mannheimer, Renato, and Sani, Giacomo. 1987. *Il mercato elettorale.* Bologna: Il Mulino.

Parisi, Arturo. 1979. "Un partito di cattolici." In *Democristiani,* ed. Arturo Parisi. Bologna: Il Mulino.

Ricolfi, Luca. 1988. "Il processo di secolarizzazione in Italia nel dopoguerra." *Rassegna italiana di sociologia* 1: 37–88.

Sani, Giacomo. 1980. "The Political Culture of Italy: Continuity and Change." In *The Civic Culture Revisited,* ed. Gabriel Almond and Sidney Verba. Boston: Little, Brown.

———. 1991. "Church Attendance and the Vote for the DC." *Italian Politics and Society Newsletter,* Fall, pp. 14–19.

Sciolla, Loredana. 1988. "Dimensioni della secolarizzazione." *Rassegna italiana di sociologia* 1: 5–36.

THE SUNSET OF CHRISTIAN DEMOCRACY

Edmondo Berselli

In two years the Christian Democratic Party (DC) has come dramatically near disintegration as an organized political force. These years began with the parliamentary elections of 5–6 April 1992; although the DC hit an all-time low—dropping below 30 percent of the vote—it maintained a relative majority. It would be incorrect to consider the extremely profound DC crisis simply as a crisis of party organization. It is due to a loss of political inspiration, a sociocultural "relaxing," an inability to renovate its leadership and get back in touch with public opinion. In fact, it is the crisis of a political system which is in a parallel and equally intense process of socioeconomic transformation; the DC is paying the highest price precisely because of having been the mainstay of this system and social order. The events of the *annus mirabilis*—1989—which radically altered the international context to which the DC had been in the habit of referring, naturally had a decisive role. In order to understand how the earthquake developed that shook the foundations of one of the most stable systems of the West and one of the parties that seemed effectively immovable, it is necessary to take a few steps back.

THE PARTY OF THE MEDIOCRE GOVERNMENT

In the course of the 1980s the DC was profoundly transformed. Even for many citizens not prejudicially hostile toward it, the party had become a political entity of such indistinct outlines that it ended up nonjudicable. Its superimposition on wide bands of Italian society, as well as its profound interlacing with the political and institutional system, impeded a precise investigation of individual subjects and limited the "political discourse" it offered the country. For example, people had only vague ideas about what the DC's programs were regarding the South, the tax system, government administration, health services, or the "accelerators" of financial troubles. They were equally uncertain about what type of political product it intended to hold up for public opinion, except that it would not be a future directed toward conserving the status quo in the certainty that nothing would ever change.

The Italian problems were so vast—from the very high rate of public debt to the extemely low standard of public services—that to ask for precise responses from the political class was fruitless.[1] One risked receiving a mechanical ideological response because Italian parties were not in competition over how to manage the country. They were therefore unwilling to submit for collective judgment the concrete measures adopted in response to social and economic problems. However, the parties were bitter rivals on the level of fundamental statutes, prejudices, and constitutive idealism.

On 18 April 1948, after a very hard electoral campaign, the parliamentary elections revealed the defeat of the Socialist-Communist popular front, which had been hegemonized by the PCI. From this date on the DC generally offered Italians a "horizon of freedom"—not without a certain blackmail rhetoric.[2] This was a noteworthy objective in itself. But after the first years of the government, in which the framework of contemporary Italy was built, all attempts at rationalization became lost opportunities, and government programs were changed into a series of suggestions which were largely redeemed by their practical execution and the assessment of their efficacy.[3]

In short, it was proven hard to drag the DC into explicit discussion of government activities. One had to accept the "take it or leave it" that it proposed regarding the Italian system. This, however, was not without consequences for the party's identity. If it was accepted that the DC actions took place within a generic space, characterized by a fundamental disinterest in the concrete and stringent terms of governing, the image of the DC administration was revealed as incessantly indirect laissez-faire, directed above all toward guaranteeing an average continuity of the country's conditions, but with very scant or no effective priorities of management.

If a neutral observer had assessed what the DC attitude was toward the "contents" of the government, the choices and decisions to adopt, s/he would have deduced that the DC management style consisted of subordinating all actions to an exclusively political concept in which the effort to maintain consensus (rather than the empirical objective) was prevalent. This diluted every "negotiation solution." Once the antisystem position of its biggest rival, the PCI, was changed, the cultural poverty of the DC would be manifest. A party limited to supporting the welfare of the largest possible number of voters does not seem to stand as a candidate with the arrogance for governing in the years following the European transition, globalization, and into the twenty-first century. It could perhaps have laid claim to a more consummate paternalistic wisdom concerning the velleities of political trends, a habit and a control of the government machine that others did not possess, but it would have been "found out" as having no meaningful points of view as incisive choices became urgent.

THE PARTY OF FACTIONS, THE HOMEMADE ALTERNATIVE

It was not fortuitous that ultimately the internal articulation of the party was also weakened. In appearance distinctions persisted, were sharpened, proliferated. But if this had been true when the identity of "faction" was evoked in the realm of contractual or dividing negotiations, it would not have been equally true when the internal DC lineups were defined forming coalitions related to the operation of party leadership. In this sense, the multiple "souls" of the DC, the subparties in it, in the most recent period appeared reduced to a minimum, consolidated into lineups that were not easily distinguishable. In addition, if the value of the factions (as an expert within the DC world wrote) "was in their ability to increase, spread, radiate the presence of the parties in a democracy that granted to them, and only to them, the function of link between society and institutions, it assisted in the meantime in forming a popular 'final sentence' against the 'partyocracy,' in which all differences concerning the parties or their internal factions actually evaporated."

There had certainly been a historic friction between the center and left DC, but by now it involved almost exclusively the "physiological" problems of internal leadership, on one hand, and, on the other, the inherent questions of the relationship with the other two major parties, the Socialist Party (PSI) and the PCI (then Democratic Party of the Left, PDS).[4]

It is no secret that the fortunes of the DC for a long time depended on its capacity to present itself as continually alternative to itself in a political system blocked for four decades by the democratic uselessness of the PCI. The rotation of the so-called "thoroughbreds" (the most visible leaders), negotiations among the factions, the breaches and rebalances during congresses guaranteed the incessant mise-en-scène of a transformist show which seemed to function with the certain efficacy of a surrogate model of authentic political alternation.[5] This very articulated system of representation and power allowed, on one hand, the absorption of all centrifugal thrusts, and, on the other, a shift to the outside (meaning to the allies of the government) of its conflicts and tensions.

The breakup of this alternative system of parthenogenesis was brought about above all by the accession of the Socialist secretary, Bettino Craxi, to prime minister in 1983–87. The "decisionism" of Craxi and the stress that he placed on governability produced at least two effects. First, it demonstrated that the science of government was not instilled by divine will in the DC. In addition, it revealed the weakness of the consociational strategies on which the DC had built its position and that consisted of considering every ally potentially replaceable—and therefore blackmailable—and of negotiating every action with the Communist opposition in parliament.

Taking advantage of its decisive role in the constitution of every government alliance (despite its modest electoral force), the PSI was able to produce rather good results for long stretches. Toughly negotiating its presence in the government, thanks to its image as a government party with the key to the alternative future in its pocket (namely an alliance of the left with the Communists, once they had been electorally reorganized and accepted Socialist leadership), the PSI was able to collect unusual political dividends. Above all, it succeeded in the original and effective task of blocking every initiative to limit its power. The traditional DC propensity to resolve what would have been precluded by the limits of consociational government alliances with the opposition—"winking at" the PCI at its convenience—was blocked by Socialist vetoes, which were supported ideologically by a very violent polemic against the Stalinism of the PCI and its nondemocratic soul. In addition, the "race to the center" inaugurated by Craxi placed the PSI in direct contact with the non-Catholic DC electorate and intensified the rivalry felt by the Socialists toward the DC. At the apex of his fortune, in the mid-1980s, Craxi appeared as head of the government and head of the opposition, in a position to systematically wring power from the DC.[6]

HOW TO RESPOND TO CRAXI

The DC response to the Socialist "rival partner" was developed in two times and in two ways. In the first case it was of an ideological nature and assumed the figure and political characteristics of a representative of the DC left, Ciriaco De Mita.[7] "Intellectual of Magna Grecia," according to a well-known definition by the industrialist Gianni Agnelli, who censured him with certain "thought tortuosities," De Mita, secretary of the DC from 1982 through 1988, was not in reality a banal politician. He had some absolutely respectable convictions—e.g., that it was necessary to resolve the Italian anomaly (namely, the democratic deficit of a political system lacking alternation), and that the government and institutional appartus of the country suffered from a lack of competition among political groupings, all of which legitimate themselves through competing to assume the responsibility of governing.

However, from the theorem of alternation also came some factious corollaries which appeared less appreciable to the PSI. For example, the Demitian hypothesis of electoral reform, borrowed from political scientist Roberto Ruffilli, had the serious defect that it was intolerable to Craxi, as the construction of two large alternative lineups seemed structured purposely to zero out the PSI's position, the Socialist "power of interdiction." De Mita considered Craxi delegitimated from a democratic point of view precisely because the PSI, a party of the minority, justified its role of arbiter with the quality of the electorate that it represented.[8]

Naturally there were many conflicts between the two parties. The period of the "program government" (1988–89), led by De Mita, ambitious on a general level for its technocratic aspects, in reality left the strategic question of the relationship between the DC and PSI unresolved. And it was difficult to believe that precisely during the period in which Craxi was returned by a landslide in the 1987 elections, intoning the leitmotif of governability, the DC passively accepted the Socialist competition for the occupation of the political center.[9]

While competition from the PSI mounted and Craxi was able to speak of a Socialist long wave, the DC's second response to the Socialists took the form of a strategic alliance, hinging on Craxi, on one side, and Andreotti and Forlani on the other. Why did this change in conduct on the part of the DC occur, under the banner of "making a virtue of necessity?" Beginning with the 1987 parliamentary elections, it was not difficult to foresee that if a "DC spirit" were to exist, it would not fail to bear fruit. Such a spirit, the existence of which could be deduced from the behavior of the party from De Gasperi on, was always oriented toward cooptation of the allies.[10] In brief, the DC alternation of the postwar period characterized at least three strategic choices: 1) after the breaking of the constituent pact that also included the PCI, the constitution of centrist governments with the involvement of the minor lay parties occurred; 2) at the end of the 1950s, when, in the wake of the economic miracle, the opportunity arose to integrate part of the non-Marxist working class with the democratic state, the model of the center-left was developed which at the beginning of the next decade brought the PSI into the government; 3) during the season of the Red Brigade's terrorist offensive (and in a period of very serious and oppressive socioeconomic crisis), Aldo Moro defined "national solidarity," a large majority (lasting from 1976 to 1979) founded on the involvement of the PCI of Enrico Berlinguer.

These three solutions can be discussed on the level of the true ends that caused them. However, it seems impossible to attribute them simply to an instrumental design. Better yet, there certainly exist characteristics instrumental to the distribution of power, to softening potential and effective opposers by inducing them to get their hands dirty through association with government practices. But we cannot ignore an aspect of democratic sincerity on the part of the DC which was intensely felt within the party. In any case, to be brutal, in the choice between a monopoly of power and its division, the DC has always been inclined toward the latter.

It was easy to foresee after the 1987 elections that De Mita's theorizations and radicalism did not constitute the ideal background for adequately playing the game with a PSI that appeared the winner. De Mita showed himself to be a leader too weak to control the inevitable friction of the new situation; too ideological and therefore predictable, De Mita was a prisoner of his own political designs. For this reason, at the end of 1988 De Mita entered the last DC congress as secretary and left seriously and glaringly defeated. The congressional sacrifice of De Mita, hatched in the name of political realism, did not constitute an internal coup de main. It was rather a shrill signal, directed at the PSI, that from now on the match for political hegemony would be played on a completely different field—no longer based on programs or lofty planning, but rather on the integral rediscussion of an entirely political agreement.

At the end of the last decade, then, the DC began to reorganize around the figures of Giulio Andreotti and Arnaldo Forlani. Andreotti, "Giulio the star," seven-time head of the government, was a specialist of the day to day, able to manage every situation, endowed with a freedom from prejudice that was considered only a symptom of cynicism by his detractors, but for his supporters it tended to resemble the endowment of a statesman. As a brilliant Italian journalist wrote, Andreotti's special characteristic was "the ability to turn situations and things to his advantage, from television to the center-left, the advancement of Communists or their crisis, the ambitions of Craxi or Spadolini."

As for Arnaldo Forlani, the essential words in his vocabulary were "union" and "cooperation" of political forces. For the new couple in DC power, every internal conflict in the government coalition was an occasion for mediation. If during the De Mita era the conflicts with the PSI were fundamental, an echo within the government alliance, with the advent of the Andreotti-Forlani team the leader of the PSI found himself in front of a wall of rubber apparently meant to absorb all thrusts, to block every offensive, to round off all corners. At the same time, however, it quickly became clear that this consummate ability to manage the political alliance of the government, particularly in economic policy, was dramatically insufficient for the necessary reconstruction of the country.

CATHOLIC QUESTION, CATHOLIC QUESTIONS

It was said that Andreotti was not the entire DC.[11] If the DC objective had consisted simply of enduring, it is likely that the Andreotti methods (summarized in his formula "Power wears out those who don't have it") would have been the most suitable for attaining it. But a large party like the the DC—precisely because it was also an agglomeration of groups, each of which was endowed with its own ethical-political statutes—could not be reduced to daily administration. The "liberal" Catholics were not able to accept that the DC had completely become a type of branch business functioning to ensure a day-by-day management that seemed ruinous in the long run. The "social" Catholics could not stand to see the party degraded to a lay parody of itself. Those who had always been Andreotti's enthusiastic supporters, the intransigent Catholics of the integralist communion and liberation movement, signaled a marked pacifist and anti-American shift immediately after the outbreak of the Gulf War, making evident the large variety of positions in the party.[12] In short, there was the sensation that in the future some fundamental questions could emerge with unsettling results for the unity of the party. These questions related to the rooting of the DC in the country and to the complex interaction of the party and the segments of civil society tied to it. One of the principal questions concerned the status of a party which expressly referred to the Christian vision in a period of social transformation that widely and profoundly secularized Italian society. In brief, the DC itinerary from the 1970s on had caused the party increasingly to identify itself on the side of government rather than on the level of confessional and religious expression.

On the left, the so-called "Catholic discomfort" had bloomed again well before the Gulf crisis and the war against Saddam Hussein. We should remember the "Palermo experiment," a political laboratory of markedly clerico-populist features led by Leoluca Orlando, then one of the most visible figures of the DC left. Orlando would soon have left the DC, but at the beginning his exile from the party and the subsequent launching of the Network movement were assessed as politically marginal phenomena, exactly as other experiments of political secession from the DC had been marginal and disastrous in the past. However, it was in no way marginal that the

Andreotti DC was not able to neutralize the Palermo heresy through the classical contractual game of political concessions and compensations in which it had traditionally been the master.

Still less marginal was the pacifist surge in the traditional Catholic element of the DC. This was significant not so much because it effectively set the premises for dividing the party but because it opened for discussion—perhaps for the first time—the effective DC representativeness of the Catholic world. On the topic of the Gulf War even the average Catholic voter, who did not harbor particular sympathies for the left, found a new and substantial difference between the position assumed by the DC as a party of the government and that of consistent sectors of the Catholic hierarchy and environment. One had the impression that some ties were loosening conspicuously. For once, the Catholic component of Italian society, with its natural quietism, found itself instinctively closer to the left's cries for peace rather than to the DC and the government position under DC leadership.

Against this background, the drift to the left became more marked in many Catholic lobbies, associationism, welfare communities, sectors of voluntary service, in the world of Catholic youth, and the old social Catholicism in the unions. The against-the-war stance rendered notably more precarious a relationship that had been in crisis for some time (at least beginning with the repealable 1974 divorce referendum, which caused a fracture in the Italian Catholic world), but which at the time seemed to cut a player out of the game. This player was the principal instrument through which the course of Italian political evolution had served to hold a place open for social Catholicism—the left DC. Compared to other times, there was a sharp sensation that the spectre of differentiation in the Catholic world now constituted the basis for a pulverization of political Catholicism that would lead to the total disintegration of as much unity as the DC had embodied.

THE NORTH WIND

By a type of conspiracy of history, precisely during the Gulf War the PCI's dissolution took place in Rimini. This party was reborn as the Partito Democratico della Sinistra (PDS), renouncing the Marxist tradition and explicitly accepting the rules of liberal democracy. It was the conclusion of a process started in November 1989. In the wake of the wave of emotion caused by the crumbling of the Berlin Wall, the secretary of the PCI, Achille Occhetto, announced that the moment of complete change had arrived for the PCI, from its name to its symbol.[13]

The end of the "Communist threat" struck at one of the fundamental trumps of the DC—its function of blocking an antisystem force. An accurate assessment of this would have called for a very rapid renovation effort. However, such an effort was not even begun. At this time, the most evident threat to the DC came from the "aggression" of the Lega Nord.[14] For a state party like the DC, the wedge inserted into the political system by the leader of the league, Umberto Bossi, was more insidious, as it was aimed at the heart of the DC power system, which is based on a process of income redistribution in welfare and patron/client terms. It also targeted the heart of the DC electorate, the middle classes that had traditionally found refuge in DC arms.

Moreover (and this aspect has been insufficiently assessed), the league obtained its most striking results in Lombardy and other regions of the industrial North, where for some time there had been a rather low approval rating for the DC. (If we take as a point of reference the 1990 regional elections—the last before the big political earthquake—the gap in the DC vote between North and South was almost 12 percentage points: 30 percent in the North versus 41.8 percent in the South.) This was not without consequences. First of all, an extremely marked imbalance between the DC foundation in the North and electoral performance in the South became evident. Within the political machine it is usual to adapt to challenges along the line of least resistance. It could thus have been expected that to maintain its consensus levels, the DC would be obliged to hold tightly to the South. In this case, a single instrument was suitable to this end: the maintanence and development of the system of government transfers, of raining distributions, of spending without control over results. This was a consolidated policy, spread through both unproductive investments and extraordinary spending interventions and, more diffusely, with disability pensions or hirings in the local administrations—namely, with patron-client practices of income support. However, this policy of spending "for the development of the South" was now the focus of widespread rejection in the North; also, it was rendered almost impracticable by a progressive and impressive worsening of the state budget. In addition, if the DC had chosen to become the "Party of the South," its national representativeness would have been in crisis. A "southernization" of the party apparatus, simultaneous with its decline in the North following the attack of the league, would have placed in grave difficulty precisely those factions of the DC that had continued to present themselves as exponents of a modernity tempered by an avowed social spirit, put in the position of administering locally (like in many zones of Lombardy and the Veneto), supporting growth in a manner not too different from the most propagandized Emilian model managed during the postwar period by the pragmatic Communists of the North. A vicious circle was then revealed which had the predictable result of cleaving northern and southern DCs.

THE SHOCK OF APRIL 1992

The parliamentary elections of 5–6 April mark a turning point. In the desert of political proposals that had preceded the elections, the competition began to seem like a referendum for or against the government alliance. It became easy for the opposition to describe the DC-PSI relationship as an *ancien régime* to be beaten. Probably also Arnaldo Forlani and Bettino Craxi's approach to the election campaign, all to mark continuity, accepted the risk of a popular judgment of the political package constituted by the government coalition. Actually, it explicitly solicited this "verdict." Presenting the government alliance as the sole possible instrument for the management of the country and the government parties as the sole plausible interpreters of the concert of public administration in a certain sense furnished the coalition with a minor political legitimization, in which the exterior unity of the partnership could serve to mask the emptiness of the political program, the container taking the place of the contents. If nothing else, a rather clear assessment was asked of the electorate: vote either yes or no for the government.

A more intense shock than had been predicted came from the ballot boxes—a slap to the government, small caresses for the traditional opposition. Almost 8 million Italians deposited an antisystem ballot, choosing an area of protest (Lega Nord) or frontal antagonism with respect to the liberal democratic parties (Movimento Sociale—namely, the neofascists—to the right and Rifondazione Comunista—namely, the paleo-Marxists—to the left). The major parties saw their foundations collapsing, as in the case of the DC and PDS, or they suffered the burning disappointment of a stalemate, as did the PSI. Moreover, the Lega Nord had made its way to the head of the line, dividing the national delegation and southernizing the two principal parties of the government. The first of those defeated, DC secretary Arnaldo Forlani, showed that he understood the sense of the vote very well and resigned at the National Council meeting convened ten days after the vote. But at this point a seemingly incomprehensible situation began to unfold. Except for some sectors of the left, the entire party was opposed to Forlani's resignation. The principal leaders disdainfully rejected the profoundly anti-DC idea of making Forlani the immediate scapegoat of the electoral defeat. There has almost always been a vein of subtle sadism in the way the DC treated defeated leaders, obliging them "by the spirit of service" to bear the results of defeat. In spite of this, it was acknowledged that Forlani's analysis was substantially correct. He had recognized the exhaustion of the formula based on the alliance with the PSI and put his term in office on reserve in order to permit freehanded and wide-ranging negotiation.

It is necessary to emphasize that Forlani had not been the secretary of a scattered DC. Instead he had been the director and interpreter of a precise political period, based on the cast-iron relationship with the PSI after the period of conflict managed by De Mita. If this preferential relationship entered a period of crisis, a reserve strategy would be needed as soon as possible. Clearly the DC did not have such a reserve strategy. Renouncing his office, Forlani set the party free to search for contacts and alliances outside of the old formula and probably also outside of the axis with the PSI, of which he had always been the guardian. But the party was not ready for such an immediate remixing, and there was no leader who could have plausibly been proposed for a marked change in the political trend. Therefore Forlani was temporarily supported.

It is worth underlining a feature that was perhaps not sufficiently noted: The key point of the Italian political evolution related to the hypothesis that the thirty-year collaborative relationship of the DC and PSI had reached its limits. All the hypotheses of electoral reform formulated in that period tended, in large or small measure, to rectify the Italian "anomaly" of a political center occupied by two parties which in a zero-sum system would have had to confront each other as adversaries. The parliamentary elections brought to light that the political ecosystem, in which the collaboration between the Catholics and Socialists had developed, had been dramatically restricted over time. Both protagonists of this long collaboration were shown nude, stripped of an alternative line.

STRIKES OF THE HAMMER

Before 5 April 1992 the most violent protest against the DC had come—it would not seem paradoxical—from a Christian Democrat. And not from just any Christian Democrat, but directly from Francesco Cossiga, then President of the Republic.[15] Purified of the dross of the daily news, of the intoxication of a polemic that had reached white heat, Cossiga's behavior in the last part of his term in office can be identified on the basis of two fundamental motivations. The first was the acute perception of the necessity for profound constitutional adjustment in order to furnish the conditions of a "mature" democracy no longer blocked by ideological exclusions. The second was the individuation in parliament of two opposing fronts—one (led by the PSI) favorable to a decisive institutional leap, the other (DC-PDS) inclined toward minimizing constitutional intervention and acting with solutions of "soft change."

The strongest disagreement between the head of state and the DC occurred with a long message on institutional topics which Cossiga addressed to parliament and which was discussed in the houses at the end of July 1991. The message probably marked the final attempt at making the aforementioned two lineups emerge in parliament and of directing the institutional debate toward a confrontation which at that point, in Cossiga's opinion, could no longer be contained in the clearinghouses of the party system but had to find a popular legitimization for its breadth and its meaning, even through referendum measures.

The accusations against Cossiga for wanting to clear the path to a plebiscitary-type democracy were not lacking. But the most immediate result of the head of state's initiatives was a showy delegitimization of his original party, which was indicated as one of the factors restraining the politco-institutional renovation.

The second disrupting hammer blow came from the magistracy, with the Mani Pulite (Clean Hands) operation begun by the Milan public prosecutor's office. With the discovery of the kickback system and arrest warrants at high political levels, "the regime" (as Umberto Bossi began calling it) founded on the DC-PSI alliance started to teeter.[16] All of a sudden the interlacing of politics and kickbacks no longer appeared to be a series of isolated cases, but a generalized element constituted by government activity, as if the metastasis of party interest had integrally replaced the skeleton and organs of government administration.[17]

At first it seemed that the principal target of the magistracy's action had to be Bettino Craxi's PSI. In fact, over two years it assisted in the fracturing of the PSI and its virtual disappearance from the political scene. The dissolution was very rapid and traumatic, but a destructive element had also been inserted in the body of the DC and should have made itself felt with a relentless clockwork rhythm. But in the days following the April 1992 elections, there was not a perception that the political change had assumed an overwhelming cadence for the DC. This was so true that in the following month, as soon as Francesco Cossiga resigned a few days before the expiration of his term, the old governmental alliance, patched up for the moment, tried to elect Arnaldo Forlani, secretary of the DC, as President of the Republic. The attempt failed due to too few votes, as did a following attempt to bring the Socialist Giuliano Vassalli to the Quirinal. The Quirinal recovered for better or worse with the election of Oscar Luigi Scalfaro (who was then a second string candidate, little known politically).[18] Because of the usual question of divided balances, the DC had to cede the presidency of the council of the new government to a Socialist, Giuliano Amato, who in an initially uncertain and then increasingly decisive manner began a period of recovery of government accounts.[19]

After the summer of 1992 Forlani quit as DC secretary and was replaced by Mino Martinazzoli, elected by the party in a plebiscitary mode. Northern, curt in manner, an exponent of the prominence of the internal left, a lover of Pascal and Montaigne, an author of desolate warnings to the party ("You are like winter olives: content to resist and endure"), Martinazzoli had to master a complicated equation with two unknowns: how to radically renovate the party without losing any of its components. In the paralyzing wait to resolve this unresolvable dilemma, the new leader began to be hounded by events, progressively losing the ability to control them.

FATAL 1993

In the meantime within the party there grew the activism of Mario Segni, an exponent of a moderate DC who had initiated a strong movement to change the electoral law with a series of referenda from the proportional method to a prevalently uninominal majority system. Recalling a tradition of the progenitors of the DC, the Popular Party of Luigi Sturzo, Segni created his own group, Popolari per la Riforma, which entered the playing field with a spectacular assembly in Rome on 10 October 1992 and a congress in Milan on 23 January 1993. Actually, Segni was placed at the extreme edges of the party.[20]

It was, however, a legal case that precipitated the DC drama: news that an investigation had been opened against Giulio Andreotti on the basis of depositions given by Tommaso Buscetta, Francesco Marino Mannoia, and other Mafia "repenters."[21] The arrest warrant, sent to the strongest Christian Democrat of the Palermo magistrates, appeared to the public like a biblical sign of the times, an extraordinary symbol of the end of a power system. The man who just a few months earlier had been the strongest Italian, the personification of DC existence and perpetuity, was now dragged down from the altar, out of the sanctuary of power.

It was 27 March 1993. Two days later, while the polemic resonated loudly, Mario Segni quit the DC. The referendum leader concentrated completely on the campaign for the referenda for 18 April which would have given the final big shake to the First Republic.[22] Passage to a majority model, which would make room for a bipolar political system, seemed structured purposely for removing the DC from the center of the political picture. The role of the DC as a party that presented itself as synthesis and composition of a very broad band of classes and interests was precisely the topic of discussion.

The DC, however, had been not only the party at the center, the fixed star, the pillar and mainstay of every coalition. It had also been the cement of the very particular Italian socioeconomic development, interpreter and executor of a model that kneaded together the labors of small and medium-sized industry and union protection, a welfare state that was simultaneously "socialism of the middle classes" and patron-client welfarism, unguided modernization and protected backwardness at the expense of the common good. It was awareness of this type which led Martinazzoli to his pensive hesitations. The DC leader understood that a DC which overcame the conservative temptation of the right, presenting itself as the southern counterpart of the Lega Nord, with an implicit or explicit proposal of coming to terms with Umberto Bossi, would have given rise to a very strong repercussion to the left. In an analogous way, the arrangement in an equally crowded and indeterminate "area of progress," hegemonized by the PDS, would have provoked a schism on the right on the part of whoever intended to occupy the moderate politico-electoral space. The DC was changing from clearinghouse to combustion chamber.

There was an opportunity during the national DC council convened in June in which Martinazzoli spoke more explicitly than usual, underlining the need "not so much of renewing relationships with the political forces but of attempting a large-scale reconciliation with society." Behind these words a belief could be heard: the DC's fate was tied to its capacity to rise again in its entirety—that is, to reinvent itself as something completely new and completely the same.

As soon as he launched the idea of a constituent assembly for the end of July 1993, which should have begun the transformation of the DC into a new popular party, Martinazzoli set about the prodigious business of holding the body of the DC together while at the same time giving it a new soul, defying the probable result of not healing the body nor saving the soul. While everything appeared in frenzied movement, Martinazzoli discovered a single card left to play: to be still, even immobile, offering at the most a bit of a beauty treatment as if it were surgery, mediation as if it were stringent choice, silence or muttering as if it were a parting word. Perhaps in his heart of hearts he was indulging in the illusion that the First Republic had not completely declined and that at the height of an extraordinary political upheaval it would have been possible to address to the sunset of the DC the prodigious biblical invocation, "Stop, oh sun."

Martinazzoli entered the 23 July constituent assembly convinced that the DC, or the new popular party, had to continue to be a party of the center, even if the uninominal majority electoral system defined the center as a position of contention among the lineups and not a stable trench or stronghold. He continued to think of the DC as a fundamental guarantee of national unity threatened by the Lega Nord. After a thousand remarks, he seemed to have convinced the assembly that a "German" future had been inscribed in the DC genetic code: the DC of the future could be a party like the CDU of Helmut Kohl—of popular-conservative stamp, but not alien to the modernizing spirit. The assembly approved Martinazzoli's plan unanimously. The old DC heart refused to pay any price to change its own body. In the new popular party the entire DC, excluding no one, would have to be reincarnated.[23]

The fact is that this solution came extremely late, as the party appeared to be an expanding galaxy, dilated by a thrust toward outer space that threatened to disintegrate it forever. New leaders like Rosy Bindi had launched the DC of the Veneto toward the left, reintroducing visions of solidarity and giving voice to the new (or old) Catholic-social tendencies that had never stopped looking to the left. Other factions of the party were feeding temptations of the right, proposing themselves as interlocuters of the Lega Nord. Still others, like the director of the DC newspaper *Il Popolo,* Sergio Mattarella, declared themselves disposed to making a radical political experiment of the DC, knowingly denying the risk of the DC becoming a party of simple minority testimony.

In all probability the "German party" would have been a viable option as long as Mario Segni remained in the DC. But the referendum leader left, and the times seemed to impose a clear choice: right or left, without verbal acrobatics and without transformisms. In any case, the DC was losing its principal historic prerogative—being the political instrument of the democratization of the Italian middle classes, to which it had offered in the postwar period a shelter from the nostalgia for the right and the Communist danger. For the DC the polarization of the popular vote that was being sensed was extremely serious because it sent the moderate voters in the direction of the Lega Nord and the extreme right and the fringes of social

Catholicism toward the left. A political panorama with a hole in the middle began to emerge, in which two lineups would not remain to fight for the moderate voters converging on the center; rather the voters of the center would dash off blindly looking for someone to represent them. An eventuality of this type could prelude a society in part broken up and dispersed among extremist irrationalities and in part constrained (by paradoxical but philosophical repercussion) to find in the PDS—that is, the ex-Communists—a factor of national cohesion and democratic continuity. The DC had to find a way to restructure into a political force newly able to obtain the consensus of citizens inclined to "normal" modernization without adventures. In view of this objective, however, it would be necessary to sacrifice the old DC, with its corruption and its patronage system, and also with its limits of "Catholic party," and to make it the melting pot of something else. Instead Martinazzoli succeeded in appearance only in transferring the entire DC "army" to the new popular party: saving a seat for centrist and "solidarityist," liberal and welfarist, the right and the left. At this point numerous DC horses (no longer completely thoroughbreds) gave the impression of supporting the secretary in order to set him up as a champion, displayed in the front line for the last battle, an inevitable weapon against attacks from the outside and very advantageous cover for the thousand conflicting strategies of the various rear guards.[24]

The Vatican hierarchy collaborated in this potentially suicidal outcome. Although it accepted in theory the end of the dogma called "political unity of the Catholics" (naturally the unity is meant to be under the DC shield), in reality the hierarchy made short shrift of every solution other than Martinazzoli's, beginning with the heresy of Mario Segni, head of the Popolari per la Riforma. But between the end of 1993 and the beginning of 1994 it was no longer a question of ecclesiastical support for the DC, and not even of the agreement among its heads, and even less of its ability to find allies.[25] All hypotheses became possible: the breakup of the party, with the fracture and subsequent game to the death between right and left; an anonymous diaspora which would bleed the party, forcing it to a rapid death; the "surrender" to Segni's Popolari; a chaotic attempt to constitute a new political formation, completing in a breathless manner the process which had been announced by Martinazzoli and which had substantially slipped from his hands.

CONCLUSIONS

Actually the surrender to Segni had already happened. All the components of the DC in the period preceding the spring 1993 parliamentary elections indicated the referendum leader as their candidate for the premiership. The last discussions in the party, heated and violent, concerned the political arrangement of the new DC: conservative party or (as De Gasperi said) "party of the center that marches toward the left?" The future of the DC still seems conditioned by a "past that does not pass," by the misunderstandings that throughout the postwar period were at the root of DC fortunes and that today seem to constitute the virus of its dissolution. Today there no longer seem to be any alternatives. The DC of the future can attempt to survive in only two ways: positioning itself on the right side of the political spectrum or splitting into two branches, one on the left, one on the right. But as always there is a third way: not resolving any misunderstandings, repeating the destiny of the French MRP after the end of the Fourth Republic—i.e., remaining a momument to itself, with the probable result of being crushed by two lineups in formation, ailing heart of a political system which, while it assumes the characteristics of a less imperfect bipartisanism than before, refuses the DC vocation of continuing to be the mirror of the country as a whole.

NOTES

1. One of the most accurate pictures of the problems of an economic policy that leads to a continual and growing public sector indebtedness is in L. Campiglio, "Illusioni di richezza, rischi di declino," in *La riconquista dell'Italia,* ed. Fabio Luca Cavazza (Milan: Longanesi, 1993).

2. A thorough discussion of the role of the parties in Italy during the Republican alternation is found in P. Scoppola, *La Repubblica dei partiti: Profilo storico della democrazia in Italia (1945–1990)* (Bologna: Il Mulino, 1991).

3. In a famous book by the political scientist Giorgio Galli, the Italian political system was defined in 1966 as "imperfect bipartisanism," which discounted the presence of two large alternative parties, the DC and the Communist Party, in a system blocked by the Marxist, pro-Soviet, and anti-Western tendencies of the latter, which rendered government alternation impracticable.

4. For a picture of the entire Italian development in the postwar period, see P. Ginsborg, *Storia d'Italia dal dopo guerra a oggi: Società e politica 1943–1988* (Turin: Einaudi, 1989); from a leftist perspective, the English historian highlights the deficit of reforms that marked the Italian postwar period. See also S. Lanaro, *Storia dell'Italia repubblicana: Dalla fine della guerra agli anni novanta* (Venice: Marsilio, 1992), which offers numerous ideas for framing the political alternation within the profile of the history of the culture, and A. Lepre, *Storia della prima repubblica: L'Italia dal 1942 al 1992* (Bologna: Il Mulino, 1993).

5. M. Follini, *L'arcipelago democristiano* (Rome and Bari: Laterza, 1990). This book is an attempt to interpret the composition of the DC by factions after the secretaryship of Ciriaco De Mita. In *La DC al bivio* (Rome and Bari: Laterza, 1992), the same author individuates the premises of the DC crisis after the events of 1989 in the assertion "of forms of opposition that cultivate words of a moderate order and contest the DC's center space" (p. 28).

6. For a critical "balance-sheet" of the PSI during the Craxi era, see the conclusion of G. Sabbatucci, *Il riformismo impossibile: Storie del socialismo italiano* (Rome and Bari: Laterza, 1991); E. Berselli, *Il PSI del movimentismo al temporeggiamento* (Bologna: Il Mulino, 1991); M. Rhodes, "Il declino del 'onda lunga' e la fine del craxismo," in *Politica in Italia,* ed. S. Hellman and G. Pasquino (Bologna: Il Mulino, 1993; also 1992). Valuable and detailed information is found in W. Merkel, *Prima e dopo Craxi: Le trasformazioni del PSI* (Padua: Liviana, 1987), while a debate on the PSI as party of the left is found in V. Foa and A. Giolitti, eds., *La questione socialista: Per una possibile reinvenzione della sinistra* (Turin: Einaudi, 1987).

7. See G. Baget Bozzo, "De Mita, o l'utopia della politica pura," *MicroMega,* no. 3 (1989).

8. "The objective was to block the PSI in the majority, creating, thanks to the electoral system, a situation fixed by Craxi: either subject to previous confirmation of the penta-party (the government alliance formed by the DC, PSI, and the three 'lay' parties), which signified a priori the hegemony of the DC, or press to the left on the PCI, destined in this case to prevail politically over the PSI by the sheer force of votes. The quality of the agreements became the sole political measure, while the PSI had so far founded its role in the government alliance on the quantity of its votes, as representative of the most dynamic and creative part of the country" (Baget Bozzo, p. 111).

9. *Ibid.*

10. Alcide De Gasperi, "the Chancellor," who died in 1954, was the most prestigious politician the DC produced in the postwar period. Head of eight governments between 1945 and 1953, De Gasperi, author of the breakup of the national unity that included the Communists, always sought to obtain the collaboration of the minor parties of liberal and social-democratic tendencies. For an interpretation of this political figure, see P. Scoppola, *La proposta politica di De Gasperi* (Bologna: Il Mulino, 1977).

11. M. Mafai, "Andreotti fra craoce e palazzo," *MicroMega,* no. 2 (1990).

12. See M. Donovan, "Il pacifismo cattolico e la guerra del Golfo," in *Politica in Italia,* ed. S. Hellman and G. Pasquino (Bologna: Il Mulino, 1992).

13. One of the best analyses of the difficult transition from communism to a liberal approach is P. Ignazi, *Dal PCI al PDS* (Bologna: Il Mulino, 1992). For a summarizing reflection on the alternation of the Communist Party, see M. Flores and N. Gallerano, *Sul PCI: Un'interpretazione storica* (Bologna: Il Mulino, 1992).

14. Founded in Lombardy by Umberto Bossi as a local movement, not without xenophobic and anti-South elements, the Lega Nord at the beginning of the 1990s rapidly became the strongest party in various regions of northern Italy, conquering vast sectors of the traditional DC electorate thanks to a very strong polemic against the parties and their welfare and patron-client policies, appealing for mobilization against excessive federal tax pressures founded on the division of the state into three republics. Among the few scientific analyses of the Lega, see Ilvo Diamanti, *La Lega: Geografia, storia e sociologia di un nuovo soggetto politico* (Rome: Donzelli, 1993); R. Mannheimer, ed., *La Lega Lombarda* (Milan: Feltrinelli, 1991); S. Allievi, *Le parole della Lega* (Milan: Garzanti, 1992), is useful in formulating ideas on the cultural identity of the league movement. Contributions of great interest focusing on the disintegrative tendencies in Italy are G. E. Rusconi, *Se cessiamo di essere una nazione* (Bologna: Il Mulino, 1993), and R. Cartocci, *Fra Lega e Chiesa: L'Italia in cerca di integrazione* (Bologna: Il Mulino, 1994). On the historic differences among the various Italian regions, see R. Putnam, R. Leonardi, and R. Nanetti, *Making Democracy Work: Civic Tradition in Modern Italy* (Princeton: Princeton University Press, 1993).

15. Cossiga was elected 24 June 1985, in the first round of votes, with a wide majority collected by the maneuverings of Ciriaco De Mita. According to predictions, he had to emerge as the symbol of a certain dusty institutional drabness, and in fact for five years he played the part of the jurist president, devoted advocate of the correctness of institutional progress, convinced of the possibility of again leading the political conflict within the existing constitutional structure; in the end, when he was convinced that it was necessary to arrange a profoundly different institutional order, he was revealed as an absolutely unexpected dividing principle.

16. In the public's eyes, the investigation started in February 1992 with the arrest of Socialist official Mario Chiesa. Afterwards Albergo Trivulzio was condemned for having pocketed kickbacks as administrator of a Milanese municipal board. The discovery of incredibly widespread corruption caused the mass media to coin the term Tangentopoli (Kickbackopolis), which spread into common usage, while the magistrates of the Milan public prosecutor's office, and in particular Public Prosecutor Antonio Di Pietro, acquired immeasurable popularity.

17. Perhaps the most acute analysis of the Italian political upheaval following the trauma of Tangentopoli is by the historian Luciano Cafagna, *La grande slavina: L'Italia verso ala crisi della democrazia* (Venice: Marsilio, 1993). A detailed journalistic reconstruction, characterized by a marked opposition perspective, is G. M. Bellu and S. Bonsanti, *Il crollo: Andreotti, Craxi e il loro regime* (Rome and Bari: Laterza, 1993).

18. After sixteen votes, on 25 May Scalfaro, considered of high moral profile and outside of the partyocracy tradition, was elected head of state with the

votes of the DC, PDS, PSI, PSDI, PLI, Verdi, Rete, and Lista Pannella. The election of Scalfaro was favored also by the drama of the moment. Very shortly after his election the Sicilian Mafia hit one of the symbols of the anti-Mafia fight, the magistrate Giovanni Falcone, killing him and his wife with a spectacular attack on the highway that connects the Palermo airport and the city.

19. The support of Amato's government (which began to strike the strongholds of the Italian welfare and patron-client system—health services, pensions, government employment) was perceived by the DC as something seriously self-damaging in the long run. According to many DC exponents, the DC facilitated decidedly unpopular measures in parliament, bearing their burden before a public which was ever more indignant at the partyocracy, to the complete advantage of the opposition parties. This situation became even more visible with the subsequent government of Carlo Azeglio Ciampi.

20. Segni had his first big success 9–10 June with a referendum relative to a marginal feature of the electoral law for the Chamber of Deputies but which was interpreted by the public as an opportunity to strike at the parties. The referendum, in which 62.5 percent of the voters participated, was approved by 95.6 percent (see P. McCarthy, "Il referendum del 9 giugno," in Hellman and Pasquino, eds., 1992 ed. Before the 5 April 1992 election Segni proposed a "pact" to political representatives, the subscribers of which (who were numerous) were pledged to support the referenda for electoral change, or, in any case, the process of electoral reform.

21. One year before the start of the investigation of Andreotti, on 12 March 1992 an event of extreme drama took place: the head of Andreotti's faction in Sicily, Salvo Lima, accused by his opponents of ties with the Mafia powers, was assassinated by the Mafia. Many believed that Lima's murder was a vendetta against Andreotti, by now unable to make the magistracy subject to conditions and even constrained to approve clearly anti-Mafia laws.

22. The electoral referenda of 18 April 1993 concluded with a landslide victory (more than 82 percent) for those who wanted to change the electoral system in the direction of a majority model.

23. A nearly immediate check of the risks that the DC ran with the majority system occurred in the local government elections in some large cities in 1993 with the double round system of balloting. In June, the DC suffered crushing defeats in Milan, Turin, Catania, and numerous other cities. At the beginning of December, in Rome, Naples, Genoa, Venice, Trieste, and Palermo the DC defeat was even more ruinous. In the large Italian cities Martinazzoli's party did not even succeed in reaching the second ballot, and in some cases (e.g., Rome and Naples) it consigned its own electorate to the MSI, a formation of the extreme right which was always excluded from the political game because of its neofascist character.

24. For a comprehensive picture of the Italian situation and perspectives in the period of major politico-institutional crisis, see Cavazza, ed. See especially the last section, dedicated to political change, edited by E. Berselli, L. Ornaghi, and V. E. Parsi.

25. The last appeal for political unity of the Catholics under the banner of the DC was made by Cardinal Camillo Ruini, president of the Italian bishops, in an inaugural lecture on 23 September 1991 at the meeting of the permanent council of the episcopal commission. Thereafter, the Church supported Martinazzoli but in a position different from the bishops; this in fact marked the end of the precept of political unity of the Catholic world. On more than one occasion, Pope John Paul II spoke favorably of the pluralism of Catholics, noting that the crucial problem for contemporary Italy consisted of "not losing its soul in pluralism and not losing pluralism in unity."

THE LEFT AND THE TRANSFORMATION OF ITALIAN POLITICS

Gianfranco Pasquino

THE PROBLEM AND THE OPPORTUNITIES

At the threshold of the Second Republic, the Italian left appears to be facing some of the old problems. Unexpectedly, it is also enjoying some new opportunities. The major problem of the Italian left plagued it throughout the First Republic: internal divisions, conflicts on strategies, diverging viewpoints on whether and how to propose its candidacy to the government of the country.[1] In addition, a fundamental problem has recently surfaced. Almost suddenly, the left has been confronted with a crisis of identity. In essence, to belong to the left in Italy has always meant to nourish expectations of change, to work in the hope of a socialist transformation, to believe in solidarity and to utilize the state for collective purposes. Italian leftists were proud to be identified as such with reference to their lifestyles, their commitment to politics, even their personal integrity. The Communists, in particular, though politically distrusted because of their Moscow affiliation, were highly respected as honest, hard-working, reliable, and capable individuals. Perhaps all these qualities made them even more redoubtable in the opponents' eyes. While a certain idea of the left and of what it means to be a leftist still lingers, in Italy as well as in Europe, there is no longer a strong, cogent leftist identity. Indeed if anything is still strong and cogent on the left, it is the need to recreate such an identity. The new opportunities for the left, offered by political and institutional developments, cannot by themselves satisfy this need, which is ideological and (so to speak) existential. Nevertheless, the almost complete dissolution of the center parties and above all the terminal crisis of the Christian Democrats (DC), the most powerful organizational machine of the old regime, have paved the way for a promising and possibly lasting political realignment favoring the left. The new electoral laws, some already implemented for the popular election of several mayors, seem to offer important insitutional opportunities as well as powerful constraints for the progressive electorate to coalesce. Where party leaders might stick and succumb to their selfish political ambitions and personal jealousies, their progressive and left-wing voters seem to indicate a remarkable propensity to reward credible candidates and coalitions. A taste of national government was even savored for eleven hours by three ministers of the Democratic Party of the Left (PDS). Because of their competence, they had been appointed by the incoming prime minister, Carlo Azeglio Ciampi, to the government created at the end of April 1993. A scandalous vote of the House of Deputies intended to prevent the judges from further investigating former prime minister Craxi's illegal activities immediately prompted their resignation in protest against a parliamentary majority still willing to rescue the protagonists of the systems of corruption. The path to the government, still uphill, is, however, finally open even to the PDS, traditionally discriminated against when its name was the Italian Communist Party (PCI). More than just an opportunity, those few hours in the government seem a harbinger of things to come again soon.

There is a preliminary difficulty in analyzing the Italian left today. Its composition—that is, the inclusion and exclusion of some components—is in itself a political decision. The very definition of what is or should be left, identity crisis notwithstanding, has to be considered more than just a scholarly problem. It lies at the heart of any political strategy and struggle. How can one mobilize and reconcile a diversified electorate resorting just to issues of candidates, offices, power? Still, definitions count because they circumscribe or enhance the political and electoral appeal of leftist and progressive ideas, leaders, and organizations. There are those who say that the leftists and the progressives no longer coincide in Italy—or perhaps for that matter in most European countries either. Tentatively, one can say that not all Italian leftists are progressives, such as Rifondazione Comunista, a splinter party which emerged out of the transformation of the PCI into the PDS. Its leaders and supporters are definitely leftists and almost as definitely would not be considered progressives. They seem bent on preserving their Communist past and making the PDS their enemy on several issues, resorting to traditional and worn out Communist jargon. And not all the progressives—such as the Greens, some sectors of the Republicans, and Mario Segni's followers, the Popolari (most of them former Christian Democrats)—can be and would like to be defined as leftists. Indeed many among the Greens reject any resort to spatial positioning. They stress they are neither right nor left. Moreover, there are some political groups, such as La Rete (Network), founded by the former Christian Democratic mayor of Palermo, Leoluca Orlando, which cannot be located along the left-right continuum. Nevertheless, they would consider themselves progressives, though not leftists. Finally, there are the Socialists. At this point, they would defy any classification, especially if one looks at their public policies and governmental alliances. They themselves would reject the label of leftists in favor of reformists. Some would say that while in government (1980–92), they followed and enacted neoconservative policies. Therefore, even their classification as progressives is somewhat controversial, so that they seem suspended in a very uneasy political space. This suspension goes a long way toward explaining their present crisis. The fact is that the entire Italian political alignment is undergoing dramatic changes spurred and accompanied by significant electoral and institutional reforms, and the Italian left is caught in this whirlwind.

Be that as it may, I believe that it is still appropriate to accept and utilize a spatial definition of the left in Italy. For analytical purposes, I will consider leftists all those who sit to the left of the speakers in the Italian parliament. At present, these parties and groups are (from left of center to left) the Socialists, the Greens, the Network, the PDS, and Rifondazione Comunista. A different matter, involving a precise value judgment, is the classification of the progressive alignment on important institutional and political issues, above all on the groups' willingness to draft a common program and present common candidates. A flexible, though widely shared, definition of the progressives along these lines would almost always exclude Rifondazione Comunista, often exclude the Network, and very often include most of the Greens, most Republicans, some sectors of the Socialists, and some left-wing Catholics (Social Christians). Once influential Radical leader Marco Pannella's position has become less clear in recent times, though on the issue of civil rights he most often takes a progressive stance. One may thus conclude that by all accounts the Italian left is in transition. Actually it is as divided as ever. Potentially it is stronger than it ever was. It is looking for new organizational forms. It is obliged to formulate new programs and shape innovative policies. It must transform itself while the political system is being transformed. It can be characterized as the only potential coalition capable of withstanding the brunt of the growing and aggressive Lega Nord and its political ally, Berlusconi's Forza Italia.

In order to overcome the most glaring divisions and most damaging conflicts, a partially successful attempt to create what is called a left-center coalition has been launched under the name of Democratic Alliance. Its purpose is to become an umbrella organization providing a safe haven for all progressives. It aims at the formulation of programs, the coordination of policies, the promotion of activities, and the selection of candidates. Mayoral candidates of Democratic Alliance already won offices in Turin and Catania, as well as in several other less important cities, in June 1993. That is, coalitions including the Popolari of Mario Segni, the Republicans, the Greens, and the PDS have proven capable of winning conspicuous majorities of votes. In contrast, a coalition made up of the PDS with Rifondazione Comunista and the Network, but without support from the Popolari, badly lost in Milan—partly because the opponent was the very powerful candidate of the Lega Nord. In December Democratic Alliance candidates swept all major cities from Genoa to Venice, from Rome to Naples, from Trieste to Palermo. This explains why there is an ongoing intense debate within the PDS on the issue of electoral and political alliances. And Segni has insistently requested that the PDS drop any alliance with Rifondazione Comunista and to a lesser extent with the Network as a precondition to its joining forces with the Popolari and the other progressive parties and groups. Once more, as often in the political history of the Italian left, the harshest decisions have to be made by the PDS. Indeed no diagnosis or prognosis of the Italian left is possible or useful without starting from the role played and to be played by the PDS.

THE PDS

There is no doubt that in postwar Italian history the Italian Communist Party was, for better or worse, both an object of admiration and an element of contradiction within the left. The left—specifically the Socialists (PSI) and Social Democrats (PSDI)—feared the PCI's organizational capabilities and militant party devotion and discipline. At the same time, for any reformist policy, the PSI and PSDI needed the support of the industrial working class and the lower popular strata which made up the electorate and membership of the PCI. Encumbered by its ties with the Soviet Union, the PCI could never represent a real governmental alternative to the DC. Too often it was willing to trade its parliamentary presence and discipline for resources necessary for the activities of its organization and the gratification of its reference groups. This so-called consociational practice helped the party to grow but at the same time trimmed its oppositional profile. It was dropped at the end of the 1980s, when Craxi frontally challenged the PCI. In the meantime, slowly—probably too slowly—detaching itself from the Soviet Union, the PCI finally broke with the Communist Party of the Soviet Union following the military coup in Poland in 1981. Belatedly, it was obliged to change its name and symbols when the Berlin Wall collapsed in November 1989. Nonetheless, this momentous change took a long time to be implemented. The new party was not inaugurated until February 1991, after an overdrawn, intense, and bitter confrontation. This delay allowed the internal opponents to get organized throughout the country. Some of the opponents (as noted) left the party and created Rifondazione Comunista, which soon captured one-tenth of the PCI's more active members and more than one-fourth of the Communist electorate. Other opponents remained within the party and created their own faction: the Democratic Communists.[2] It took a while for the new PDS to become a recognized and relatively cohesive party. Even today the Democratic Communists still constitute an internal, cohesive, rather sectarian opposition. On most issues, they do not share the views of the party secretary and fight the decisions after a debate and majority vote. On other issues, the secretary is sensitive to their requests and criticisms. Consequently, the party is unable to steer a clear line. For instance, on the extremely important issue of the electoral referendum (April 1993), the Democratic Communists rejected the official decision reached by a very sizable majority of the PDS and destroyed whatever party discipline was left within the PDS. They went so far as to create a special ad hoc committee to campaign for the no vote. In essence, they were advocating the defeat of the official position of the party in favor of incisive reforms of the proportional system. Needless to say, this internal division of competing factions represents one of the major problems of the new PDS. It creates continuous tensions. It prevents the formulation of clear policies. It gives public opinion the image of a divided, ineffective, unreliable organization. It wounds the credibility of the secretary himself.

There are today three recognized factions and one subfaction within the PDS. The countervailing faction to the Democratic Communists is the Reformists, led by Giorgio Napolitano. The Reformists are presently rather weak, first because their leader has been elected speaker of the House of Deputies and cannot play an active role in political battles, and second because their most important political option has been destroyed by the events. The Reformists believed in the possibility of constructing a joint party of the left, mending the 1921 rift of Leghorn, when the Communists abandoned the PSI in order to establish their own pro-Soviet organization. The Reformists, a minority within the PDS, thought that in a new workers' or labor party their political role would be greatly enhanced. The disgraceful disarray in which the PSI has fallen has all but shattered this option. Moreover, the Reformists' recent presentation of political ideas and programs has proved very limited, almost nonexistent.

The third faction within the PDS is an undeclared one led by the PDS secretary, Achille Occhetto. Understandably, it is a centrist faction. In recent times, it has moved toward a tactical reconciliation with the Reformists, in both the choice of policies and the search for alliances if not in official declarations. Within the centrist faction there is a subfaction, politically positioned on the center-left, led by the whip of the PDS House parliamentary caucus, Massimo D'Alema. Everybody within and outside the party is well aware that D'Alema is Occhetto's challenger and potential substitute. He has characterized himself as the party leader who most encourages party pride and would like to acquire a sort of new hegemony by the PDS on the entire Italian left. The goal is rather ambitious, especially because the political, organizational, and ideal resources do not seem to inhabit the PDS any longer. Moreover, D'Alema's leadership qualities are seriously questioned outside the PDS.

There is no doubt that Occhetto retains an important role and enjoys some charismatic recognition within the party. There is no comparison, however, with the almost sacred quality with which previous Communist secretaries were endowed—above all Palmiro Togliatti (1893–1964) and Enrico Berlinguer (1922–84). Moreover, Occhetto himself is responsible for having encouraged (or compelled) the previous lackluster secretary, Alessandro Natta, to resign in 1988. Therefore, he has created a precedent (so to speak): Communist secretaries do not have to die in office any more. Consequently, Occhetto's own position is no longer sacred and not necessarily for life. He can be challenged. So much so that D'Alema has been obliged several times to deny his intentions, though he cannot hide major differences of opinion and strategy. Even though Occhetto still draws a lot of legitimacy from the courage he showed in transforming the party in a timely fashion, he remains on trial at all times.

Recent events have considerably strengthened Occhetto's personal position and that of the PDS. For one thing, the PDS seems to be the only nationally organized party, even though it remains rather weak in several areas of southern Italy. According to most opinion polls, it has become the largest party in Italy today. About 20 percent of the voters would support it. The PDS's ranking is due fundamentally to the decline of the Christian Democrats, who have lost so many possible votes as to drop below the PDS. What counts more, however, is that recent elections have shown that the PDS has overcome some of the classic Communist problems. The most important of these was that the PCI had been unable to attract political partners in addition to the Socialists. Therefore, if and when the Socialists wanted to play power games—and this was predominantly the case throughout the 1980s because of blatant and deliberate anti-Communist policies by Craxi—the PCI would remain isolated and excluded from power even at the local level. The June and December 1993 mayoral elections in several important cities seem to indicate that a new political season is blossoming for the PDS. The party has constructed and participated in different political coalitions. Some of these have combined the old and new left—i.e., Rifondazione Comunista and Network. Some coalitions were created around a modern center, including the Republicans and the Popolari, as well as the nonfundamentalist Greens. In other cases, even when the PDS was left alone, its popular candidates proved to possess strong enough vote-attracting capabilities to be elected mayors. (It is interesting to note that left-center coalitions were by far more successful than purely leftist coalitions. The obvious implication is that the PDS was often asked to choose between Rifondazione—which for many PDS members and leaders means the old comrades—and the Popolari—for some PDS members and leaders just polished conservatives.) Electoral success has temporarily strengthened Occhetto's position. It has also posed some unavoidable strategic problems for the PDS. Among these are two new developments on the Italian left. The first is the decline of the PSI. The second is the reform of the electoral laws, accompanied by the emerging imperative for the creation of electoral and political coalitions.

THE ASHES OF THE PSI

The once very powerful PSI is now in shambles. Its very survival as a national political organization seems in doubt.[3] Its leader (and former prime minister) Bettino Craxi is under investigation by the judiciary for corruption and several violations of the law on the public financing of political parties. At the beginning of 1993, Craxi was obliged to resign as party secretary after an excessively prolonged tug-of-war which practically ruined any chance of a smooth succession. Indeed the succession struggle has been so rough that the PSI has had two secretaries in less than six months (January–June 1993). Both secretaries had previously held top offices in the trade union movement. This fact alone suggests that there was no line of succession within the PSI since Craxi was suspicious of any potential challenger. It also indicates that it was impossible for party members to reach an agreement on a party politician. The first of the new secretaries, Giorgio Benvenuto, was ousted in a stormy and confused meeting. He has since left the PSI and created his own group, Socialist Renaissance. The present secretary, Ottaviano Del Turco, is trying to distance himself and the party from an embarrassing past without arousing too much dissent within the ranks of Craxi's die-hard supporters. There are still many Craxiani allied with parliamentarians and local officeholders who want to survive politically and not be purged by the relatively new leaders. For the time being, Del Turco cannot afford to purge. Hence he simply hopes that those who are indicted will voluntarily stand aside. In the meantime, former prime minister Giuliano Amato is apparently playing his own political game, waiting in the wings and hoping to create a sort of center-left pole of attraction.

In spite of a sizable flow of kickbacks, the PSI is bankrupt. Most important leaders and former ministers—among them Gianni De Michelis and Claudio Martelli, but the list is extremely long—are under investigation. At this point, their political careers appear all but terminated. Finally, all 1993 electoral results proved extremely disappointing for the party. It was almost impossible for the PSI to recruit attractive mayoral candidates. With a few exceptions in minor areas, none of the PSI candidates was elected. Socialist representatives have all but disappeared from important city councils. In Milan, the cradle of Italian socialism and Craxi's stronghold, a city whose mayors were Socialists for most of the postwar period, the PSI struggles just to remain afloat. In the elections of April 1992, the PSI polled 14.5 percent of the votes. Most surveys indicate that no more than 4 percent of Italians are now inclined to vote for the PSI. Since the new electoral law for the House of Deputies requests that parties overcome a 4 percent national threshold in order to obtain parliamentary representation, the PSI is running a serious risk of being absent from the next parliament.

It is not simple to explain in a few words how the patrimony of votes and power accumulated by the PSI in fifteen rambling years could be destroyed in less than one. Nonetheless, one convincing explanation can be offered. When Craxi took over the PSI in 1978 many Italians wanted to go beyond the skewed bipolar competition between the DC, the party which was always in power, and the PCI, the party always in the opposition. The DC looked, and was, corrupt; the PCI looked, and was, sterile. The Socialists seemed to offer a way out: modern and Western-oriented, less ideological and technocratic. They challenged the way of governing of the Christian Democrats—i.e., incessant mediations and *decisionismo,* a sharp decisionmaking style. The PSI challenged the PCI bureaucracy, intent on protecting its accumulated political resources and preserving its veto power—for instance, on labor issues—by offering the image of a deregulated socioeconomic system. It is difficult to estimate how many Italian voters actually believed the promises and propaganda of the PSI and Craxi, but very slowly a number of them shifted their vote toward the PSI.

In too many local areas, however, Socialist politicians represented the past. Especially in the South, the growth of the party was not a product of modernity, but of a traditional patronage system managed with arrogance and brutality. Here old party notables and new career politicians joined forces to amass political power. It was especially in the South that the PSI made some spectacular electoral gains. It is now clear that the electoral and political growth of Craxi's party was extraordinarily artificial. It was not based on a carefully cultivated electoral realignment. It was not constructed on a sound organizational effort. It was not buttressed by a redefinition of the Socialist political culture. The nineteenth-century French thinker Pierre Proudhon could not be used to replace Karl Marx nor to provide answers for the restructuring of the welfare state and the rethinking of Keynesian economics. The growth of the PSI proved in practice to be essentially due to an unscrupulous utilization of governmental power. Socialist supporters, friends, and sponsors were rewarded and made rich with public money.[4] Socialist electoral and political gains were the products of blackmail: "More power to the Socialists or political and governmental instability" militated against all governmental partners—specifically the Christian Democrats. It is true that some Christian Democrats were all too inclined to accept this blackmail, provided they could retain their own considerable power. They were definitely not minor, meek, and inexperienced partners in the patronage and spoils system. Socialist success was also the product of blackmail against entrepreneurs, who were obliged to pay kickbacks in order to work for the state and local governments.

There was a shared political motivation among the various groups who willy-nilly supported the PSI. It was that only the Socialists (and the Christian Democrats) could prevent the coming to power of the Communists. Once the Berlin Wall collapsed and the Communists completely changed their party, international affiliation, and domestic policies, this overriding anti-Communist motivation was no longer tenable. Almost every major political and socioeconomic actor felt liberated. The reactions were such that the political construction erected by the Socialists fell like a sand castle.

Day after day the political and legal irresponsibilities of the Socialists are being uncovered. They will embarrass the present and future of the party and negatively affect all party and parliamentary careers. Moreover, there was no fallback strategy since Craxi had destroyed all alternatives and eliminated all opponents. His ruthless domination of the party machine had rewarded only his faithful yes-men and relatives. (His son was the secretary of the Socialist Federation of Milan, and his brother-in-law had been the mayor of Milan.) Understandably, this style of leadership has created many internal and external enemies. This explains why the party collapsed so quickly and why the new secretary had to come from the outside. By all standards it will be extremely difficult to reconstruct a viable Socialist political organization, especially in times of political acceleration. Obviously the plummeting of the PSI and its eventual disappearance from the Italian party landscape constitute very serious damage to the image and overall strength of the Italian left. If a progressive left is not socialist, what can be its political and cultural underpinnings?

ELECTORAL REFORMS AND POLITICAL OPPORTUNITIES

The proportional electoral system utilized throughout the postwar period has been profoundly reformed. In practice, it has been essentially eliminated. Thanks to two electoral referendums, held in 1991 and 1992—which the Socialists adamantly opposed—the Italian parliament has been compelled to approve new laws for city councils, the Senate, and the House of Deputies. These rather complex laws are analyzed in detail elsewhere in this volume. Suffice it to say that all the mayors of cities with more than 15,000 inhabitants are to be elected through a runoff majority system. The winning candidate will enjoy a secure and stable majority since he/she carries 60 percent of the seats in the city council.

This has meant that the usually fragmented Italian left has been obliged to construct political coalitions, identify winning candidates—rarely purely party candidates—and offer common platforms. In some important instances, these coalitions and the winning candidates have been the products of collaboration on the left—specifically between the PDS and some centrist, moderately progressive forces, such as the Republicans and the Popolari, under the aegis of the above-mentioned umbrella organization, Democratic Alliance.

Moreover, the laws for both the Senate and the House—that is, first-past-the-post systems with limited proportional elements to be applied in single-member constituencies—will impose changes on the left, its leaders, and its actual and potential voters. To be more precise, party organizations may retain some control over channeling the vote. Party activists may still be significant in turning out the vote. But party symbols and labels will have to be blurred so that support for candidates can come from several organizations. The decisive factor will in all likelihood be the candidate him/herself. Obviously these electoral changes are bound to impinge upon the Italian left in ways which cannot be precisely identified but only tentatively explored.

To put it in American political science jargon, this transformation amounts to the emergence of candidate-centered politics. In a country where party politics has been dominant and oppressive for more than forty years, this transformation amounts almost to a revolution. For the Italian left it is a frontal challenge. Always jealous of its differentiated traditions and always relying on its competing organizations, the Italian left will now be obliged to coalesce. The alternative may not necessarily be to perish. It will certainly be to continue losing national elections. Since the new electoral systems encourage a sort of bipolar competition in single-member constituencies, a political space is created for a U.S.-type liberal left capable of reaching out to all the progressives in every constituency. This would be a sea change for the Italian left. Understandably, the very awareness that this change is in the making has produced tensions and controversies within the classic Socialist-Marxist left and among those who challenge the old power system, such as Mario Segni and Democratic Alliance.

The decision to create alliances (and which alliances) and to coalesce around candidates (and whose candidates) is particularly difficult for the PDS. For different reasons, Rifondazione Comunista and Network will have serious problems in joining any alliance they cannot lead or in blurring—even more, jettisoning—their strong identities. After all, Rifondazione strives to characterize itself as a true Communist party, the only party protecting and representing the interests of the working class, the real and adamant social opposition. Nonetheless, everybody in Italy is familiar with what has traditionally been Communist flexibility. No doubt Rifondazione will make no exception to this flexibility when it comes to the need to join alliances in order to survive as a party and to reacquire access to parliament. Network is a rather fundamentalist antiparty movement. It expresses a sort of moralist rejection of the old political system. No doubt it will have serious problems finding electoral allies. Due to the terms of the new electoral system, for both Rifondazione and Network the search for allies has quickly become a matter of sheer survival. This awareness has pushed them to looking for an acceptable relationship, first with each other, next within the left at large, fundamentally with the PDS.

The choice of electoral and political alliances is a somewhat more complicated matter for the PDS. Any clear-cut decision will prove tougher than it seems. After all, the PDS is the best placed party, politically and electorally, of the left. At this point, it can reasonably hope to inherit the votes of minor left-wing groups and even of many Socialists. It is the only party of the left which can convincingly present itself as a governmental alternative. Still, it does not have enough political strength by itself to win seats in many single-member constituencies outside its remaining strongholds in the Red Belt regions: Emilia Romagna, Tuscany, Umbria, Marches, and the recent addition of Upper Latium. This sober realization explains why there are two conflicting positions within the PDS. On the one hand, there are those who believe that the PDS cannot renounce nor dilute its newly shaped identity. It should not run the risk of delivering votes to the Rifondazione Comunista cousins, ready to exploit any shift to the center by the PDS and revive their "Communist purity" propaganda and appeal. According to this view, the PDS alone should decide if, when, where, and with whom to create electoral coalitions. It ought not to tie its hands prematurely to just one option, even less to a centrist option. On the other hand, there are those who argue that for the PDS to play the new electoral game without alliances amounts almost to committing suicide. In any case, it is as risky as playing roulette. According to this view, the PDS should exploit the favorable circumstances and behave magnanimously to create left-center coalitions and participate in them even when (for instance) mayoral and parliamentary candidates do not come from its ranks. Only coalitions of this kind—including the Republicans, the Social Christians, the Greens, and those few acceptable and clean Socialists—are likely to be credible as governmental alternatives in the eyes of the electorate. Only coalitions of this kind are truly national and therefore may challenge the Lega even in the North. Exclusively coalitions of this kind may win a majority of seats in the next parliament. The reasoning is that from now on Italian politics will be coalition politics, and the PDS has the splendid opportunity to build coalitions from a position of strength. Coalition politics will require a restructuring, a redefinition, a streamlining of its party organization. Candidate-centered politics will challenge the entrenched party bureaucracy because it is clear that a potentially winning candidate must go beyond the classic borders of purely partisan appeals. Therefore, in most areas the winning candidate cannot be a party candidate. This painful awareness explains the resistance of the already widely trimmed, though still powerful, party apparatus. For most in the PDS apparatus, candidate-centered politics coupled with coalition politics effectively represents the end of their political ambitions and career projects. It may seem exaggerated to give so much attention to these "personal" elements. However, the real stuff of Italian postwar politics as a whole has been woven by career expectations and constructions. A true and inflated stratum of "professional" politicians developed in Italy, thanks also to the existence of mass parties and a proportional electoral representation system. The abandonment of proportional representation and the decline of mass parties have opened up the possibilities for a profound and positive transformation of Italian politics. On the left, the resistance to this transformation is made up of a complex mixture of partisan commitments and subcultural identities, personal ambitions, and political projects. The mixture must be quickly reshuffled in order to become more appealing and more effective.

PROGRAMMATIC RENEWAL—OR THE LACK OF IT

Institutional and political changes design the framework within which the Italian left will be obliged to work from now on. In order to attract the number of voters indispensable to produce a governmental mandate, the left must show itself capable of offering those voters well-formulated programs and viable solutions, attractive can didates, and credible governing teams. The Italian Communist Party has always committed some of its best energies to writing programs. At best the results have been mixed, often disappointing, though perhaps the proof of the program is in the making. On the other hand, the practice of local Communist governments has been comparatively successful.

The latest product of the PDS is a dense, intelligent, comprehensive, ambitious volume drafted by a highly respected political economist.[5] Because the Democratic Communists rejected the very idea that the PDS should propose a governmental program, only the political introduction to the volume was ever discussed. It is not clear whether it was approved or not. In any case, the entire program was soon put aside and forgotten. The fact is that once more PDS internal disunity has deprived the party, and the left, of a useful instrument through which to counter the few simple and simplistic ideas being put forth by the Lega Nord. It is well known that the entire European left is struggling to cope with its inability to go beyond its historical successes: Keynesian steering of the economy and the welfare state.[6] The Italian left is no exception. Worse still, both the Italian variant of Keynesianism and the Italian type of welfare state were imbued by the Christian Democrats with significant patronage and clientelist elements. Before creating any new Keynesian project or welfare program, the Italian left will be obliged to get rid of all the degenerations of the past. This is why the PDS has decided to emphasize two major reforms: the fiscal system and regional governments. (Again, we cannot provide the details of these reforms here.) The slogan sounds old and revered: "No taxation without representation." Intuitively, one cannot relaunch the economy and above all create more jobs if the state is unable to extract more resources in a fairer way from its citizens. One cannot reform the state and its bureaucratic apparatus unless regional governments are given more power, precise functions, and autonomous resources in many fields, uppermost among them in the health system.

Obviously there is much more to the legislative program of the PDS than just these two extremely important reforms. However, the sad fact is that neither the PDS nor the Italian left as a whole have been capable of popularizing their proposals in these two fields. They have formulated programs and indicated solutions. Their most aggressive competitor at this point, the Lega Nord, has fabricated slogans and catchwords. However, since the Lega claims to be what is new in Italian politics, its mobilizing power looks greater. The Lega credibly portrays itself as never having been involved in running the political system or exercising governmental and parliamentary power. Therefore, it can deny any responsibility for the Italian socioeconomic and political crisis. Topped with a smashing criticism of *partitocrazia* and the party system as such, Lega slogans and protests appear to carry the day, at least in large northern areas. Of course, the Lega may just represent the last embodiment of Italian *trasformismo*. That is, it might be willing or perhaps obliged to trade its parliamentary votes for some selfish socioeconomic gains and exemptions. Still, the Lega presents itself as the major challenge to a slightly growing left, particularly since the left has not yet been able to present itself as a cohesive and programmatic alternative to the past.

All this said, the Italian left has never been so close to the governmental threshold. However, it will successfully make the transition from the opposition to the government only if and when it shows the ability to transform and improve itself in order to transform and improve the political system. It must solve cultural and organizational problems. It must reach a satisfactory synthesis between the honorable Italian tradition of mass participation and the U.S.-style political imperative of candidate-centered politics. Otherwise, it will remain a confused ensemble of fragments in search of an unlikely unity. And its electoral and political victory will be even more unlikely.

NOTES

1. I have analyzed the fragmentation of the left in "The Italian Socialist Party: An Irreversible Decline?" in *Italy at the Polls: The Parliamentary Elections of 1976*, ed. Howard R. Penniman (Washington, D.C.: American Enterprise Institute, 1977), pp. 183–227.

2. The two best analyses of this transformation are provided by Stephen Hellman, "The Difficult Birth of the Democratic Party of the Left," in *Italian Politics: A Review*, ed. Stephen Hellman and Gianfranco Pasquino (London: Frances Pinter, 1992), vol. 7, pp. 68–86, and Piero Ignazi, *Dal PCI al PDS* (Bologna: Il Mulino, 1992).

3. An excellent up-to-date account is offered by Martin Rhodes, "The 'Long Wave' Subsides: The PSI and the Demise of Craxismo," in *Italian Politics: A*

Review, ed. Stephen Hellman and Gianfranco Pasquino (London: Frances Pinter, 1993), vol. 8, pp. 66–82.

4. I am pleased to have identified and analyzed all these elements a long time ago: "Modernity and Reforms: The PSI between Political Entrepreneurs and Gamblers," *West European Politics* 9 (1986): 120–41.

5. Michele Salvati, *L'Italia verso il duemila: Analisi e proposte per un programma di legislatura* (Rome: Editori Riuniti, 1992).

6. A comprehensive overview of the changes in party programs of the left in Europe can be found in Richard Gillespie and William A. Paterson, *Rethinking Social Democracy in Western Europe* (London: Frank Cass, 1993).

QUESTIONS AND ANSWERS ABOUT THE LEGA NORD

Renato Mannheimer

The Lega Nord is one of the principal protagonists of the Italian political system today and plays a significant role in political debate at the national level. Its importance has grown enormously recently due to electoral results. The Lega gained 0.5 percent of the national vote in 1987 and 8.7 percent in 1992. No other party made such progress. Indeed the success of the Lega corresponded to a decline among most of the traditional political forces. The Lega was fourth in electoral popularity—after the Christian Democratic Party (DC), the Democratic Party of the Left (PDS), and the Italian Socialist Party (PSI). Unlike other forces, the Lega's electorate is concentrated almost exclusively in northern Italy, where it won more than 20 percent of the vote. Its popularity is greatest in Lombardy, where one out of every five voters supports it, and it attained almost 30 percent of the vote in Como, Sondrio, and Varese.

The increasing popularity of the Lega has been confirmed by the results of subsequent local elections in several areas of the North. In the municipal elections of Monza in December 1992, for example, the Lega had 32 percent of the vote—up from 20.4 percent in April 1992. In the elections in Varese, held at the same time, the Lega obtained 37 percent—compared with 30 percent just a few months before. In Varese the Lega has formed the local government and has appointed a mayor. In Milan in June 1993, the Lega won approximately 40 percent of the vote and here too named the mayor.

This increase in Lega approval has manifested itself in a territorial expansion that we could describe as an oil stain. The last local elections, in December 1993, appeared to signal a lull in this expansion: the Lega was not able to win a coalition for the mayors in Genoa, Trieste, or Venice. Nonetheless, the Lega retains a high level of popularity in the traditional strongholds and holds great importance for the current political scene. Its characteristics are thus worth knowing. To this end I chose to answer a series of questions, almost always the same, that I am asked by friends and foreign colleagues concerning the Lega phenomenon.

1. Which most general medium- and short-term social and political processes have framed the electoral success of the Lega Nord?

The cause of the earthquake that led to an extensive redistribution of the electoral vote among the parties lay in the expansion of the "dissimilar vote." As defined by M. Caciagli and A. Spreafico, this means choices directed toward nontraditional political forces.[1]

The increase in the dissimilar vote emerged in two ways. First, the percentage of votes for nontraditional parties almost tripled, from 5.7 percent in 1987 to 14.5 percent in 1992. Second, there was an increase in the number of votes due to the electors' growing discontent. The number of nontraditional parties increased; dozens of new players presented themselves on the electoral market, profiting from the existence of an ever-increasing number of votes from those desiring something different from the usual.

This trend has been defined by many long-term factors, including a decline in the traditional political subcultures—which for some time characterized and determined electoral choices in Italy—and in general a certain decrease of salience of the left-right dimension, on which some of the traditional parties principally based their vote choice. Surveys show that during the last ten years a process of estrangement from—and at times contempt for—the traditional parties has been added to this long-term phenomenon. All this brought on a growing detachment on the part of the voter from the political forces for which s/he usually voted.

Voters began to consider the possibility of casting their ballots for different political forces. The so-called potential electoral mobility progressively increased, thereby increasing interest in political events. In particular, as highlighted above, this voter "availability" favored all new forces presenting themselves in the electoral arena. For a time, whichever force succeeded in assuming an image of novelty (the Hunters' Party, the Motorists' Party, etc.) succeeded in obtaining a certain number of votes.

It is important to note that these phenomena caused some of the most significant changes in the characterisctics of the Italian electoral system. In particular, both actual and potential mobility increased dramatically. A more intense competition developed among parties (which increasingly could not count on their traditional backers), and the role of political communication became much more important than in the past.[2]

2. *Among all these new forces, why was it the Lega that knew how to garner so many more votes than the others?*

The reasons for the Lega's enormous electoral success are the topic of a heated debate among scholars and observers. In short, the principal emerging interpretations are the following:

a) The Lega knew how to appropriate and exploit feelings of membership and territorial identity that during this period reemerged in growing portions of the population, partly as a result of the fall in importance of party memberships and traditional subcultures. The erosion of the Communist and particularly the Catholic subcultures in some ways permitted the reemergence of a feeling of identity and pride of membership in the northern Italian region, the political importance of which was therefore dramatically increased and largely evoked and underlined by the Lega.

b) The Lega represents a distancing from and a protest against the traditional parties. Since its beginnings, it has sought to present itself primarily as the antithesis of traditional parties, and central to its stance was the image of being different from them. The difference was demonstrated both in content and in its sometimes vulgar and unrefined language. However, it was precisely this commonness that appealed to a good part of the electorate as being nearer to itself and different from "traditional politicalese." This permitted the Lega not only to gather votes limited to specific issues, but also to profit from the more general sentiment of dissatisfaction with the traditional parties. In brief, the Lega knew how to profit from the population's preexisting sentiments, and on these it built its fortune. The appeal to territorial identity is in a way instrumental to the desire to send, through votes, a strong signal of detachment from the parties.

c) The Lega is a product of the process of secularization of society as a whole. Thus above all it has attracted the most lay votes already in the popular parties and of the DC in particular.

Many more less important interpretations may be added to these three. It is rare that a voter chooses the Lega for only one of these reasons. They are in reality interlinked, with varying relative importance. It is precisely the relative importance of each that scholars debate. I believe that the most important by far is the second—i.e., the Lega as protest formation. As noted, in the Milan June 1993 mayoral elections, approximately 40 percent of the electorate voted for the Lega. In this case, this was a choice based on the absence of other alternatives more than a decision in favor of the program of the Lega. In recent weeks, the Lega's leader, Umberto Bossi, has underlined, in both the content and language of his statements, the different nature of the Lega.

In brief, despite the Lega's being considered a territorial party from the point of view of the distribution of its voters, it is not territorial if one considers its proposals, which are only in part tied to the local dimension and which certainly do not constitute the fundamental reason for its voters' support or for its electoral success.[3]

3. Who are the Lega voters?

The Lega had its first successes among voters in the "white" zones of Lombardy, in medium and medium-small cities—predominately male, with mid- to low-level educations, middle-aged, self-employed (shopkeepers, artisans), or employed (blue- and low- or mid-level white-collar workers). Later the Lega progressively broadened its base to include a public in all social and economic classes.

Today the Lega's characterizing trait is its extraordinarily composite structure. That is (as was the case for a long time with the traditional popular parties), the Lega's electorate covers all social strata, even though they are motivated by different reasons and interests. The middle classes with mid-level educations still predominate, though much less so than before. Age is an important characteristic of Lega supporters. Most striking (confirming a trend seen, for example, in an October 1991 poll) is increased support from young people (both certain and potential) and the number of younger voters continues to increase. According to a November 1992 survey in Milan, more than 30 percent of the city's under-twenty-four age group votes Lega, while nationally 15 percent does.

As for the party provenance of its voters, it has been shown that the Lega owes its initial successes largely to the ex-DC electorate. However, from the beginning, and still more so today, the Lega has garnered votes from other parties as well, including those of the left. One notes a continuing prevalence of ex-DC supporters, but much less than earlier.

4. Is the Lega a right-wing party?

The notion that the Lega is a phenomenon of the right is quite widespread. Journalists, commentators, and politicians frequently point to the Lega as the "new right." Is this definition correct? An initial response may be based on an interpretation of the political space in terms of the traditional left-right opposition. Many Lega leaders claim that it stands outside the classical left-wing conflict, which it considers outdated and which it rejects. More recently, Umberto Bossi stated that right and left coexist within the Lega and that at the time when the movement must govern, these two wings would separate.

How are things in reality? Is the Lega right wing, left wing, centrist, or what? The answer is relatively complex, in as much as it requires defining the subject to which we refer (the Lega in general? its leadership or a part of it? the voters? the sympathizers?) and also what we use to assess left or right (the subjective perception of the *leghisti* or the non-leghisti? the type of political choices [but which ones]? the judgments of commentators?).

Let's begin by considering the opinion of Lega voters. In three different surveys—one conducted in October 1991 in northern Italian regions and two in 1993 in Milan—voters were asked to indicate their political positions along a left–right continuum.[4]

A first interesting fact is the percentage of those polled who refused to place themselves on the left-right continuum. However, our data show that the rejection of the conventional political space is not as common among Lega party supporters as such declarations would have us believe. When asked to pinpoint their position between right and left, the percentage of "certain" Lega voters who were able to do so without difficulty was only slightly lower than that of other party supporters. Instead a failure to pinpoint their position is quite common among voters who refuse to indicate their party of choice (34 percent). This is due to the widespread tendency in Italy not to declare one's political preference. This behavior, found in about 30–40 percent of those polled, does not seem more common among the Lega voters than among those of other parties.

In the second of the studies here examined, we note a general increase in the percentage of those polled who refuse to locate themselves in the left-right dimension. This trend is largely due to the diffusion of the choice of not placing oneself in the electorates of the PDS and, still more, of the Verdi (Green Party) and the Lega. It is important to note that the latter two political forces characterize themselves and are frequently considered by scholars as outside of the left-right dimension. We must specify that the results of the three surveys are not completely comparable for various reasons.[5] Moreover, what was demonstrated for the electorate as a whole and for the Lega and Verdi gives weight to the hypothesis that in general, but more specifically among the voters of these two political forces, the left-right dimension appears in some way less an instrument of expressing voter orientation.[6]

This does not mean, however, that the term "left" is not used to orient oneself when casting a ballot. To the contrary, various studies have shown that, especially in the current magmatic situation or in the absence of other terms for judging candidates, the left-right continuum still represents one of the most used instruments in electoral choice. Yet even if it is employed in lieu of knowledge of other elements of the competition's platform, in and of itself this criterion appears increasingly less suited to representing the voters' opinions and political orientation. But the fact remains that the majority of those polled, including leghisti, position themselves in the left-right continuum. We can therefore examine the prevailing orientations of the Lega electorate in regard to this dimension. The results are shown in Figures 1–3. In these figures the "political space" is subdivided from the extreme left to the extreme right. On average, the Lega electorate positions itself roughly around the center of the left-right continuum. In this respect Lega supporters seem to bear most resemblance to the Christian Democrats, who also position themselves around the center.

In 1991 a similarity appeared in the central positioning of Lega and Greens voters. In both 1993 studies, however, the Greens electorate shifted much more to the left. This was most likely due to the different territorial point of reference and the type of alliance in the competition for the direct election of the mayor of Milan. Moreover, to a large extent the Lega-Greens similarity is more apparent than real. While the members of both parties on average consider themselves at the same point on the line, the distribution within the electorates of the two parties is very different. While the large majority of the DC electorate is located at the center (in 1991, 67 percent considered themselves in one of the two central positions, 53 percent in May 1993, and 79 percent in November 1993), Lega voters (and Greens voters in 1991) are much more widespread. The variety in the distribution is much higher than for the DC: only 33 percent of the leghisti in 1991, 23 percent in May 1993, and 20 percent in November 1993 position themselves in the center. While both parties have experienced a decrease over time of supporters who place themselves in the center and a major differentiation within self-positioning has taken place, for the Lega this phenomenon is decidedly more accentuated. From this point of view, there is no doubt that the Lega electorate presents characteristics different from those of the DC in spite of the similarity of self-positioning by the voters of these two political forces.

In sum, the Lega's structure is composite and far from homogeneous. This will be confirmed below.[7] However, analyzing the temporal trend of the data, one notes a progressive increase in the percentage of Lega voters considering themselves center-right. Within the scenario of a rather varied composition, the Lega electorate tends increasingly to this area of the political picture.

As noted, the subjective self-positioning of the voters is only one among the many methods of measuring the traits of a political force. It would be worthwhile to try to define positioning by considering some elements of content—e.g., issues of the Lega discourse on autonomist themes from both a fiscal and political-administrative viewpoint and questions on extracommunity immigration in Italy. (It does not interest us here to establish whether these statements truly and correctly represent the movement's political line; it suffices that they are shared by the public leghista.) Indeed the degree of agreement with statements in these areas is much higher among the leghisti than among the voters of other parties. Thus while less than half (43 percent) of a complete sample group is "very much in agreement" with the statement that "The majority of tax money that we pay in our region should be used here," almost two-thirds (63.6 percent) of Lega voters strongly agree. Furthermore, 19 percent of the complete sample states that it agrees that "It is better that the North be separate from both central and southern Italy." Among

Figure 1

Distribution of Lega, DC, and Greens Electorates along Left-Right Continuum: Northern Italian Regions, October 1991

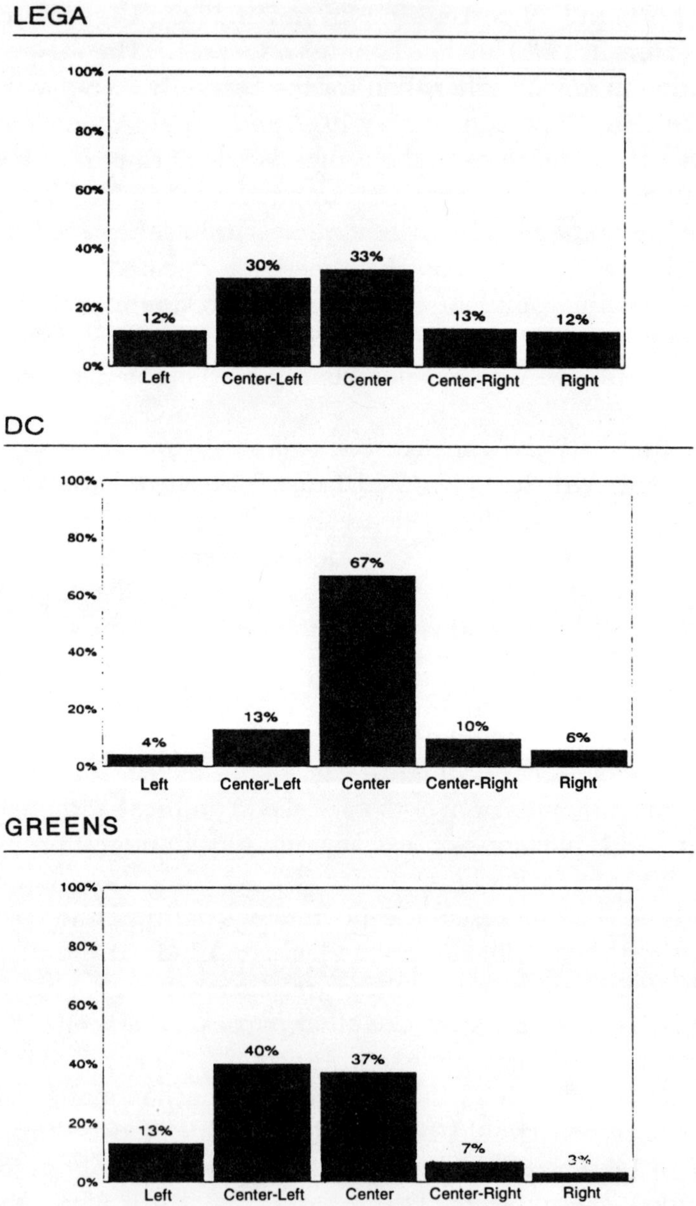

Figure 2

Distribution of Lega and DC Electorates along Left-Right Continuum: Milan, May 1993

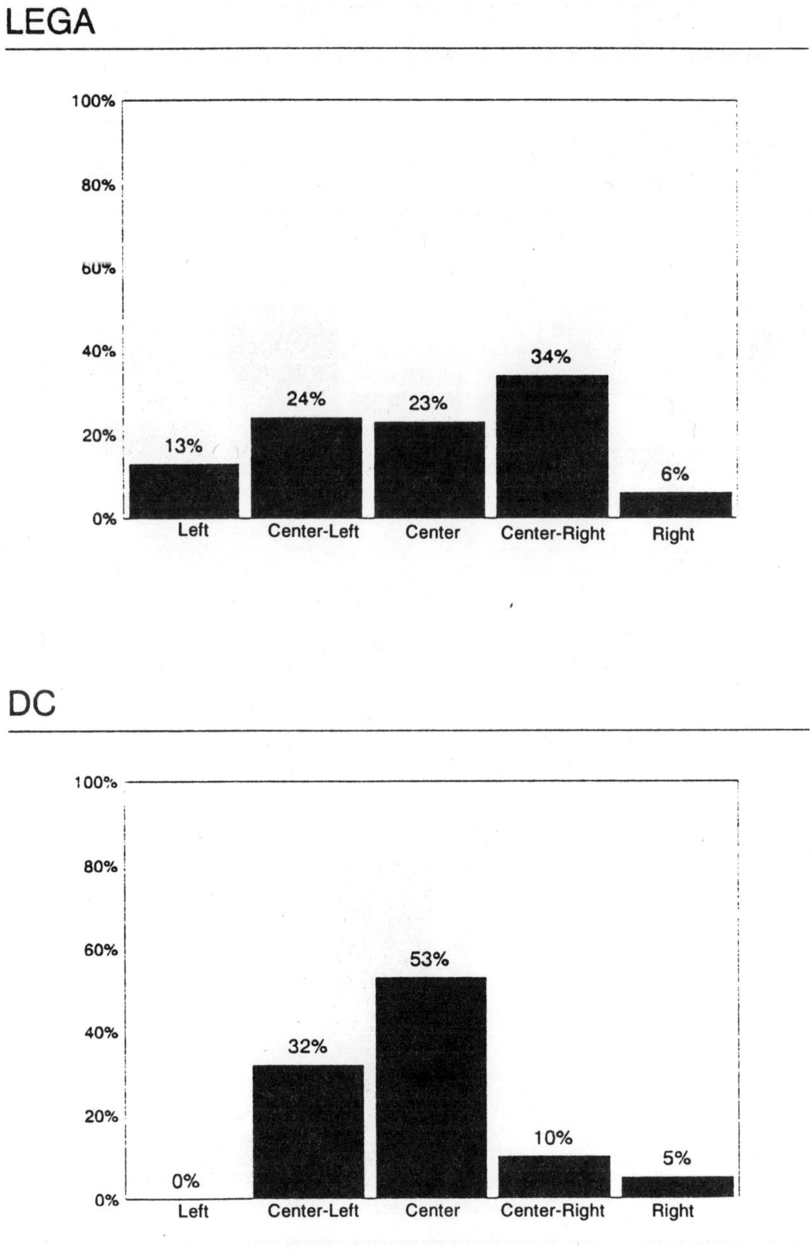

Figure 3

Distribution of Lega and DC Electorates along Left-Right Continuum: Milan, November 1993

LEGA

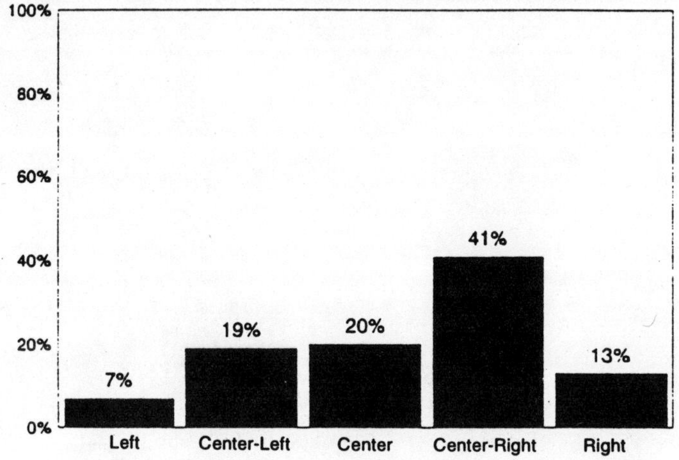

DC

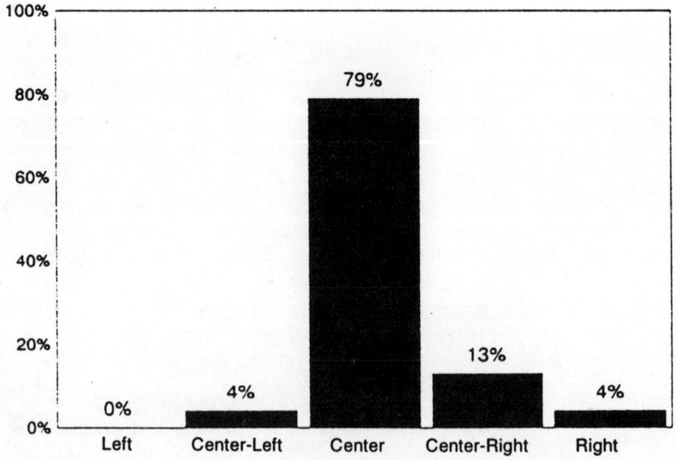

leghisti this percentage rises to one-third (34 percent). Finally, while less than one-fourth of the general sample (22 percent) agrees that "So many immigrants are a problem," more than one-third (34 percent) of the leghisti agree with this statement. In some measure, therefore, these statements demonstrate some of the opinions that characterize Lega voters and distinguish them from the rest of the population.

Are these right-wing convictions? It is difficult to say definitively considering them in and of themselves. As noted, the content of the left-right opposition has progressively extended from economic themes (from which it derived) to many other social themes. Regarding the latter, it is not always easy to understand the criterion defining one choice as left wing and another as right wing. From the viewpoint of people's beliefs, it would seem that the three Lega statements mentioned above are largely shared by a public that considers itself right wing. In fact, in an examination of the level of approval of these statements among those who position themselves to the left, center, and right, approval appears to be much higher among those who consider themselves right wing.

Can we then say, consistent with the trend demonstrated by the subjective self-positioning noted above, that the leghisti are right wing? Only to a certain measure. The fact that these statements are shared by more than the mean of all leghisti, independently from their self-positioning on the left-right continuum, would suggest a specifically "leghist" connotation for these beliefs. In brief, there are (many) leghisti who, although considering themselves left wing or (more frequently) of the center, adhere to beliefs that are (also) shared by the majority of those who, leghisti or not, consider themselves right wing. Consequently, even if among all the leghisti the three statements are shared by a higher percentage than among the rest of the electorate, they appear still more popular in the subgroup of leghisti considering themselves to be right wing. In some way, then, these statements reveal a double connotation: right wing in as much as they are approved in general by those who consider themselves right wing, leghist in as much as they are approved by the leghisti, regardless of how they define themselves.[8] It could thus be hypothesized that the opinions that distinguish the leghisti position them in some measure in a dimension all their own that is only partially covered by the left-right opposition.

5. Is the Lega a racist or intolerant party?

In the first years of its existence, the Lega certainly championed sentiments of intolerance, especially toward southern or foreign immigrants. It seems improbable that these were the principal reasons for party members' support, but it is certain that these sentiments were frequently stressed by Lega leaders. Furthermore, various analyses and polls have shown that among the more militant leghisti, a strong sentiment of intolerance was present in general, not only toward immigrants, but also toward anyone different. However, some studies demonstrate that within the Lega's general core of party members this intolerance is much less present. Moreover, Lega leaders soon realized that these aspects were counterproductive to their movement. Consequently, intolerant tones have recently been sharply attenuated, so that today they are much rarer than earlier, although they have not completely disappeared .

The closed attitude toward "what is different" within the Lega's electorate is still a much discussed matter. Some, especially outside observers, consider that even today the Lega is characterized by a certain degree of social intolerance. Others, particularly Lega leaders, strongly deny the existence of such phenomena. So it is worth taking a closer look, if only briefly, at survey responses on this topic.

The people interviewed were given two sets of questions about the degree of trust or "irritation" they felt toward four social groups (among them politicians and southern Italians). The electorate is subdivided according to attitudes toward the Lega. There are three categories: the "certain" voters intend to vote for the Lega in the next elections; the "potential" voters have no other party allegiances and will consider the Lega when deciding for whom to vote; and the "others" do not vote for or consider the Lega and therefore are outside the market.

The responses to the questions on trust and irritation are basically the same not only for certain and potential Lega supporters, but also for the others interviewed. The degree of trust or irritation is similar through the whole sample, without differentiating the Lega electorate from the others. For example, politicians inspire the least trust from all those interviewed. This has now become almost commonplace, a view shared by voters of every party, though to a different extent.

The intensity of these feelings is, however, distinct. For all four social groups—and much more toward politicians and southern Italians—irritation increases from the others to potential Lega supporters and reaches its highest level among the certain supporters. In other words, Lega supporters are less trusting than the rest of those interviewed toward all four categories—even toward the inhabitants of their own region (though to a hardly perceptible degree). In sum, an attitude of generalized closure develops as the intensity of support for the Lega increases. The percentage of respondents who declare "much" or "some" trust in at least three (or all four) of the groups sharply decreases from others to potential to certain voters.

In regard to "irritation," the values of the Lega supporters are identical to those of the others except toward Sicilians and (to a much lesser degree) blacks. But here again the Lega voters seem more closed. The percentage of respondents who feel "much or some irritation" toward a significant proportion of the groups indicated is generally quite low but still increases (though to a small extent) as support for the Lega gets stronger.

Thus Lega supporters would seem to be more closed toward "different." However, although this distinction exists, it is less important and less statistically significant than other elements in differentiating Lega supporters from other voters. In a discriminating analysis, Lega electoral opinion was set as a dependent variable and various attributes, attitudes, and orientations considered so far as independent variables, allowing us to more specifically examine the impressions that have emerged in the preceding pages.

The analysis once more showed the importance of the trend toward territorial autonomy, also from the economic-fiscal factor. This dimension was found to be the most efficient in distinguishing the voters of the Lega from those of other parties. The next factor in order of importance was mistrust of politicians and southern Italians and the role of youth. A sense of regional belonging was much more limited. On the whole, the analysis allowed 78 percent of the Lega voters to be classified, which is 28 points better than a random assignment. Of course, there are numerous errors, mainly due to the complex nature of the Lega electorate.

It should be noted that while we have been able to trace an average profile of the Lega voter (a relatively young individual, of average cultural position, mainly from the independent middle class, with little interest in politics, rather closed toward the "different" and the exterior in general, and sensitive to autonomous themes [especially of a fiscal nature]), the multiplicity of the features and attitudes emerging suggests that a much more varied picture lies behind this description. As already pointed out, the choice of the Lega vote does not depend on a single characteristic, but it is determined by the simultaneous presence of a series of attitudes, characteristics, and orientations, some of which we have tried to describe here.

6. What is the future of the Lega?

Various "cores" exist within the Lega, differing in their socioeconomic components and in some of their attitudes and opinions, but to a large extent united in their negative attitude toward the traditional parties. This composite nature of the Lega electorate was already highlighted in other analyses of even a few years ago. However, it is certain that the inner division and differentiation of the Lega's electorate has gradually intensified with the extension of the Lega's electoral base.

And what of the future? It is well known that a composite electorate is common to almost all other mass parties. Each of these has or has had a "bonding factor" (religious, ideological, or other) which in some way has contributed to holding party members together in spite of strong internal differentiation. But the bonding factor of the Lega—which, as we have seen, appears to be not so much a sense of territorial belonging as antagonism toward the traditional parties and/or the defense of a large number of (often contradictory) interests in some way connected to the territorial dimensions—seems much weaker than the ties that have held other political groups together in the past.

Bossi is quite aware of this state of affairs. On one hand, he is gradually abandoning the "pure local roots" dimension of his movement (he has felt it is a "provocation") to take on a more political tack with "national" responsibilities, to some extent transforming the Lega into a party like the others. On the other hand, he anticipates that if the Lega were to assume government responsibilities and thus make choices, its supporters would split (as in the past) among left, right, and center groups, as has traditionally happened to parties.

Certainly in the political world the Lega must face the inevitable difficulties connected to the process of the institutionalization of movements. As is known, this process involves the intensification of organizational problems and those of managing political and non-political personnel. In addition, the Lega today can count less on the amount of volunteer work supplied by many of its sympathizers and activists.

There is then the question of competition from other political forces. For quite some time the Lega has enjoyed a role of particular importance—in fact, a monopoly position—among the new forces, which centered their platforms on opposition to the traditional parties. Today the picture appears to have changed. For one thing, other political forces, which up to this point had been absolutely incapable of responding to the Lega, have begun to react and attempt to win back the voters' trust. For another, important new political forces are springing up that position themselves as direct rivals of the Lega. The most significant is the Forza Italia movement, inspired by Silvio Berlusconi, the most important Italian businessman in the arenas of television specifically and media more generally. It is impossible to predict the Lega's fate in the coming months. The current state of the Italian political system is in fact so fluid as to render irrational any prediction on its future evolution and that of its players.

This article is the result of ongoing research at the Institute for the Study of Public Opinion in Milan. An abridged version is in *The End of Post-War Politics in Italy*, ed. Gianfranco Pasquino and Patrick McCarthy (Boulder: Westview Press, 1993).

NOTES

1. M. Caciagli and A. Spreafico, "Introduction," *Vent'anni di elezioni in Italia, 1968–1987* (Padua: Liviana, 1990). See also G. Sani, "La de-strutturazione del mercato elettorale," *Rivista italiana di scienza politica*, December 1992, pp. 539–65, and I. Diamanti and G. Riccamboni in *La parabola del voto bianco: Elezioni e società in Veneto 1964–1992* (Vicenza: Neri Pozza, 1992), p. 173.

2. It is useful to emphasize that the phenomena here described are exclusively Italian, but they have nonetheless occurred in varying degrees throughout Western Europe. Extensive electoral volatility, the increase of distrust in the traditional parties, and the consequent success of the new parties have in fact been observed in the majority of European nations.

3. Naturally it is difficult to establish with certainty the reasons behind the Lega's electoral success and consequent efficacy, especially between 1990 and 1992. Certainly—as has emerged from a series of qualitative polls conducted among voters—the crumbling and fall of the Communist regime influenced many moderates to vote for parties that presented themselves as "bulwarks against communism," particularly the DC.

4. The first poll was conducted by the Eurisko Society as part of a survey of the Osservatorio Politico Italiano, under the direction of Renato Mannheimer and Giacomo Sani as part of a project partially funded by the CNR. The data are for Valle d'Aosta, Piemonte, Liguria, Lombardia, Veneto, Friuili Venezia Giulia, Trentino Alto Adige, and Emilia Romagna and consist of 903 cases. The second poll was conducted by Abacus in May 1993, with a sample group of 801 resident voters in Milan. The third poll was conducted by ISPO in November 1993, with a representative sample group of 1,023 Milanese citizens of voting age.

5. Differences could also depend on the increase in feelings of hostility toward parties in general, notable in the period between studies here considered. Beyond the different areas of reference, there are differences in the survey methods—the first study was conducted in person and the others via telephone—and consequently in the formulation of the questions posed.

6. Within the Socialist electorate there is also an increased number of refusals of voters to position themselves on the left-right axis, but this datum is not considerable given the small number (n = 13) of those polled who in 1993 opted for this party.

7. For the Greens in 1991 one can note a phenomenon analogous to the predisposition for the left that in some ways prefigures the 1993 makeup of this political force.

8. One of the widest distributions of the positioning on the left-right continuum of leghisti voters is also indicated by a higher measure of the standard deviation of self-positionings, which gives an indication of the scope of the dispersion around the mean value. Piergiorgio Corbetta agrees with the conclusion of the "non-reducibility of the Lega to the left-right schemata" in an analysis of highly refined methodology based on the results of the exit polls of the 1982 political elections (P. Corbetta, "La Lega e lo sfaldamento del sistema," pp. 244 ff.).

BIBLIOGRAPHY ON THE LEGA LOMBARDA

Allievi, S. 1992. *Le parole della Lega.* Milan: Garzanti.

Belotti, V. 1993. "La rappresentanza politica locale delle leghe." *Polis* 2.

Biorcio, R. 1992. "Dalle leghe all Lega Nord." *Il mese,* supplement to *Il gazzettino dell'economia,* 21 July.

Cesareo, V.; Rovati, G.; and Lombardi, M. 1989. *Localismo politico: Il caso della Lega Lombarda, Comitato regionale della DC.* Varese: La Tipografia Varesina.

Confalaonieri, M. A. 1990. "S'avanza uno strano soldato: Qualche idea sulla Lega Lombarda." *Ulisse* 3.

Diamanti, I. 1993. *La Lega: Geografia, storia e sociologia di un nuovo soggetto politico.* Rome: Donzelli.

Greco, M., and Bollis, A. 1993. *Carroccio a Nordest: Storia, programma, uomini della Lega Nord del Friuli Venezia Giulia.* Milan: MGS Press.

Lombardi, M. 1990. "La Lega Lombarda: Manifestazione politica del localismo." *Studi di sociologia* 4.

Lucchini, M. 1990–91. "La partecipazione militante nella Lega Nord: Il caso di Varese." Thesis, Università degli Studi di Milano.

Mannheimer, R., ed. 1991. *La Lega Lombarda.* Milan: Feltrinelli.

Moioli, V. 1991. *I nuovi razzismi: Miserie e fortune della Lega Lombarda.* Rome: Edizioni Associate.

Parisi, A. 1992. "Leghe leghisti legami." *Polis* 2.

Pasquino, G. 1991. "Una Lega contro i partiti." *La Rivista dei libri* 2.

————. 1991. "Meno partiti più Lega." *Polis* 3.

Revelli, M. 1993. "L'identità negata: Dove nasce la doppia faccia del Leghismo." *Il Manifesto,* 16 February.

Ricolfi, L. 1993. "Politica senza fede: L'estremismo di centro dei piccoli leghisti." *Il Mulino* 1.

Rovati, G. 1992. "L'equilibrio in frantumi: La Lega Lombarda alle elezioni." In *Partiti storici e nuove formazioni,* ed. G. Galli and D. Comero. Milan: Angeli.

Rusconi, G. E. 1992. "Prendere la Lega sul serio." *Micromega* 5.

Segatti, P. 1992. "L'offerta politica e i candidati della Lega." *Polis* 2.

Vimercati, L. 1990. *I Lombardi alla nuova crociata.* Milan: Mursia.

THE MOVIMENTO SOCIALE ITALIANO

Piero Ignazi

INTRODUCTION

For at least sixty years, from the 1920s to the 1980s, Italy was the point of reference for the entire European extreme right. In the postwar period, with the exception of the flare-up of the NPD in 1966–69, no other party achieved the electoral successes of the Italian neofascists, the Movimento Sociale Italiano (MSI; see Table 1) or organized so many activists and established so many local structures. The MSI, in fact, is the only party of the extreme right in Europe to boast an uninterrupted presence in parliament from the first legislature until today, with almost always more than 5 percent of the seats. Added to this are the one-hundred-odd regional, provincial, and municipal councilors and forty-four mayors elected by direct suffrage in the partial local government elections of May and December. This large representation capacity also reflects an organized force of vast proportions. The official data continually declare membership exceeding 100,000 and more than 1,000 territorial sections. In addition, the MSI makes use of numerous parallel organizations—from youth, student, and women's groups organically tied to the party to veteran, immigrant, ecological, sport, and cultural organizations and the like. The MSI, then, is an important part of the Italian party system and, as we will try to illustrate, has a political culture much more articulated than appears superficially. Before tackling this crucial knot, which constitutes the point on which the MSI's future turns, we want to frame it within its historic development, beginning with its foundation.

Table 1

Votes for MSI in Chamber of Deputies, 1948–92

Year	Percent
1948	2.0%
1953	5.8
1958	4.8
1963	5.1
1968	4.5
1972	8.7
1976	6.1
1979	5.3
1983	6.8
1987	5.9
1992	5.4

Source: Official data, Ministry of the Interior.

HISTORIC PROFILE OF THE MSI

BEGINNINGS

The MSI was created in December 1946 through the initiative of a group of young ex-fascists supported in the shadows by some heirarchs of the old regime. In the immediate postwar period there were various attempts (tied to the numerous recidivist journals) to aggregate the ex-fascists, but the MSI asserted itself quite early as the point of reference for the entire "nostalgia" sphere. The new party was declared, first in veiled forms, then ever more explicitly, heir to fascism in its final version, that of the Italian Social Republic (RSI), the Republic of Salò formed in northern Italy by Mussolini after his removal from office and the armistice declaration in the fall of 1943. The reference to the Republic of Saló implies a precise politico-ideal choice—namely, the recall to the socializing, anticapitalist, antibourgeois principles of the Verona Charter, the programmatic manifesto drawn up in 1944 at the Ninth Congress of the Fascist Republican Party (Partito Fascista Repubblicano—PFR) which represents the quintessence of the fascist movement—and, at the same time, the rejection by those fascists of the Central South who had not followed Mussolini in his last venture. This choice was in contrast to the component of the fascist regime characterized by a bourgeois, moderate clerical, and conservative approach. These two components found expression in the MSI in organized factions that opposed each other repeatedly in the internal political battle.

In this period of development the MSI had to confront—and untie—the knot of acceptance of the system born from the ashes of fascism and of open participation in political life. Since 1945 groups of ex-fascists had promised spectacular initiatives and exemplary (at times also terrorist) gestures; but these initiatives, as much as they were covertly supported by the party (the members of terrorist groups were in many cases also party activists), conflicted with the legalistic inclination, the desire to practice politics openly. However, a declaredly neofascist party had to either chose the path of clandestineness and resistance or accept (and adjust itself to) the rules of the new regime. Its survival depended precisely on its ability to show that it was as legalistic as was possible. In fact, already in 1947 the MSI had decided to present itself at the local government elections of Rome, obtaining 4 percent of the votes in spite of the inevitable difficulties of running the election campaign. This result positioned it as a gathering point for the entire "nostalgia" world. In addition, to facilitate the installation of the MSI, to hide a potential competitor from the political scene, the Party of the Average Man (Uomo Qualunque) was created. Appealing to the resentment of those eliminated, to the desire of the petit bourgeois for a quiet life and their intolerance of the new (broad) role of the parties and resistance rhetoric, this movement obtained 5.3 percent of the vote nationally but 9.4 percent from Rome southwards in the 1946 elections to the Constituent Assembly. In reality, the MSI and Uomo Qualunque moved on very different tracks, but the reference electorate was substantially the same. This gave rise to the fierce competition between the two parties at the parliamentary elections of 1948.

At these elections, just one and a half years after its constitution, the MSI succeeded in presenting itself in all constituencies as proof of the rapidity of its territorial infiltration. However, while in the South the party was able to develop its election campaign undisturbed, in the North this was almost impossible due to the reactions of the antifascist forces. The memory of the civil war of 1943–45 was still too vivid to allow a "turning of the page." The election results confirmed this geographic split. The MSI garnered more than two-thirds of its votes in the South, and all six elected parliament members came from southern electoral colleges.

This territorial imbalance in the distribution of consensus determined a new order among the internal components of the party and consequently its political choices. The initial managing group, composed of young ex-RSI adherents, had supported a fascism socialized and open to the left, in contrast to the conservative establishment of the "hierarchs" which had not followed the fate of Il Duce to the bloody end. Given the election results, the tough polemic against the "traitors," to whom membership was directly barred in the first statute, was destined to be smoothed out. Since the ideological division between "socializers" and "corporatists" also reflected a geographic division of North and South, it was difficult for the Saló-ist managers (of the North) to skip over the fact that the electoral reservoir of the MSI was in the South. In fact the influx of ex-leaders and managers of the National Fascist Party and the organized growth of the party almost exclusively in the South in 1950 brought a change at the peak of party leadership: the new secretary, Alfredo de Marsanich, exponent of the moderate faction, embodied the ideal of continuity with the past regime, as he had been a minister of the fascist government.

CONSOLIDATION AND MODERATION

With the change in leadership, the MSI abandoned its most openly antisystem resolutions and advanced the strategy of inclusion in the system, which it continued for two decades until the early 1970s. The to-the-death opposition to the system was replaced by an ever more explicit offer of support for the majority party, the Christian Democrats (DC), to which the MSI presented itself as a national force for the defense of common interests: Christian civilization and the battle against Communist materialism. This policy of moderation manifested itself with a) an electoral alliance with the monarchists; b) a declaration of adherence to the Atlantic Pact, against which the neofascist members of parliament some years earlier had joined in furious battle; and c) an agreement with the DC, passed over at the last moment, for a candidacy at the municipal elections of Rome in 1952. The "Americanophile" attitude contradicted one of the leit motifs of neofascist propoganda until then—the iniquity of the peace treaty—just as disposability toward the new democratic regime was poorly adapted to the repeated proclamations of faithfulness to the fascist ideal. But these contradictions did not block a very strong advance in the local government elections of 1951 and above all 1952, particularly in the South, where the MSI obtained 11.8 percent and (with slates shared with the monarchists) the control of some large cities like Naples and Bari. A success of this magnitude was vital for the MSI because it diffused the threat of its dissolution proposed by the minister of the interior. The party had grown too much to be dissolved without creating incidents and tensions.

Overcoming this obstacle, the MSI was able to nationalize its presence and increase its electoral gains in the 1953 elections (from 2 to 5.8 percent). From the mid-1950s—in particular after the Milan Congress of 1956, in which the socializer faction, led by Almirante, attempted a final assault on the secretaryship and lost by just seven votes—the MSI fully developed its strategy of inclusion in the system. The director of this operation was the new secretary, Arturo Michelini, who remained at the head of the party until his death in 1969. In spite of the fact that the MSI leadership was firmly in the hands of the moderate component, the party was anything but united, and the most radical faction was well rooted in the youth groups, which constituted a strong point of the MSI. In fact, in the 1950s the student organization Giovane Italia, the university organization FUAN, and the Raggruppamento Giovanile Studenti Lavoratori (RGSL) recruited approximately 10,000 members. The university organization, in certain faculties of the central-southern universities, was the first of its kind and as an activist youth presence was inferior only to those of the Communists and Christian Democrats.

At the end of the 1950s the MSI achieved its major political successes, reaching the threshold of the government. First, together with the liberals and monarchists, it supported some Christian Democrat governments and finally, with its deciding votes, the 1960 Christian Democrat government of Tambroni. This agreement represented the culmination of the policy of inclusion but also confirmed its impracticability. The prospect of a clerico-fascist government triggered a series of protests, the epicenter of which was Genoa, where the MSI Congress was convened at the time. The reaction of the left—which culminated in bloody piazza confrontations and some deaths, first in Genoa, then in Reggio Emilia and Rome—drove the MSI back to marginality.

CRISIS AND MARGINALIZATION

This defeat had a twofold effect on the MSI. On one hand, it resuscitated the internal opposition; on the other, it favored the successive development of organizations of the extreme right, external and in opposition to the party. But while the former aspect was congenital to the party, the latter represented a prominent change in the camp of the extreme right. Until the early 1960s, in fact, the MSI had a monopoly on the political representation of the extreme right. With the exception of the Movimento Politico Ordine Nuovo (MPON) movement created by a group of secessionists led by Pino Rauti on the day after the Milan Congress of 1956, no small political grouping among the many that sprang up under the initiative of leaders disappointed in or dissenting from the party has had political visibility. Instead, after the defeat of 1960, the MSI gradually lost the ability to control in this area. The incessant reproposing of inclusion, even after the first governments of the center-left (DC plus PSI and lay parties), demonstrated its inability to adapt to new circumstances. Consequently, new organizations arose and developed plans alternative to those of the MSI. Their point of departure was the recognition of the unreliability of the MSI, by now unable and/or unwilling to engage in a revolutionary battle against the system, as implied in a politics of compromise and blackmail with the Christian Democrat power. This analysis, pitiless but not without truth, accompanied a new interpretation of Italian political reality and the international context. The "Red Threat," in spite of détente, was more alive than ever, as it had only changed tactics. It was trying to penetrate all the nerve centers of society, thus undermining it from within, and at the same time attacking the European stronghold from the peripheries of the postcolonial world which were subject to the strategy of Soviet domination. In order to confront this "underhanded aggression," it was necessary to identify the "healthy organs" of the nation and get ready for the "inevitable" final fight with the Reds. From this ensued contacts with sectors of the armed forces, from which the MSI had always been excluded and to which it had never turned because of the end of the civil war: all the high officials claimed resistance "credits."

Between the end of the 1960s and the beginning of the 1970s the MSI was at the low point of its electoral history—only 4.5 percent at the 1968 elections—and lost the ability to influence the DC; at the same time, it lost the hegemony of the extreme right. As proof of this last change, there was a marked flourishing of groups and movements—some of them ephemeral, others prominent—from the paraputschist National Front of Junio Valerio Borghese and Rosa dei Venti to radical to terrorist ones, Avanguardia Nazionale (AN) and MPON. All these groups offered an outlet for the urgent demands for order, for a reaffirmation of traditional values, and for physical protection, deemed necessary by sectors of the bourgeoisie frightened by social tensions. For the first time the MSI was not the natural channel for these demands.

THE NATIONAL RIGHT

With the death of Michelini and the return (after twenty years) of Almirante to the leadership of the party, a new period began that saw an organizational restructuring, a replacement of leaders, and the plan of achieving the same aims set by Michelini—i.e., leaving the ghetto and gaining credibility as a potential government partner with the DC—with more articulated tactics and an ideological refinishing. On the organizational level, the party was equipped with a central structure of full-time officials, the youth organizations were fused into one organism (the Fronte della Gioventù), the role of the local leaders was emphasized, and at the same time the decision-making process was strongly centralized, both between party leaders and periphery and on the central level, where the secretary assumed a role like Caesar. On the ideological-strategic level, the MSI attempted to play the role of a modern right, presenting itself as less nostalgic of the past, gathering the monarchists' castoffs and opening itself to those who did not belong to the fascist subculture.

Precisely to accentuate this change, of course, the party added the suffix "National Right" (Destra Nazionale) to its name.

The new strategy also provided for a renewed antagonism with "Communist subversion." In this way the MSI succeeded in reclaiming a good many of the radical dissidents who had fed movements like MPON and AN. Therefore, the party offered itself as a well-trained defender of the silent majority and at the same time a respectable and renovated potential ally of a moderate coalition. At the same time, an ideological-cultural renovation was attempted (journals like *La Destra,* study centers like the Institute of Corporate Studies, and the homonymous journal were started) and conferences were organized with a new quality and diversity of participants—all of this to minimize the association with fascism and win legitimacy in the political and electoral arena.

In spite of the sensational electoral successes of the 1971 local government elections and the parliamentary elections of 1972, where the MSI hit its historic high point (8.7 percent), and the organizational expansion (approximately 200,000 members), this strategy did not lead to concrete results. Its internal contradictions—superficial and openly instrumental ideological revision, inability to control the most militant fringes of the party, and its youth organizations conniving with the most violent groups of the radical right—and the containment policy of the DC, preoccupied with the effusion of votes for the MSI, led the National Right strategy down a blind alley. The electoral defeat of 1976 (-2.6 percent) provoked an uprising of the supporters of the renovation and of agreement with the DC; the split that ensued led to the National Democracy Party, which, in spite of the adherence of more than half of the parliamentary group, vanished in 1979.

THE PROTEST PARTY

The departure of the most moderate component brought a distinct shift of the party toward postions of major protest against the system and, more important, relaunched the figure of Pino Rauti, who had rejoined the MSI at the beginning of the 1970s. Rauti gave life to a faction that was a veritable laboratory of plans and ideas united by the aim of conquering the obsessive return to the past. The point of departure of the Rautian group was the crumbling of liberal-bourgeois and Marxist ideologies, together unable to respond to the needs of contemporary societies and above all the younger generations. Capitalism, with its reduction of every relationship to market terms, destroyed the possibility of an authentic and spiritual community life; standardization, consumerism, and alienation—no longer subversion or communism—were the crucial problems. The influence of the new right, rather transparent in the Rautian approach, was a true ideological-cultural innovation for the MSI.

In this special climate the "Hobbit camps"—summer youth camps in which the new Rautian tendency was expressed—were organized. The militaristic and sullen atmosphere of similar earlier initiatives left the entire field open to discussion, which was interwoven with an irony and self-irony (unknown before), directed at the study of the cornerstones of a new policy and aimed at overcoming the often bloody confrontation with leftist movements in the name of a common "otherness" with respect to the system. New key words entered the MSI's lexicon, such as advocacy of civil liberties (*garantismo*), civil rights and minority rights, and comparison. New interlocutors were privileged—the young and the southern middle class instead of the northern industrial bourgeoisie—and the anti-Communist appeal opened the doors to opposition to the system. However, the MSI abandoned none of its traditional ideal heritage. But inspired by the decline of ideologies and by the dissent of youth and the growth of consociationism (the years of the Historic Compromise), it added new content and was characterized as a protest party. The enemy to beat was no longer communism but "the regime." All the parties, beginning with the DC, were responsible for the Italian crisis; therefore there was no longer a silent majority to defend, but rather the protests of the young and of southerners to support.

The distinct change in strategy would seem to lead the MSI to a flirtation, even more dangerous than in the past, with the radical groups that at the end of the 1970s saw a final season of violence. But the panorama had changed for the radical and terrorist right as well. Indifference to the MSI was replaced by open hostility, so much so that it united all the other parties. The "armed spontaneity" of the post-1977 years knew neither strategy nor allies: terrorist acts, the battle against everybody and to the death constituted the only practicable political action as a potential revolutionary spur. In the years 1977–79 the violence was rekindled and there was an increase in attacks both claimed (a high of 146 in 1979)and unclaimed (a high of 367 in 1978). The principal groups of this period—Costruiamo l'Azione, Terza Posizione, and the Nuclei Armati Rivoluzionari (NAR)—were differentiated from historic groups of the radical right like the MPON and AN by the incredible bloodiness of the actions, by extraneousness to every political plan, and by the abandonment of the nationalist and anti-Communist issues on which the MPON or AN had legitimated themselves. In spite of some persisting gray areas of connivance (for example, a headquarters of the Roman Fronte della Gioventù, meeting place for young party members and terrorists), the MSI was not contaminated by this last terrorist wave. The new recruits moved outside the neofascist orbit, and, more important, the party did not suffer the consequences of their actions, contrary to what had happened in the early 1970s.

DEPARTURE FROM THE GHETTO

In the 1980s the MSI's role in the Italian party system changed radically. In reality the MSI did not modify its strategy of protest and opposition to the regime and maintained (with some difficulty) both the traditional nostalgic referents and alternative and "community" perspectives of the Rautian group (more the "modernizing" goals of a new component that was forming in the party). The changes, then, took place outside of the MSI and without any contribution from the party. The first change had to do with a different approach to the phenomenon of fascism. The militant and resistance interpretation, which placed fascism in a type of nefarious cesspool, was replaced, thanks to the pioneering work of Renzo de Felice, by a more problemmatic vision. Historic research, cultural debates, and anthological exhibitions—beginning with that on the 1930s (Annitrenta) organized by the municipal administration of the left in Milan in 1982—interpreted and at the same time influenced a vision more detached from fascism. All this did nothing to revitalize a nostalgic profascist sentiment (not even within the MSI)—even though this new climate was greeted with satisfaction—but rather allowed a less Manichean vision of the two prewar decades.

A second change was the end of the *anni di piombo,* years of terrorism and political violence. From 1969 to 1982 there were 351 killed and 767 wounded; two-thirds of these were victims of the right (attributing to the radical right unclaimed massacres such as that of the Bologna station, in which 85 were killed and more than 200 wounded). But while in the early 1970s terrorist violence had been a prerogative almost exclusively of the right, beginning in 1977 it was divided equally between left and right, creating a spiral of violence—and above all daily microviolence—which embittered the political conflict. At the beginning of the 1980s the neofascist world as much as the extreme left (in particular the daily *Continuous Battle*) called for laying down arms and practicing tolerance and respect for the adversary. Thus a period of violence and total opposition ended.

Thus at the beginning of the decade, by virtue of the historicization of fascism and the deradicalization of the political conflict, the MSI was able to leave its ghetto. Paradoxically, this favorable trend—which was also evident in the good results at the 1983 elections—placed the MSI in difficulty because the party had not promoted this new climate. In a sense it suffered because it was not equipped ideologically and culturally for the new period which had begun. There was no strategy for integration and full legitimization in the system. On one hand, it did not renounce its identity—fascism; on the other, the innovative Rautian views (weakened by the party's expulsion of the group that then represented the "new Italian right") placed it outside of the liberal-democratic representative system. In the end the MSI had to choose whether to abandon part of its ideal and cultural identity and fully accept the system or to maintain the perspective of an alternative regime, be it corporatist or community. The MSI remained mired in this dilemma, which was aggravated by an electoral drop in 1987 (5.9 percent: -0.9 percent) and the almost simultaneous loss in 1988 of its historic leaders—beginning with Almirante, who had left his post the year before to his probable very young successor Gianfranco Fini—and the reemergence of very strong internal competition. This was the sore point around which turned the internal debate on the role of the party in the system. Although still paying homage to system alternatives, delineated also with a plan for a new presidential-type constitution, the true clash focused on the alliance strategy: agreement with the DC or the lay parties and the PSI to break the Christian Democrat-Communist duopoly.

THE 1990s

A turning point in 1990, the election of Rauti to secretary of the party, originated from this state of dissatisfaction. Rauti was one of the last historic leaders of the party (at sixteen he had fought in the RSI) and had traversed various periods; at the end of the 1970s he had devised a melange of fascist-MSI elements with those of the new right. The policy proposed by Rauti was extremely innovative, however. First, the party had to abandon all references to the "right," as fascism was a revolutionary, not a conservative, movement. Therefore, the MSI, rediscovering more authentic origins, had to place itself on the left and try to attract the Communist electorate. Second, the "pseudo-values" of Western Americanized society—agnosticism, materialism, hedonism, egoism, and consumerism—were refuted and replaced by authentically spiritual values. In addition, hostility toward capitalism was accentuated, as were anti-Western, anti-American, pro-Third World and pro-Arab sentiments.

The traditional neofascist political culture—authoritarian, conservative, and petit bourgeois—was thus replaced by an anticapitalist, anti-Western, and leftist culture. The most marked novelty was the recognition and valorization of all types of differences, in terms of both values, ideas, and plans, and in a cultural and racial sense. Willy-nilly Rauti thus introduced elements which were irreconcilable with the neofascist cultural tradition, including tolerance and the right to dissent, the acceptance of differences, and environmental protection. In short, it was an acceptance of modernity. Thanks to these cultural acquisitions, the MSI, contrary to the other parties of the European extreme right, vehemently denounced racism (even though some youth fringe groups indulged in confrontations with Jews and immigrants of color).

The Rauti secretaryship was evidently a digression. After a series of impressive electoral setbacks (at the 1990 local government elections the party plummeted to 4.0 percent, the worst result in its history), in the summer of 1991 Rauti was replaced by Fini. However, the change was more one of tone and strategy than of political culture. In other words, the new leadership abandoned a recall of the disappointments of communism and a claim of the space to the left; dropped its most vehemently anti-American and anticapitalist tones; and, reproposing itself as a traditionalist and national "right" force, tried to interweave contacts with moderate and Catholic sectors but did not overturn the antixenophobic and tolerant approach. However, the "comprehensive" attitude toward immigrants—or at least the decision to not use this issue as a spearhead of MSI politics—gave space to the Lega Lombarda (now Lega Nord) that for some years had emphasized the problem of immigrants (including those from southern Italy). In reality there was no competition between the MSI and Lega because these two parties were opposed on the Lega's fundamental issue, federalism: the MSI was, in fact, the national and nationalist party par excellence. Secretary Fini reintroduced all the arguments and classic claims of the neofascist nationalist repertoire: rights to the territories ceded to Yugoslavia after World War II; the Italianness of South Tyrol (an issue over which the MSI had broken off relations with the Republikaner, abandoning the group of the Euro-right at the Strasbourg parliament); a more incisive role in the former colonies; strengthening of the defense system, etc. Not by accident, the MSI traditionally obtained its best results in border towns, sites of grudges and nationalist claims, like Trieste and Bolzano.

The endurance of the MSI in the "earthquake elections" of 1992 (scarcely 0.5 percent less) after the debacle of the historic formations in some sense proved the existence of a faithful electorate sensitive to the classic claims of the party. The reintroduction of the nostalgic image, even though supported by a more moderate and problematic one, allowed the maintenance of a certain electoral consensus. Actually, the antiparty surge that upset the Italian political panorama, bringing about the disintegration of the PSI and the vertical crisis of the DC, could not have done other than benefit a political formation of the opposition. Thus the MSI succeeded in slowing the descent down the slope of marginality and in recouping consensus not only in electoral terms, but also as an organized force. According to official data the party declared an increase of 30,000 members from 1991 to 1992, as well as a continuing capacity to attract young people (approximately 6,000 members of the Fronte della Gioventù and good results in some university elections).

Looking toward the next elections, to endure with the new majority system, the MSI gave life to Alleanza Nazionale, an open and external group whose aim was to make political offerings of the right desirable to a broader electorate. In preparation of this plan, the MSI began to rather timidly pose the question of its identity: be faithful to fascism or abandon the founding ideology in favor of a prosystem conservatism?

THE NEOFASCIST IDENTITY

What is the political culture of the MSI today? Is it still a fascist party? The ideal references and political mythology still express a very strong attachment to fascism. However, the MSI always explicitly declares itself the legitimate heir of historic fascism. The statement at the 1982 congress by Giorgio Almirante, historic secretary of the MSI, is well-known: "Fascism is here!" This exclamation brought an ovation from the onlookers. Nonetheless, some empirical data on the values and beliefs of the intermediate leaders of the party (culled from a study on the delegates at the sixteenth congress of the party in 1990) reflect a more variegated image and call for a more accurate assessment.

First we will illustrate the prevailing attitudes toward the political system. Given the declared historic "otherness" of the MSI in relation to the democratic political system and its values, we should expect a high rate of alienation. In fact, the denial of the system is an identifying element of the neofascist political culture. However, there are many nuances in the various indicators of this attitude. The first indicator takes into consideration the alternation between a strategy of cooperation and external contacts and one of radical opposition to the system; the latter, the "tried and true," prevails with 58.9 percent versus 41.1 percent. A second indicator concerns the degree of proximity to or distance from other parties. It is evident that an attitude of strong antagonism unites all the parties in an identical, mass rejection. The percentage of those whom they assign the minimum value possible (score zero) is highest or very high for practically all the parties except the Greens and Socialists—the Greens because they are considered new and not prejudicially antifascist, the socialists because they had been among the promoters of the MSI's departure from the ghetto (Table 2). These figures bring to light a general feeling of alienation and closure toward the outside that reinforces the preceding datum on which strategy to follow. The third indicator was furnished by questions on methods of political action that were neither conventional nor legal. The acceptance of such forms of protest was widespread. Almost half declared they favored the individual reduction of taxes and bills and supported sit-ins and the occupation of vacant buildings or factories; approximately 20 percent also supported tougher actions like wildcat strikes and clashes with the police and other demonstrators. This militant tendency, however, is kept within bounds; when responding to an explicit question on the adoption of violent methods, approximately half rejected violence (but one-fourth consider it a practicable route).

In sum, from the neofascist leaders two types of attitudes seem to emerge: in one, antisystem attitudes prevail—an orientation favorable to protests (even violent ones), a total lack of esteem for and absolute distance from other parties, and radical opposition to the system; the other supports cooperation and collaboration with the system and the other political players.

Table 2

Degree of MSI Proximity to or Distance from Other Parties (0 = maximum distance; 10 = maximum proximity)
(Percent)

Party	Zero Value
PCI	64.6%
PSDI	63.4
PRI	62.4
DC	55.6
PLI	51.7
PR	47.2
Greens	22.6
PSI	20.2

Source: Offical data, Ministry of the Interior.

The politico-cultural reality of the MSI is rather more complex than this traditional dichotomy, however. An analysis of responses on a series of topics grouped in five scales of attitude (clericalism, militarism, racism, anti-Westernism, and authoritarianism) furnishes a profile with much more jagged contours (Table 3). Although the neofascist leaders declare themselves in large measure Catholic (79.3 percent), they do not intend to impose Catholic values upon society. Less than half demand obligatory religious instruction, and scarcely one-third believe that an education based on religious principles is indispensible. Some typical notions on militarism—from military spending to the national military service as a locus for the formation of men—have been shelved; instead support for defense training persists, expressed in the desire to maintain the Euromissiles. In foreign policy the anti-American and national-European positions are predominant. The United States is overwhelmingly judged an imperial power, more than two-thirds unconditionally support the Palestinian cause, and an equal number demand a major role for the European countries in NATO.

The question of racism is thornier. Xenophobic and racist attitudes were banned from neofascist politics in a courageous and costly political choice. Nonetheless, the leaders have rather radical positions on this topic: both the fear of immigrants submerging national identity (80.5 percent) and support for the forced repatriation of illegal aliens (62.1 percent) show the degree of xenophobia. The only contradiction concerns increasing aid to the Third World, which is promoted by 54.9 percent of the leaders. This expulsion-aid dualism brings the MSI near to other parties of the extreme right, like Scandinavian progressive parties and the Belgian FN, which also favor such solutions.

The last scale concerns degrees of authoritarianism-liberalism. The topics that draw the most agreement concern discipline as a pillar of society, the crumbling of traditional moral values as evidenced by pornography, and the authoritarian education of children. There were also rather severe judgments on the legalization of abortion and strikes by public employees. For all the other topics, the scale swings to the liberal side. The opinion against the death penalty and against the discrimination of homosexuals prevails by a small but significant number. The support is broader for advocating civil liberties in police matters (55.8 percent deny the idea that the

Table 3

Values and Beliefs of MSI Leaders/Cadre, 1990

(Percentage of those who claim to agree with each issue)

Religious education indispensable	33	Immigrant fertility is threat to national identity	79
Obligatory religion at school	44	Repatriation of illegal aliens	60
Religious base for rites	66	Too many public employees	28
Right or wrong, the country	58	Privatize industry and services	49
Supervision of former colonies	59	Don't pay taxes	34
No to the influx of foreign capital	41	Don't control monopolies	3
Creation of European army	74	Drug addicts in jail	47
United States is imperialist	94	Yes to the death penalty	39
Increase military spending	25	Fire public employees who strike	44
No to conscientious objection	42	Men have sole decision power at home	23
Military service as "school of life"	23	Discipline based on social order	74
Foreign army intervention, even without allies' consent	65	Parents do without obedience of children	56
There are superior and inferior races	46	No public displays of homosexuality	33
Financial power in the hands of the Jews	44	Prisons are too comfortable	35
Immigrants are cause of crime	14	Police must be able to interrogate without too many restrictions	28
Special schools for nongifted children	12	No aid to drug addicts	5
No social protection for immigrants	46	The family is the pillar of society	90

police should have a free hand), for equality between men and women, and for an understanding attitude regarding drug addicts.

This embryonic acceptance of liberal elements, tied to both the dubiousness of the views of the "new right" and to an opening to modern society and its problems, forged a political culture in which a timid acceptance of diversity was mixed (with some difficulty) with traditional authoritarian approaches (with particular reference to immigration). In addition, these new and "modernizing" elements of the neofascist political culture supplemented a "rust-proof" faith in the original identity—namely, the fascist ideology. As mentioned above, the MSI did not renounce any of its historic referents: Mussolini, Evola (the most rigorous thinker of the tradition, radically hostile toward democracy, liberalism, and the market economy), Gentile (the official philosopher of fascism), and Spiriro (the theorist of corporatism) are still the references for the neofascist cultural pantheon. The party produced no critical reworking in either historiographic or politico-ideological terms. Only on the problem of corporatism did a small group of intellectuals, uninfluential in the party, conduct an interesting critical study.

Is the MSI still a fascist party? Yes indeed, but it would be simplistic to close with such a final judgment. Although nothing has been reworked in manifest and official terms, MSI leaders are bearers of a vision that by now poorly reconciles with fascist authoritarianism. In addition, the parliamentary and institutional political practice of almost fifty years has inevitably weakened the subversive and antisystem position of the national and local neofascist political class. This "adapting to the (democratic) environment" has not, however, produce a leap large enough to speak of a new "a-fascist" party. The recent plan to modify some characteristic traits of the party with the constitution of the Alleanza Nazionale could prove a mere embellishment or could produce a new party. But in this case—as in other examples of radical renovation (French PS in 1971, German SPD in 1959, and Italian PCI in 1990)—to be credible, modifications must be traumatic and painful.

CONCLUSIONS

The MSI has traveled far from the other parties of the European extreme right owing to the conditions under which it was created (immediately after the war), its dimensions (a small, broadly based party), and its cultural course (faithfulness to fascism and inclusion of some ideological traits of the new right and the postmaterialist political culture). For example, the principal theme on which these parties built their fortunes—immigration—never had any particular salience in Italy. Official data demonstrate an upswing in recent years but underestimate the number of immigrants by at least one-third due to the large number of illegal aliens. The number of foreigners grew from 298,700 in 1980, to 423,000 in 1985, to 781,100 in 1990, to 896,800 in 1991 (equal to 1.6 percent of the population). In any case, the attitude of the Italians toward this phenomenon is in general rather tolerant. Italy is historically a country of emigration, and this has left its mark on popular culture. A survey in 1992 polled sympathy or antipathy toward social and ethnic groups. Only 4.8 percent claimed antipathy toward foreigners in general—practically a lunatic fringe and nothing more. "Extracommunity" immigrants garnered 16.4 percent hostility—specifically, blacks (10.9 percent), Arabs (18.0 percent), and Jews (10.5 percent). These are extremely low figures (especially if compared with those of other countries) which demonstrate that (with some sensational exceptions), the general climate is not favorable to xenophobic policies. In the last parliamentary elections the immigration issue was completely absent from the election campaign. Also, anti-Semitism, an issue to which the groups of the extreme right and also some fringe youth groups of the MSI are more sensitive, did not create particular anxiety—notwithstanding some demonstrations in Rome and other cities; in these cases the responsibility lay with small groups of skinheads or micro-organizations of the radical right (Meridiano Zero, Movimento Politico Occidentale). In reality, once the immigration question was "discovered" around 1990, conditions were ripened for its introduction into the political agenda, but the issue very quickly returned to obscurity. This is attributable to the deliberate refusal of the MSI, led by Pino Rauti, to make the chords of xenophobia vibrate. This position was followed, after some initial wavering, by Rauti's successor, Fini. The political entrepreneur eager to play the xenophobic role was essentially missing. The role in that period was occupied (temporarily) by a new player, the Lega Nord, with explicitly xenophobic messages.

Thus the MSI today is eccentric in comparison to the panorama of parties on the European extreme right. It proudly refers to its fascist past, to being the keeper and champion of its traditions, but at the same time, it is driven by a desire to not become sterile as a merely political alternative to the regime, which it continues to proclaim. In fact, middle-level leaders and part of the managing class consider themes extraneous to the neofascist ideological patrimony, although this has still not produced a coherent cultural and ideological design. Therefore traditional identity and new interests stand together in the MSI, still characterizing it as a party of the nostalgic extreme right, but one which is much more disposed toward change.

What will be the future of the MSI? Its return to the guidance of its most traditionalist component, embodied by the young secretary Gianfranco Fini (until 1991), rivitalized the conservative, mildly nostalgic soul of the party. However, this recovery of tradition comes with an attempt at cooperation not unlike that undertaken by Almirante in the early 1970s. But there is a marked difference. Then the ideological renovation was guided by the leadership and was perceived as purely tactical cosmetic surgery, and the activists were completely extraneous. In this case the cooperative efforts were not only shared but promised by many of the activists and middle-level leaders. This modernizing political culture, open and problematic in the face of many social and civil issues, constituted an attempt to give life to an aggregation that would overcome the confines of the MSI. The spur to modifying the MSI was twofold. On one hand, the change in the electoral system from proportional to partially majoritarian highlighted the necessity of escaping isolation and adopting coalition strategies. Without alliances with other parties and moderate movements the MSI's "booty" of votes could become useless. On the other hand, the results of recent local government elections—first in May, then much more sensationally in December 1992—demonstrated that the MSI is in a strong position to catalyze consensus beyond the usual area of membership. In December it won nineteen municipalities, of which four were provincial capitals (Latina, Chieti, Benevento, and Caltanisetta), all in the Central South. In two important centers, Rome and Naples, the MSI candidate—the national secretary, Gianfranco

Fini, in Rome and the Honorable Alessandra Mussolini, niece of "Il Duce," in Naples—reached the second ballot against the candidate of the left and gained more than 45 percent of the votes. The necessity of ensuring representation in an electoral area that does not identify completely with fascism and the imperative of allying with others in order to not vanish in a majority electoral system drove the MSI to transform itself into the Alleanza Nazionale. However, as already mentioned, only a clear and definite revision of its original traits, those of direct fascist derivation, will allow the MSI to be an acceptable partner in broader coalitions.

3. *American Intervention after the Cold War.* Robert W. Tucker. $3.95

4. *Crisis in the Balkans.* Eugene A. Hammel, Irwin M. Wall, and Benjamin N. Ward. $6.95

CENTERS FOR SOUTH AND SOUTHEAST ASIA STUDIES

MONOGRAPH SERIES

32. *Scavengers, Recyclers, & Solutions for Solid Waste Management in Indonesia.* Daniel T. Sicular. $16.50

33. *Indonesian Transmigrants and Adaptation: An Ecological Anthropological Perspective.* Oekan S. Abdoellah. $14.95

34. *Thai Music and Musicians in Contemporary Bangkok.* Pamela Myers-Moro. $22.50

35. *In the Shadow of Change: Images of Women in Indonesian Literature.* Tineke Hellwig. $22.00

OCCASIONAL PAPERS

15. *The Penis Inserts of Southeast Asia: An Annotated Bibliography with an Overview & Comparative Perspective.* Donald E. Brown, J. W. Edwards, & R. P. Moore. $6.00

16. *Patterns of Migration in Southeast Asia.* Ed. Robert R. Reed. $19.50

17. *Bridging Worlds: Studies on Women in South Asia.* Ed. Sally J. M. Sutherland. $17.50

18. *Essays on Southeast Asian Performing Arts: Local Manifestations and Cross-Cultural Implications.* Ed. Kathy Foley. $14.95

LANGUAGE TEACHING MATERIALS

Introduction to Hindi Grammar. Usha Jain. $30.00

Hmong for Beginners. Annie Jaisser et al. $28.00

Devavanipravesika: Introduction to the Sanskrit Language. Robert P. Goldman and Sally J. Sutherland. $23.50

Teaching Grammar of Thai. William Kuo. $23.50

Tamil for Beginners, 2 vols. Kausalya Hart. $12.50 ea.

SINO-TIBETAN ETYMOLOGICAL DICTIONARY AND THESAURUS PROJECT

MONOGRAPH SERIES

1A. *Bibliography of the International Conferences on Sino-Tibetan Languages and Linguistics I-XXV,* 2d ed. Randy J. LaPolla and John B. Lowe $28.00